Bible Readings
On The
Progressive Development of Truth
And Experience
In The
Books of the Old Testament

by

Hannah Whitall Smith

First Fruits Press
Wilmore,
Kentucky c2018

Bible readings on the progressive development of truth and experience in the books of the Old Testament.
By H.W.S.

First Fruits Press, © 2018

ISBN: 9781621717829 (print), 9781621717836 (digital), 9781621717843 (kindle)

Digital version at http://place.asburyseminary.edu/firstfruitsheritagematerial/149/

First Fruits Press
B.L. Fisher Library
Asbury Theological Seminary
204 N. Lexington Ave.
Wilmore, KY 40390
http://place.asburyseminary.edu/firstfruits

Smith, Hannah Whitall, 1832-1911.
  Bible readings on the progressive development of truth and experience in the books of the Old Testament / by H.W.S. – Wilmore, KY : First Fruits Press, ©2018.
  401 pages ; cm.
  Reprint. Previously published: Boston : Willard Tract Repository, 1878.
  ISBN: 9781621717829 (pbk.)
  1. Bible. Old Testament--Criticism, interpretation, etc.
  2. Bible. Old Testament--Theology. I. Title.

BS1171.S63 2018   221.7

Cover design by Jon Ramsay

asburyseminary.edu
800.2ASBURY
204 North Lexington Avenue
Wilmore, Kentucky 40390

First Fruits
THE ACADEMIC OPEN PRESS OF ASBURY SEMINARY

First Fruits Press
The Academic Open Press of Asbury Theological Seminary
204 N. Lexington Ave., Wilmore, KY 40390
859-858-2236
first.fruits@asburyseminary.edu
asbury.to/firstfruits

BIBLE READINGS

ON THE

PROGRESSIVE DEVELOPMENT OF TRUTH
AND EXPERIENCE

IN THE

BOOKS OF THE OLD TESTAMENT.

BY

H. W. S.

Author of "Frank, the Record of a Happy Life," "The Christian's
Secret of a Happy Life," &c., &c.

---

*" For now we see through a glass darkly : but then face to face : now I
know in part ; but then shall I know even as also I am known."*

WILLARD TRACT REPOSITORY,

BEACON HILL PLACE,

BOSTON

GRANT, FAIRES & RODGERS,
Electrotypers,
52 & 54 N. 6th St., Philada.

PREFACE.

THIS book is not meant in any sense to be a Commentary on the Old Testament. I freely confess that there are many difficult parts about which I know nothing, but before which I have learned to sit down in the silence and contentment of faith, and await patiently the day of God's explanations.

My object has been, not to explain the Bible, but simply to give, as far as I have seen it, the deep inner sense of the Books of the Old Testament, in their progressive development of truth and experience. These views have been opened to me principally through the writings and teachings of a few of the Lord's see-ers, or "seers," chief among whom I would mention the Rev. Andrew Jukes, of England; and they have been made so great a blessing to my own spiritual life, that I long to have others share them with me.

There may be very honest doubts as to the correctness of interpreting the Old Testament in this typical way, and I would not contend with these. But I have found in my own heart, and in the hearts of many others, a certain spiritual sense which has led us instinctively to accept and enjoy this application of the Old Testament Scriptures, and it is to such I speak in this book.

Nor are we without large warrant in the New Testament for this typical or symbolical interpretation, as in many instances the inspired writers there, make just such an application of the Old Testament narratives. See Gal. iv. 22–31: Heb. v.; vii.; ix.; x., &c. And notice especially the positive declaration made in 1 Cor. x. 1–11 concerning the story of the children of Israel: "Now all these things were our types;" and again, "Now all these things happened unto them for types." Our text reads "examples" or "ensamples," but the true rendering is "figures" or "types," as can be seen by a reference to the original, or to the margins of our reference Bibles.

I feel, therefore, that we are justified in seeking for this mystic sense in that, which might otherwise be of but little value to us spiritually. And I send forth these Readings to those who can receive them, with a heart-felt prayer that the Lord may use them to His glory.

H. W. S.

CONTENTS.

CONTENTS.

CHAPTER XII.

BIBLE READINGS.

---•---

INTRODUCTORY.

CHAPTER I.

IN the very beginning of my Christian life, I remember being much struck with the remark that the Bible revealed itself only to the need and the faith of those who came to it. Wondering just what this could mean, I began to read my Bible, and soon found that it was really true; that just as a science never reveals its secrets except to its students, so neither does the Bible. And I discovered that the only really necessary things for the understanding of it, were the felt need of its teachings and a childlike faith to receive them. I feel sure that any Christian who will come to its study with a believing heart, will grow in its knowledge far faster than with any amount of mere critical study. And no matter how little talent we may have, nor how small may be our capacity of critical research, we can all possess these two absolutely necessary requisites of need and faith, and may all expect, therefore, to have in time its deepest secrets revealed to our prayerful search.

The following series of Bible lessons is the result of this sort of experimental study. They do not undertake to be critical nor exhaustive in any sense whatever. What I wanted in my own studies was to get at the inner life of the Bible, and to see what secrets it would reveal to my soul. And these lessons are simply the supplies which I have gathered out of this inexhaustible storehouse, for my own pressing and especial personal needs. Doubtless many others have gathered far richer supplies; but perhaps those which have been so unspeakably precious to my own soul, and so wonderfully suited to my needs, may be found also to meet the needs of some others. I have no desire to insist upon my own views to the exclusion of any others. I may have made many mistakes, and may have left out very important links. I am sure many others know far more about this precious Bible than I do. But I will give to my readers the best I have, and trust to their charity to cover the multitude of faults which, no doubt, will be very patent to any who look for them.

In coming to the study of the Bible, the first and most important point of all to be settled is as to the position we are to assume toward it. Do we come as students, or as critics? If the former, then we may confidently expect, as I have said, that all its wonderful treasures of wisdom and knowledge will be one after another unfolded to our gaze. If the latter, then we shall most certainly find it a sealed book, hiding its secrets in unfathomable mysteries. When God speaks, man has nothing to do but to believe and to submit. The grand question then is, Has God spoken, and is this book really His revelation to us?

For the readers of these pages it is not necessary to go into an argument to answer this question. It has to them, doubtless, been answered long ago. And if not, the answer must be found elsewhere, as I am writing from the stand-point of an absolute conviction that this Book is God's own Book, containing an authoritative and inspired record of His mind and His ways. We must come to it, then, with this one only thought, that He has spoken and that we must believe. Whether we understand it or not, is no matter; whether its revelations look reasonable or consistent, or even possible, is of no account. He has spoken, and we must believe what He says. We must receive it just as it is, and where we cannot understand, must set it down to our limited power of comprehension, and be content to wait until the eyes of our understanding are enlightened by the Divine Spirit, and we are made able to comprehend the "wondrous things out of His law."

I do not mean, however, to ignore or look down upon

the honest doubts of earnest seekers. I know too well experimentally what these are, not to know that they must be met with loving sympathy, rather than with scoldings or contemptuous condemnation. And if it will help any soul in this direction, I am quite willing to confess that the difficulties and questionings of the generation to which I belong have not left me unmolested, and that I know what it is to have been compelled to lift up the shield of faith against many an assault of doubt, that has seemed to come like an army to overwhelm me.

But I have never found argument to help me here. The devil can out-argue any human reasoner or human reasoning, and there is nothing I am sure that pleases him more than to engage an earnest soul in a debate of this kind, in which he is so likely to come off conqueror. Doubts, are to be overcome not by reasoning, but by faith. " I will believe ; I choose to believe," have been the weapons with which I have conquered in many a fierce battle. For the will has far more to do with our believing than most people think. The will is king in our nature, and what the will decides, all else must submit to and follow. And if we will put our will in this matter over on the believing side, and *choose* to believe, turning resolutely away from every suggestion of doubt, I know from experience that we cannot fail to get the victory in the end. This will sound unreasonable to human philosophy, but nevertheless it is a *fact*, and to me it is a fact that attests the divinity of the Bible more than anything else. For unless the Bible were a divine book, no effort of will in believing it, after once doubts had entered, would amount to anything at all. When once we have seen cause to doubt a friend, no effort of will to trust again will help us. In all human relations we must have proofs of trustworthiness before we can trust. And if the Bible were a human book, it would require human proofs of its authenticity and authority before it could be believed or rested on. But to believe God, requires no proofs and no reasonings, only a choice of the will. For when the will is thus put on His side, *He* takes possession of it by His Holy Spirit, and in a divine way which is an omnipotent way, independent of any proofs, He convinces the soul of the truth of that which it has thus chosen to believe.

It may seem like stepping off of a precipice into an apparently bottomless abyss. But it is safe to step, because God is there, and will receive us.

> " Nothing before, nothing behind :
> The steps of faith
> Fall on the seeming void, and find
> The rocks beneath."

Such steps would be fatal indeed, if taken where no rocks were. But because God IS, and is in His truth, there is no risk. He that will do His will, by thus obeying His command to believe His word, SHALL sooner or later know of the doctrine, whether it be of God or not. I am as sure of this as of my own existence.

But perhaps some one may refer to I Cor. xii. 3, "No

man can say that Jesus is the Lord, but by the Holy
Ghost," as a proof against this.   In answer, I would refer to the case of the man with the withered hand.   The
Lord Jesus told him to stretch it out.   But without divine power, he could not.   He did not, however, make
this a reason for not doing it, but obeyed the Lord, and,
as he obeyed, the power was given.   He did not have to
wait for the power, the power was waiting for him.   And
so the blessed Holy Ghost is always waiting for us.   He
is given as a help, not as a hindrance.   He is always
ready, and the moment we put forth our will to obey
God's command, He is at once there to make it possible
for us to obey.

In Romans i. 17, there occurs a sentence concerning
God, which may perhaps explain my thought.   It is said
that " He calleth those things which be not as though they
were."   And it means that by this very calling, the
things which were not, came into being.   As we read
elsewhere, " He spake and it was done ; He commanded
and it stood fast."   Being God, He could thus by His
creative word say, "Let there be," and straightway
there was.   And since He is God, we can also—in obedience to His command, call those things which be not
as though they were, because His creative power is
pledged to bring them into being, and is able to do it.
If we therefore will but put ourselves in the line of His
command and say, " I will believe, I *choose* to believe,"
He will create the faith of which He has thus said, " Let
it be," and we shall find ourselves actually believing.

To me this is practical, because I have tried it and proved it to be so in my own case, in many a stress of doubt.

But believing does not always mean understanding, nor does it mean seeing the whole of the thing believed. There are many true believers of the Bible, whose faith is each one equal in strength to the others, and yet whose seeing capacity is so different, that it hardly seems like the same book to one as it does to the other. And from this cause arises, I think, most of the difficulties caused by the great differences of opinion as to Bible truth among honest believers.

A moment's reflection will convince us that in our different understandings of God's Book, we are all like people climbing up a high mountain to see the view, and whose views would of course differ according to the different degrees of height to which we might each have reached. The man at the foot of the mountain, who had just begun to climb, would have a very limited view ; true as far as it went, but hedged in on all sides by the surrounding obstructions in the shape of forests, bits of rising ground, clumps of bushes, a high piece of rock, or even a turn in the river or the road. And unless his knowledge were greater than his view, he would call the river a lake without any outlet, and declare that the road ended at that turn, and say there were no fields or hills beyond those boundary lines. But as he climbed higher his view would become more and more extended. Soon he would see the country beyond, and the distant windings of the river or road, and the dividing lines, so strongly marked at the foot of the mountain, would gradually flatten into the surrounding landscape, until they would be almost lost to sight in the wideness and the grandeur of the extended plain spread out before the climber's vision. And so on and on, as the mountain was climbed, stretch after stretch of the landscape would unfold to his wondering gaze, until finally, when he reached the top, he would see as far as human eyesight could reach, over hill, and valley, and forest, and river, one grand sweep of land, and water, and sky, a view limited only by his own powers of vision.

One can see at a glance how different is the view seen from the top of a mountain, to that seen from the mountain's foot, and can easily understand that should two gazers, looking from these two widely separated stand-points, undertake to compare "views," they would find that although they had been looking in precisely the same direction, and over the very same landscape, their descriptions of what they saw would widely differ.

And it is in this progressive way I believe, that we learn to understand God's truth. So that we can easily see how, even between honest and earnest students, there may be a great difference of "view," simply arising from the difference of stand-point from which we look. And this may well make us diffident about asserting that our view is the only true or complete one, or from feeling that those who do not see just what we see, are not looking at the landscape at all. Let us rejoice in what *we* see, but rejoice also in what our brother sees, and be ready to listen to him, lest perchance he may be higher up than we, and may have things to tell us which we greatly need to know.

Let us come then to our study of the Bible in a spirit of childlike and receptive faith, asking to have the eyes of our understanding opened that we may behold wondrous things out of God's law. And then it may be given us to be indeed among the see-ers of truth, who see for other men, and whom men therefore call their " seers."

I desire to have it thoroughly understood that in all I may say in this book I am only giving my " views ;" that which I can see from the stand-point I occupy. If others see differently, I am quite prepared to admit that their stand-point may be higher and their view more extended, and will not contend with them on account of it. I can only give to my readers that which I have, and I trust that the view which has helped me, may help also some others whose needs may be like mine.

———————

There are many different ways of studying the Bible which are very interesting and valuable, but perhaps the one which has interested me the most has been to take it up book by book, as though each book were only a chapter of the one Book. We have been too much accustomed I think to look upon the Bible as merely a collection of books by different authors, thrown together promiscuously under one cover. Whereas it really is one continuous Book, written by one Author, with a reg-

2

ular beginning and middle and ending, and a progressive development of truth all through from beginning
to end. That the several chapters of this book were
written by different penmen offers no difficulty to this
view, for while the men were many, the God who inspired them was One, and He merely used them as His
instruments to record, not their mind, but His own. Our
Bible is to us as really God's book as though He had
written it with His own hand in heaven, and handed it
down to us. And as Gaussen so truly says in his book
on Inspiration, " Whether the writers recite the mysteries of a past more ancient than the creation, or those
of a future more remote than the coming again of the
Son of man, or the eternal counsels of the Most High,
or the secrets of men's hearts, or the deep things of God ;
whether they describe their own emotions, or relate
what they remember, or repeat contemporary narratives,
or copy over genealogies, or make extracts from unin-
spired documents,—their writing is inspired, their narratives are directed from above. It is always God who
speaks, who relates, who ordains or reveals by their
mouth, and who, in order to this, employs their per-
sonality in different measures, for the ' Spirit of God has
been upon them,' it is written, and His word has been
upon their tongue."

We may therefore reasonably conclude that there is
no chance in the arrangement of the contents of this
Divine book, but that the Divine Author had a regular
plan in its arrangement, and has developed the truth to

us in its pages in a regularly progressive order, beginning with the birth of all things in Genesis, and ending with the final consummation of all things in Revelation. And although we may not see this plan because of our ignorance and blindness, we must none the less believe that it is there, and that as we grow in knowledge, we shall more and more be able to discover and comprehend it.

The objection may be made to this, that the order and arrangement of the books of the Bible was settled by a council of men. But this does not reach the case at all, for the Divine Author of the book was living when this council met; and we cannot for a moment suppose that He, any more than any other author, would have left His Book to chance, or failed Himself to see that it was all arranged according to His own mind and will.

We may confidently expect, therefore, to see unrolling out before our careful study a wonderful plan of progressive development of truth in our wonderful Book, and to find each succeeding step linked on to the ones behind it and before it, in a way that will give us a far wider grasp of Divine truth, than any piecemeal study of the Bible could ever do, valuable and delightful as that is.

And, first, there seem to be three great epochs developed in the Bible: that of childhood, that of youth, and that of manhood. The childhood of our race is represented by the patriarchal period, when, as it were, the race was in leading-strings. They did not know much

about law, but were like children in the nursery, guided
by their parents. Then comes the period of youth, represented by the Jewish nation—aware of law, struggling
against it, trying to keep it, and continually failing. And
last of all comes the period of manhood, represented
by the history of the Church, when the soul rejoices in
the law, and finds a power to keep it; when law is
obeyed, not because of its penalties, but because it is
recognized as being the best and highest good.

This much as to the grand outlines of the Bible. We
will next consider it more in detail; and I think we
shall find that each separate book takes us forward a
definite step from the one before it, and links itself to
the one beyond, and that each book has, as it were, one
central thought or idea running through the whole of it,
which is developed in this one book in a way it is in
no other. I mean that just as the chapters in any book
on science take up, one after another, separate and progressive steps or aspects of that science, while all are
linked closely together, so it is here; and also that each
book might have a heading, as we have to chapters in
any other book, giving us in a few words its central
idea.

The book of Genesis and the book of Revelation, the
beginning and the end of God's record, present us with
many strange likenesses and yet contrasts. They both
treat of the same subjects; but, while one gives us these
things in their beginnings and their failure, the other
gives them to us in their wonderful consummation and

eternal triumph. As, in a logical discourse or a carefully-prepared book, the author will, at the beginning, state his subjects, and then at the end will come back to the same statements with all the added light that has been thrown upon them by the progressive developments between; so, in this book, we come back in Revelation to the things spoken of in Genesis, only with all the added light and development that the intervening chapters of the book have progressively revealed.

We open the book on a garden in Genesis (ii. 8), and close it on a city in Revelation (xxi. 9, 10). We see the garden a home for one man, we find the city has become a home for nations. Rev. xxi. 24.

In Genesis we read of the creation of the sun and moon to give light to the world (i. 16, 17); in Revelation we read, "And the city had no need of the sun, neither of the moon, to shine in it; for the glory of God did lighten it, and the Lamb is the light thereof" (xxi. 23).

In Genesis we read, "In the beginning God created the heaven and the earth" (i. 1); in Revelation, "And I saw a new heaven and a new earth, for the first heaven and the first earth were passed away" (xxi. 1).

In Genesis we are told that "the gathering together of the waters called He seas" (i. 10); in Revelation we read, "And there was no more sea" (xxi. 1).

In Genesis the curse was pronounced (iii. 17); in Revelation we are told, "And there shall be no more curse" (xxii. 3).

In Genesis sorrow, and suffering, and death are intro-

2*

duced (iii. 16-19); in Revelation we read, "And God shall wipe away all tears from their eyes, and there shall be no more death, neither sorrow nor crying, neither shall there be any more pain; for the former things are passed away" (xxi. 4).

In Genesis man was driven away from the tree of life: "So He drove out the man; and he placed at the east of the garden of Eden cherubims and a flaming sword which turned every way to keep the way of the tree of life" (iii. 24); in Revelation nations are welcomed back to this tree: "In the midst of the street of it, and on either side of the river, was there the tree of life, which bare twelve manner of fruits, and yielded her fruit every month; and the leaves of the tree were for the healing of the nations" (xxii. 2).

In Genesis we have the marriage of the first Adam and his bride (ii. 18, 21, 22, 23); in Revelation we have the marriage of the second Adam and His bride: "Let us be glad and rejoice, and give honor to Him; for the marriage of the Lamb is come, and His wife hath made herself ready" (xix. 7).

In Genesis Satan, "that old serpent," makes his first appearance (iii. 1); in Revelation he meets with his final doom (xx. 1, 2, 7, 10).

We see, therefore, how closely linked together, even in their contrasts, are the beginning and the end of the Bible. And we cannot but conclude from this, that between these two there must lie a regular and progressive plan which shall lead us surely, and by very definite steps, from one to the other.

CHAPTER II.

THE Old Testament seems to me something like a great picture-gallery hung with numberless pictures of divine truth. In some countries it used to be the custom for the women of the king's household to work in tapestry all the events of that king's reign, and hang them on the walls of his palace, so that every visitor, in walking through the galleries and rooms of the palace, could read from these tapestry-pictures one story after another celebrating the praises of the king. And just so, in the Old Testament, we have hung up for us a wonderful series of pictures, progressively developing divine truth. The doctrines of our faith are taught us later on in our Book; but the typical pictures of these doctrines are given to us in the early part of it, and we can only, I think, get a clear insight into the doctrines, in proportion as we study them in the light of these pictures. I believe there is not a truth revealed in the New Testament that has not its corresponding picture in the Old.

19

We will first take a rapid *resumé* of the names and order of these pictures, and then consider them more in detail.

Genesis.—The outcome of Adam, or Man, and what he is by nature. This book gives us the development of human nature under many varied circumstances, and shows how man as man, without divine help, fails under all. It is a picture of the first lesson that every soul needs to learn, and that is, the utter failure of man as he is by nature, let his circumstances or his efforts be what they may. It opens with man in the garden of Eden, and leaves him a slave in the land of Egypt Its New Testament counterpart is to be found in Rom. i. ii. and iii. 1–20.

Exodus.—Redemption and its consequences. This book finds the people in hopeless bondage, from which they had no power whatever to deliver themselves, and shows us the redemption that God accomplishes for such, by His own outstretched arm of power. It answers to the experience of conversion, or the entrance into the Christian life. Its counterpart is Romans iii. 23–31, and iv. v. and vi.

Leviticus.—The worship and communion of a redeemed people. In Leviticus we see God dwelling in the midst of His people, and making known His mind to them. It fulfils in type the words of our Lord in John xvi. 13, " Howbeit when He, the Spirit of truth is come, He will guide you into all truth." Its counterpart is Ephesians ii. 13–18, and Hebrews x. 19–22.

Numbers.—The wilderness-wandering of the redeemed, or the failure to go in and possess the land
of promise.   It answers to the experience of a Christian
who knows he is redeemed out of the land of Egypt or
the world, but who has failed to go in and take possession of the rich fullness that he sees stored up for him in
Christ.   The seventh chapter of Romans is, I think, the
New Testament counterpart of this book.

Deuteronomy.—Practical obedience, or the Consecration of those who are redeemed.   It is a second giving
of the law and a second cleansing, answering to the experience of the soul of the believer at a certain stage,
when he longs to know the power of the resurrection,
and to enter into possession of the promises.   The rules
and precepts, if this is to be done, are here given.   The
New Testament key note to this book is to be found in
Rom. xii. 1, 2; 2 Cor. vii. 1, and similar passages.

Joshua.—The redeemed in heavenly places, or the
believer entering into possession of the promises, and
realizing the victory of faith. God's people in this book
come out of the wilderness, and enter at last into possession of the land which He had promised them ; the
land from which they had been turned back forty years
before by their unbelief.   It is a picture of the believer
seated in heavenly places in Christ ; and answers to the
Epistle to the Ephesians, Rom. viii. and similar passages.

Judges.—The failure of the redeemed in heavenly
places, or the dangers which arise even in advanced

stages or Christian experience. Its counterpart is to be found in such texts as 1 Cor. iii. 1–4; Hebrews v. 12–14.

Ruth.—The union of Christ and the Church. A Gentile bride was here redeemed by her Jewish kinsman from the one who by nature had a right to possess her, and was purchased to be his wife; even as "Christ also loved the Church, and gave Himself for it." The counterpart of this little book is to be found, I think, in Ephesians v. 22–32.

The next six books of *Samuel, Kings and Chronicles*, are all really only different chapters of one book. They contain the story of the kingdom, and I would suggest that their title might be, "The Kingdom of Heaven on Earth." They are typical of that "kingdom" which exists now upon this earth, outwardly in the Church in all its branches, and inwardly in the heart of every child of God. Luke xvii 20, 21, is the key-note to these books.

Ezra and Nehemiah.—Individual faithfulness in a time of general unfaithfulness. A faithful remnant go up out of captivity to rebuild the temple and the walls of the city. The doctrinal counterpart to these books is to be found in 2 Corinthians vi. 14–18.

Esther.—God's providential care over the redeemed, even though they may be in captivity, and He may be hidden from their sight. They forget Him, but He remembers them, and cares for them. It illustrates the truth of that promise so often made by the Lord to His people, "I will never leave thee nor forsake thee."

With these books we close the historical series of pic-

tures in the Old Testament. The five books which follow—Job, Psalms, Proverbs, Ecclesiastes and Canticles,
give us, I think, the progressive development of the
heart exercises of the believer, as to sanctification.

Job.—The death of self. A righteous man is here
brought through the refining processes of God's chastening, in order to bring him to an end of the self-life, and
to prepare him for a revelation of the Lord to his soul.
It answers to Heb. xii. 5–11. It is a picture of the Lord's
dealings with a self-righteous Christian, for the purpose
of emptying him of self, that he might be filled with all
the fullness of God.

Psalms.—The life hid with Christ in God. The soul
that has been brought to the end of self in Job, is here
seen walking in "newness of life." The man who
speaks here is the man of faith, and the life revealed is
the life of trust. In Job it was all, I, me, my ; here it is
all, Thou, Thee, Thy. The Book of Psalms has sometimes been looked upon as a sort of diary kept as it were
by our Lord, for Himself and His people, in which are revealed to us the deep inward emotions of His heart, under the varied aspects of His life as the Divine Man ;
and also the feelings proper to those in whom He dwells.

Proverbs.—The submission of the sanctified heart to
the teachings and leadings of Divine Wisdom. It is our
Father teaching His children how to walk safely and
wisely through this world of sin and danger. Its New
Testament key note is James i. 5, 6.

Ecclesiastes teaches us the vanity of all earthly things

to satisfy the sanctified heart. "Vanity of vanities, saith the Preacher, vanity of vanities; all is vanity." It is the record of the solemn conviction of a soul which has been taught by Divine wisdom, and has found that the world, even at its best and brightest, is only vanity and vexation of spirit. "He that drinketh of this water shall thirst again."

The *Song of Solomon* is in wonderful contrast to the Book of Ecclesiastes. There the world is searched in vain for an object to satisfy the sanctified heart. Here the Object is found, and the heart has entered into the enjoyment of it. It is the Old Testament typical expression of the truth in Ephesians v. 23–33, of the wondrous union between Christ and the Church, which is set forth here. "He that drinketh of this water shall never thirst."

Out of all that Solomon wrote and said, only these three books—Proverbs, Ecclesiastes, and Canticles—are given us. I feel sure therefore that they are full of a far deeper wisdom than the church has yet appreciated. Some students of Scripture have thought that these three Books of Solomon's show us the three stages in the path of wisdom. The first being the *purifying* stage given us in Proverbs, where we are taught practical righteousness. The second being the *illuminating* stage, given us in Ecclesiastes where the eyes are opened to see the world as it is, and its hollow vanity is discovered to us. And the third being the *uniting* stage, given us in Canticles, where the prepared soul is joined to its Beloved in an everlasting covenant of life and peace.

Concerning this progressive development of truth in the Books of the Bible, A. Jukes says, " The form of the Word, and the wisdom of its form, is a subject which yet waits to receive that attention which is its just due. Four gospels have forced some to notice the distinct purpose of God in each gospel.   But for the rest of scripture, why its form is what it is,—why like a man, and with man, it grew from age to age—why it looks and is so human,—what connection all this has with the mystery of the Holy Incarnation,—these are questions seldom asked . . . .   But I would here notice one fact, namely, that the Word is given to us in many books or sections, each of which, I am assured is a divine chapter, with one special end, illustrating something in God and man, or the details of some relation between the Creator and the creature. . . . .   Each book has its own end, and the order and contents of all, as they describe the progressive ways of God with man, answer to His ways in every soul, for within and without His ways are one, and His works the same from age to age."

THE PROPHETS.

We come now to a distinct part of God's Book, which seems to me to be to the Old Testament what the book of Revelation is to the New.   Like that, it is a prophecy of the glorious consummation of God's purposes for His people, revealing the future glory and blessing reserved for them.   Each prophet has, I doubt not, a special part of truth to reveal, but I do not feel competent to speak

3

of these. The meanings of their names may perhaps suggest something to the thoughtful reader: Isaiah, salvation of God; Jeremiah, he who exalts or gives glory to God; Ezekiel, the strength of God; Daniel, the judgment of God; Hosea, salvation of God; Joel, he that commands; Amos, strong to bear; Obadiah, servant of the Lord; Jonah, he that oppresses; Micah, poor and humble; Nahum, a comforter; Habakkuk, he that embraces; Zephaniah, the secret of the Lord; Haggai, a solemn feast; Zechariah, memory of the Lord; Malachi, messenger of the Lord.

It is enough for our purposes to understand the general teaching of these wonderful prophecies. They refer mostly to the glorious time of Christ's second coming, when He shall appear to set up His kingdom of righteousness and peace upon earth, and "the Lord of hosts shall reign in Mount Zion and in Jerusalem, and before His ancients gloriously." At that time, which is called significantly "the day of the Lord," as though all were night until then, great and wonderful blessings are promised to the children of Israel, which are, I feel sure, to be literally and gloriously fulfilled to them in this world, in their triumphant return to their own land, and their restoration to righteousness and true holiness before the Lord. The church has been too much inclined I think to monopolize these glorious prophecies to herself, and to give them only a spiritual application. But if the blessings belong to us, then the curses must also, for it is plainly the people who had been cursed

that are to be blessed : and it seems strange that such
an unwarrantable separation could ever have been
made, as to give all the curses to the Jews, and to appropriate all the blessings to the church. I shall never forget the indignation with which a converted Jew once
called my attention to this ; and I think it is very plain
that God's chosen people have a glorious future in store
for them on this very earth, which has been the scene of
their bitter failure and downfall.

I believe, however, that while the primary application
of these books is to the Jew, they have a very blessed
typical application to Christians ; and that we who now
by faith enter into God's spiritual kingdom, enter also
into possession of spiritual blessings that correspond
very wonderfully to the temporal ones here set forth.
There is a rest that yet remaineth for God's chosen people. But we which have believed may enter into that
rest now and here, and may antedate the outward millennium, by an inward millennial experience, that can
be described in no other language so well, as in that
which is used by these old prophets to foretell the future
glory of their own nation. The spiritual mind has
always realized this, and from this cause perhaps has
sprung the mistake of monopolizing to ourselves prophecies, which have so wonderfully expressed our soul's
deepest experiences, that it has seemed hard to believe
they could have been intended for anything else.

With these prophecies the Old Testament closes, and
the dispensation of law is ended. God's first covenant

with His people has utterly failed because of the weakness of their flesh, and when next we open the Book we
shall find that a new covenant has been introduced,
which God Himself says is a "better covenant established upon better promises." "For," He says, "if
that first covenant had been faultless, then should no
place have been sought for the second. For finding
fault with them He saith, Behold the days come, saith
the Lord, when I will make a new covenant with the
house of Israel and with the house of Judah : not according to the covenant that I made with their fathers
in the day when I took them by the hand to lead them
out of the land of Egypt; because they continued not in
my covenant, and I regarded them not, saith the Lord."
. . . . "In that He saith, a new covenant, He hath
made the first old. Now that which decayeth and wax-
eth old is ready to vanish away."

The first covenant failed, not because of any weakness in itself or its provisions, for the "law was holy,
just and good." But its purposes could not be accomplished, "in that it was weak through the flesh," and
God therefore sent "His own Son in the likeness of sinful flesh and for sin," that He might "condemn sin in
the flesh," and might make it possible for the righteousness of the law to be fulfilled in us "who walk not
after the flesh, but after the Spirit."

The story of this new and better covenant will be
found in the New Testament. But before entering upon
its consideration, we will examine more in detail the lessons of the Old.

CHAPTER III.

MAN, AND WHAT HE IS BY NATURE.

Keynote: Rom. iii. 9-19.

IN the book of Genesis we have given to us, as I have suggested, the outcome of Adam, or man as he is by nature. We see here the development of human nature in many different forms of life, and its continual failure. This book gives us in type the first great lesson that every soul has to learn, and that is the lesson of its own helplessness. It shows us man tried under many different circumstances, and failing in every one, until finally the sad but sure transition is made from the garden of Eden into the bondage in Egypt

Not that there are no individual examples of faithfulness and its reward, given us in this book, but the story of man as man developed here, is one of repeated and most grievous failure. It has always seemed to me to be a very vivid picture of the experience of the awakened soul, seeking to make itself what it ought to be by continually repeated efforts of its own, and ending at last by finding itself in apparently hopeless Egyptian bondage We all of us doubtless know something of this experimen tally. We know what it is to have set ourselves to the work of our own reformation, to have been cont·nually turning over a "new leaf" on our birth-days, or at New Year's time, thinking always that each renewed effort would surely be successful, and laying the blame of every failure on some fault in our circumstances or surroundings, believing that, if these were but more favorable, all would be easy and sure. And we remember well, some of us at least, the final and hopeless disappointment when we discovered, beyond a shadow of doubt, that we were utterly helpless, and then the joy that came, when in our helplessness we threw ourselves upon the mercy of God, and found in Christ the redemption our souls had so long sought for in vain.

Of all this the books of Genesis and Exodus form a wonderful picture

The story of man's first trial and its failure, is given us in Gen. i. ii. and iii. He was created by God in inno·cence and purity, and was placed in the garden of Eden under the most favorable possible circumstances; possessing a nature inclined towards righteousness, and with every surrounding that could help to establish him therein. And yet in spite of it all, he failed most grievously, breaking the one only law that God had given to control him. and making it necessary for his own good that he should be driven out from his home in the beautiful garden, lest he should eat of the tree of life and live on forever in the fallen and sinful condition to which he had brought himself. (iii. 22–24).

In this trial and failure the whole human race was involved, and all were taught the lesson, if they could but have learned it, that man as he is by nature must always fail, and that God alone can make him stand; and there-fore this very fall was the occasion of the display of God's infinite grace provided to meet it, for at once the promise is made of a Deliverer, who should deliver the very race, whose destiny He was to share. Had man fully learned here the lesson of his own helplessness, who can say that this Deliverer would not have came at once? But much was yet unlearned, and the human race had many sad experiences of failure to pass through, before the "fulness of time" could come, when He would be revealed.

Man's second trial was made outside the garden, when he was, as it were, left to himself, without law or restraint. He might perhaps have said of his first trial, "I failed because of that one law. Let me try now a life without law, and no doubt my righteousness will assert itself." But his failure this time was even worse than at first, so that we read vi. 5, 6, "And God saw that the wickedness of man was great on the earth, and that every imagination of the thoughts of his heart was only evil continually, and it repented the Lord, that He had made man on the earth, and it grieved Him at His heart." And the result was that He destroyed man from the face of the earth (vi. vii.), leaving alive only one family, whose head, Noah, was "a just man and perfect in his genera-tions," and who, it is said, "walked with God."

With this perfect man a third trial was made, upon a renewed earth, with all the evil surroundings and influ-ences removed. And lest man might say that his last failure had arisen from the absence of any law to restrain him, a law was now given against the one especial sin that had proved his latest ruin—the sin of violence. ix. 5, 6: "And surely your blood of your lives will I re-quire: at the hand of every beast will I require it: and at the hand of man, at the hand of every man's brother will I require the life of man. Whosoever sheddeth man's blood, by man shall his blood be shed: for in the image of God made he man."

Moreover, God established with him now a covenant of promise, which secured him from any fear of a future destruction, such as had just taken place; and the human race, as it were, turned over a new leaf, and made a fresh start. But the end of this trial, like that of all the others, was a grievous failure. Men conceived the idea of climbing up to Heaven by a tower of their own building, and God, to save them from a worse failure, was compelled to confound their language, and to scatter them abroad "upon the face of all the earth." xi. 1–9.

The call of Abraham came next. God chose a man out of these scattered nations, and called him to a walk of separation to Himself. xii. 1. "Now the Lord had said unto Abram, Get thee out of thy country, and from thy kindred, and from thy father's house unto a land that I will shew thee." It is as though man might have

said then, as many have said since, that it was hopeless
to expect him to be righteous, when in association with
his fellow-men, and that a life of separation was his only
chance; and God gave him that chance. He chose
one family and made them His peculiar people, separat-
ing them from all the nations round about them, and
causing them to dwell apart in tents, and to be
"strangers and pilgrims on the earth." But even under
these favored circumstances, human nature proved
itself to be the same, and disappointing failure was again
the end. God's peculiar people became hopeless
bondsmen in the land of His enemies, and the book
that began with man in the garden of Eden, ends with
man in Egyptian bondage.

Such to my mind is one of the chief lessons of the
book of Genesis—man's efforts and their inevitable
failure. And such is the experience, sooner or later, of
every human soul. We all have to learn this lesson
before we can come to the book of Redemption. The
natural thought of the heart of man invariably is, that
we can live up to our ideal, and make ourselves what
we ought to be, if only we try hard enough, or are placed
in sufficiently favorable circumstances. And we spend
months, and it may be years of our lives, in turning over
new leaves, and making fresh starts, thinking each time
that we have now at last found the secret of success,
and attributing our failures, not to any fault in ourselves,
but always to the faults in our circumstances and surroundings. Until at last, after countless failures, we dis-

cover the secret of our own helplessness, and see that we
are in truth bound hand and foot in a hopeless bondage ;
and then to us, as to Israel, comes the glad story of
God's redemption, and our Exodus from Egypt takes
place.

The New Testament doctrinal counterpart to this
book is to be found, I think, in Romans i., ii. and iii. 1–20,
where man's hopeless and undone condition by nature
is declared to us, summed up with a description of our
bondage in these words, "that every mouth may be
stopped, and all the world may become guilty before
God." This must be known before redemption can be
declared. "They that are whole need not a physician, but
they that are sick;" and the Lord Jesus came not to call
"the righteous but sinners to repentance." It is only the
sinner that stands in the Saviour's path. It is the lost
sheep whom the shepherd goes out to seek. It is in our
weakness alone that His strength can be made perfect.

Dear readers, have you learned this lesson? Have
you gone through the sad experience of this book, and
are you ready to embrace with joy the story of God's
redemption which will be next unfolded to you? Or
are you still dwelling in the picture I have tried to draw,
seeking to effect your own redemption by your efforts
and resolutions, and fondly hoping to turn over at last
the final new leaf which shall contain nothing but a
record of righteousness? Are you in short trying to save
yourselves, or are you letting Christ save you? Only
your own hearts can answer these questions, and I pray

for your souls' sakes, that they may be honestly and speedily answered.

Throughout the story of general failure given us in this book, are mingled, however, as always in God's records, most blessed instances of individual faithfulness, which show us in beautiful pictures, the Divine ways with souls that really trust Him, and follow Him whithersoever He leadeth. In the stories of Abraham, Isaac, Jacob and Joseph, we have given to us, I think, different aspects of the Christian life. Abraham shows us the life of faith; Isaac the life of sonship and liberty; Jacob the life of legal service and bondage; and Joseph the resurrection life of victory.

Abraham's life is a wonderful illustration of the text, "The just shall live by faith." So eminent was he in this, that he is called in the New Testament "the father of the faithful," and is cited continually as the sample and pattern of faith. "By faith Abraham, when he was called to go out into a place which he should after receive for an inheritance, obeyed; and he went out, not knowing whither he went. By faith he sojourned in the land of promise, as in a strange country, dwelling in tabernacles with Isaac and Jacob, the heirs with him of the same promise. For he looked for a city which hath foundations, whose builder and maker is God. * * * By faith Abraham, when he was tried, offered up Isaac: and he that had received the promises offered up his only-begotten son, of whom it was said, That in Isaac shall thy seed be called: Accounting that God was able to raise him up, even from the dead; from whence also he received him in a figure.'' Heb. xi. 8, 9, 10, 17, 18, 19.

Isaac's life as the son and heir of his father, pictures before us the Christian's life as the son and heir of God. '' Wherefore thou art no more a servant, but a son: and if a son then an heir of God through Christ.'' Of Isaac we read that his father gave unto him '' all that he had.'' Gen. xxiv. 36. And of our portion as children of God, we are told that our Father '' hath blessed us with all spiritual blessings in heavenly places in Christ;'' and that all things are ours, for we are Christ's, and Christ is God's. The birth of Isaac was by promise, and his life throughout was a life of happy ease in his father's house, without care and without responsibility, his ways all marked out for him, and all things provided. He took no thought for the morrow, for his father took thought for him. He needed to carry no cares, for his father carried them. He had but to '' lift up his eyes '' and see, and behold all that he needed was brought to him by the arrangements of his father's love, Gen. xxi. 63–67. And so we, if we take our rightful place as children in the house of our Father, may '' go in and out '' in the happy freedom of childhood, '' careful for nothing,'' because our Father cares for us, with all our steps directed, and our paths marked out, and all our wants provided for. Our souls shall then truly '' dwell at ease,'' and we shall know what it is to be '' followers of God as dear children,'' with the unquestioning obedience and simple faith of childhood. And then, and not until then, can we understand the depth of meaning in our Lord's words, when the question was asked of Him, " Who is the greatest in the kingdom of Heaven ?" and He answered by calling a little child and setting him in the midst of them, and saying, " Verily, I say unto you, Except ye be converted, and become as little children, ye shall not enter into the kingdom of Heaven. Whosoever therefore shall humble himself as this little child, the same is greatest in the kingdom of Heaven." Matt. xviii. 1-4.

Jacob is a type of the life of legal service and bondage. He illustrates, I think, the error against which we are warned in the Epistle to the Galatians, of seeking to gain by our own works that which is freely promised us in Christ. Jacob *managed* in order to obtain the blessing which God's promise had secured to him. (Comp. Gen. xxv. 23 with xxvii.) The result was exile from his father's house, (xvii. 43), and a life of hard service in a distant country. The position of a son was exchanged for the position of a servant, and bondage took the place of liberty. I do not mean that Jacob ceased to be a son, only that he lost the son's place and privileges in the father's house, and, though still a son, was obliged to work for himself as a servant in the house of a stranger. The blessings which came to Isaac as the gifts of his father's love, came to Jacob as the results of his own wearisome labor. Isaac had but to lift up his eyes and see, and behold his wife came to him, provided by his father's care, while Jacob worked

4

seven years for his wife, and even then received her sister in her stead, and was obliged to work seven other years in order to win her at last. Gen. xxix. 16–28. Isaac's flocks and herds, and silver and gold, and men-servants, and maid-servants, and camels and asses, came to him as the heir of his father, while Jacob says of his possessions, "This twenty years have I been with thee: thy ewes and thy she-goats have not cast their young, and the rams of thy flock have I not eaten. That which was torn of beasts I brought not unto thee; I bare the loss of it; of my hand didst thou require it, whether stolen by day, or stolen by night. Thus I was: in the day the drought consumed me, and the frost by night; and my sleep departed from mine eyes. Thus have I been twenty years in thy house: I served thee fourteen years for thy two daughters, and six years for thy cattle: and thou hast changed my wages ten times." Gen. xxxi. 38–41.

Throughout Jacob's whole life management took the place of trust, as it does in the life of many a Christian, and yet he was forced to confess, as finally all such legal Christians will also be, that it was not his own labor that had brought him prosperity, but only that God had been with him and blessed him; for he said to Laban, after recounting all his wearisome years of toil, "Except the God of my father, the God of Abraham, and the fear of Isaac had been with me, surely thou hadst sent me away now empty." Gen. xxxi. 42. The lesson, however, does not seem to have been fully learned until that night on his homeward journey, when "there wrestled a man with him until the breaking of the day," and he was lamed, so that he could resist and manage no longer, but was forced to go halting upon his thigh all the rest of his life. And then, in his weakness, his name was at last changed from Jacob, a supplanter, to Israel, a prince of God, for said he, "as a prince hast thou power with God and with men, and hast prevailed." Gen. xxxii. 24-31. Jacob conquered at last by his weakness, and we too must learn that our victory can only come when God's "strength is made perfect" in our utter weakness.

Joseph's life is, I think, a type of the resurrection-life of the believer, that life which is set before us in Rom. vi. 4: "Therefore we are buried with him by baptism into death : that like as Christ was raised up from the dead by the glory of the Father, even so we also should walk in newness of life."

It is a life which, from the first, dreams of victory and rule over the things of time and sense, and which attains this rule through suffering. In a dream God revealed Joseph's future kingship to him, Gen. xxxvii. but his brethren did not believe it, and hated him for his pretensions. "Art thou greater than our father Jacob?" they asked ; and they said of him scornfully, "Behold this dreamer cometh !" Souls that live near to God can receive more of the heavenly mysteries than others, and for this they will be called "mystics," "dreamers," and not even their brethren can understand them.

But the time of Joseph's exaltation did not come at once. The road to it lay through the pit, and through slavery, and imprisonment in Egypt. Self must die before the soul can reign unhindered. We must lose our life in order to find it. Through emptying to fulness, through abasement to exaltation, is always God's order.

In his wonderful book on the Types of Genesis,* Jukes thus expresses it: "We ask the Lord that we may know the power of His resurrection and the fellowship of His sufferings. He draws us by His Spirit thus to pray. A dream of power over self and sin flits before our inward man. We think a few short stages will bring us to the end, that His love who has promised, will quickly give us the victory. Instead of this we discover fresh evil, and new forms of bondage. We seem to ourselves it may be, thrust into the pit or sold into hopeless slavery. We sink lower and lower. False accusations are made against us, and we know what it is to be 'reckoned with the transgressors;' and even to be called, 'Beelzebub,' with our Master. We are wronged, misrepresented, punished, cast out. Until at last our souls imprisoned, as it were, within walls of granite, are brought to the end of self, and the full deliverance comes. This discipline will be, I believe, both inward and outward. Our friends, as well as ourselves, will think that all is lost, and will leave us alone, perhaps, in our captivity. But could we hear the Lord

* "The Types of Genesis briefly considered as revealing the development of human nature," by Andrew Jukes. Longmans, Green & Co., London.

speak, He would tell us that all was well, that this discipline is really indispensable, and that these very trials are the chariots appointed by Him to carry our souls to the place of exaltation and triumph. And the believer that truly trusts, recognizes this, and saying continually to each thing, Thy will be done, reigns, as Joseph did, triumphant over every stage." See Gen. xxxix. 1–6, and 20–23.

Delayed for thirteen years, the dreamed-of exaltation came at last, (xli. 38–44), and Joseph became ruler over the land of Egypt. The soul that suffers shall also reign. The things of time and sense shall be put under our feet, and we shall walk conquerors through the very country, where before we have been slaves and prisoners.

Mere faith cannot do this. Joseph reigns where Abraham failed. Neither can the Spirit of Sonship alone accomplish this victory. Isaac was content to rest at home in the enjoyment of all the good things of his father's house. To Jacob, Egypt was only a place of wearisome toil and sorrowful exile. The resurrection-life alone can walk through the world a triumphant conqueror. It can be in it, as Jesus was, a royal King over all its allurements and all its temptations. It can be "more than conqueror" through Him, and can set its feet on the neck of its enemies.

Surely we know something of this. We have seen lives, lived it may be in the midst of the world's grandeur, or surrounded by its blackest sinfulness, that have been untouched by either, and have walked victoriously through all. We have wondered at it. Could we have read the inner history of such, sure I am that they would have told us that it had been by the way of inward death and of outward loss they had been brought, and that their path, like Joseph's, had been through emptying to fulness, and through abasement to exaltation.

Such are some of the lessons taught me out of this wonderful book, which has been justly called the "seed plot" of the Bible. Lessons of failure on the one hand, where nature reigns, and of grand success on the other, where God is permitted to be King. Teaching thus, even in its first chapter, the lesson of the whole Book, that we are nothing and Christ is all.

Dear reader, may I ask thee to pause here, and before thou shalt read another chapter, settle the question as to whether thou hast really learned this lesson. Because, until it is learned, no further progress of the soul is possible. We have started out together, I trust, to go through our blessed Book not only intellectually but experimentally also, and this is our first step, upon which all the rest depend. In God's pathway no one can walk but the weak and the helpless. Into His kingdom none can enter but the children and the foolish ones. His strength is made perfect always and only in our weakness.

And this means a real weakness, not a theoretical

one, and a real and actual foolishness and helplessness. It means, dear reader, that thou must so come to the end of thyself and of thy own resources, as not to know what to do next, nor where to turn. That thou must be in utter despair as to any possibility of helping thyself in any way whatever, and must come to the Lord as a poor, lost, undone sinner, with no claim upon His mercy but thy utter need.

And if in the past there has lurked in thy soul any secret thought or dream of making thyself good enough for God to save, give it all up now and forever, and out of thy hopeless slavery cry to Him, as we shall see Israel doing in our next chapter, and thy Exodus will come as speedily as did theirs.

Texts illustrating man's lost and undone condition by nature: Rom. iii. 9–19; with Ps. xiv. 1–4, and Ps. liii. 1–4; Rom. v. 12; viii. 7, 8; Is. liii. 6; Eph. ii. 1–3; John viii. 23, 41–44; Gal. iii. 22; Eph. ii. 11, 12; Jas. iv. 1–5; Eccl. vii. 20; 2 Chron. vi. 36; 1 John i. 8, 10; Jas. iii. 2; Prov. xx 9; Job. ix. 30, 31; Jer. ii. 22; Col. iii. 5–7.

CHAPTER IV.

REDEMPTION AND ITS CONSEQUENCES.

Keynote: Rom. iii. 21, 22.

REDEMPTION and its consequences, might be given as the typical title of this book. It tells us the story of God's way of redeeming His people, and the results that follow this redemption. Its New Testament doctrinal counterpart is to be found, I think, especially in Rom. iii. 21-31. Immediately following the declarations concerning our utterly lost and undone condition in the first part of Romans, to which I have referred as presenting a parallel to the book of Genesis, we are here made glad by the wondrous story of deliverance for these very lost ones, "through the redemption that is in Christ Jesus; whom God hath set forth to be a propitiation through faith in His blood, to declare His righteousness for the remission of sins that are past, through the forbearance of God; to declare I say, at this time, His righteousness, that He might be just, and the justifier of him which believeth in Jesus."

In the book of Genesis we have seen man passing, by a series of failures, out of the garden of Eden into the

44

land of Egypt, and we open upon him now in a condition of apparently hopeless bondage there. "And the Egyptians made the children of Israel serve with rigour. And they made their lives bitter with hard bondage, in mortar, and in brick, and in all manner of service in the field : all their service wherein they made them serve, was with rigour." Exodus i. 13, 14. The rigor of this bondage at last forced from the Israelites a cry for help. "And it came to pass in process of time, that the king of Egypt died: and the children of Israel sighed by reason of the bondage, and they cried; and their cry came up unto God, by reason of their bondage." Exodus ii. 23. And the Lord heard their cry and said, "I have surely seen the affliction of my people which are in Egypt, and have heard their cry by reason of their task-masters; for I know their sorrows ; and I am come down to deliver them out of the hand of the Egyptians, and to bring them out of that land, unto a good land, and a large, unto a land flowing with milk and honey." Exodus iii. 7, 8.

All this is a wonderful picture of the stages in our experience, by which we are brought to know the redemption that is in Christ Jesus. We seek first of all to redeem ourselves by our own efforts, and resolutions, and continual fresh starts, but our failures only grow worse and worse, until at last we find ourselves "sold under sin," in apparently hopeless bondage ; and then, when all hope in ourselves is gone, and our bondage has become very bitter to us, we cry unto the Lord, and

He hears and delivers us, and our Exodus is accomplished.

The way of our deliverance is wonderfully pictured in this story of the deliverance of the children of Israel. From beginning to end it was God's work, and not theirs. His right hand and His mighty power alone got the victory, and He brought them forth " with an outstretched arm, and with great terribleness, and with signs and wonders." Deut. xxvi. 8. They were helpless before the power of Pharaoh, their cruel master, just as we are helpless before the power of our master, Satan, who has bound us in a far worse slavery than theirs; and is even more determined than Pharaoh was, not to let us go. Their helplessness was their greatest claim. Like us, they did not merit redemption, but they needed it; and the Lord delivered them, not because they were worthy, but because He loved them. As we read in Deut. vii. 7, 8, "The Lord did not set his love upon you, nor choose you, because ye were more in number than any people; for ye were the fewest of all people; but because the Lord loved you, and because he would keep the oath which he had sworn unto your fathers, hath the Lord brought you out with a mighty hand, and redeemed you out of the house of bondmen, from the hand of Pharaoh, king of Egypt."

The especial points in their deliverance which contain the most teaching for us, seem to me to be found in Exodus xii. and xiv. The Lord had been dealing with their enslavers by showing " signs and wonders, great and sore upon Egypt, upon Pharaoh, and upon all his household," but as yet they had not been willing to let the children of Israel go. In chaper xi. 1, however, we read, "And the Lord said unto Moses, Yet will I bring one plague more upon Pharaoh and upon Egypt; afterwards he will let you go hence: when he shall let you go, he shall surely thrust you out hence altogether." This "one plague more," which was to prove so effectual, was the judgment of death upon all the first-born of Egypt. And from this judgment, the children of Israel were to be delivered by a ceremony, which has been accepted by the Church of all ages, as one of the clearest types of the work of Christ, given to us in the whole Bible. This type is described in chap. xii. 3, 5, 6, 7, 13: "Speak ye unto the congregation of Israel, saying, In the tenth day of this month they shall take to them every man a lamb, according to the house of their fathers, a lamb for an house." * * "Your lamb shall be without blemish, a male of the first year: ye shall take it out from the sheep or from the goats: And ye shall keep it up until the fourteenth day of the same month: and the whole assembly of the congregation of Israel shall kill it in the evening. And they shall take of the blood, and strike it on the two side-posts, and on the upper door-post of the houses, wherein they shall eat it." * * "And the blood shall be to you for a token upon the houses where you are: and when I see the blood, I will pass over you, and the plague shall not be upon you to destroy you, when I smite the land of Egypt."

The meaning of this ceremony, it seems to me, was simply this, that the lamb died in the place of the man, and that the sprinkled blood was to be a token of this fact to the destroying angel, that he might "pass over" that household. And in 1 Cor. v. 8, we are told that "Christ our Passover is sacrificed for us;" showing that He as the "Lamb of God" was slain in our place, and that His death delivers us from the judgment which has been pronounced against sin. The word to Israel was "When I see the blood I will pass over you," not when I see you, and your goodness, or your earnestness, or even your repentance, but when I see the blood. That is, their only claim lay in the merits of an offering slain for them, just as our only claim lays in the "one sacrifice" which was offered for us on the cross by our Lord Jesus Christ, "who through the eternal Spirit offered Himself without spot to God." Heb. ix. 14.

To my mind there is unspeakable comfort to be got out of the study of this type. First of all the offering was of God's arranging. He *wanted* to save the children of Israel. He was not an angry God needing reconciliation, but a loving God who longed to deliver His people, and who therefore Himself provided the way by which it could be accomplished. Just as we read in 2 Cor. v. 19, that "God was in Christ reconciling the world unto Himself, not imputing their trespasses unto them." Many people seem to look upon God as an angry Judge, whose wrath needs to be appeased, and who can only be satisfied with the blood of His Son.

But the real truth, as set forth here, and throughout the whole Bible, is, it seems to me, that God is a loving and just Creator, whose very justice towards His poor helpless creatures, has joined with His love to save us. As we read in 1 John iii. 16, "Hereby perceive we the love of God, because He laid down His life for us." And again, in John iii. 16, "For God so loved the world that He gave His only begotten Son, that whosoever believeth in Him should not perish, but have everlasting life." And again, in Rom. v. 8, "But God commendeth His love toward us, in that while we were yet sinners, Christ died for us." And again, 1 John iv. 9, "In this was manifested the love of God toward us, because that God sent His only begotten Son into the world, that we might live through Him." It would require a volume to quote all the passages where this blessed truth is set forth, and these will suffice. The fact is, God's justice and His love ought never to have been separated, for love always includes justice, and true justice cannot exist without love. And it is indeed true, if we only understood it, that, as Faber says, God's justice is a bed where we may lay our anxious hearts, and be at perfect rest.

If for a moment we will put ourselves in the place of a Creator, and realize the responsibilities of a Creator, I think we will be able better to comprehend this, and to understand the declaration in Rom. iii. 26, that God's very righteousness was declared, by the redemption He had provided in Christ, and that He was thus enabled

5

to be "just and the justifier of him which believeth in Jesus " Not just, and *yet* the justifier, as though the two were opposed, but just, and *therefore* the justifier, because the two go together. As we read in 1 John iv. 10, " Herein is love, not that we loved God, but that He loved us, and sent His Son to be the propitiation for our sins."

Another point in the type before us, that brings great comfort to my soul, is the fact of their perfect safety when in their blood-sprinkled houses. There were no " ifs " nor " buts," nor " trembling hopes," in the hearts of those Israelites, but perfect assurance of safety. " I will pass over you," was God's word, and they believed it, and were at peace. And to us His word is, expressed over and over again in a hundred different ways, that he that believeth " *hath* everlasting life;" he that believeth " *is* born of God;" he that believeth " shall not come into condemnation, but is passed from death unto life;" " he that believeth shall not perish, but shall have everlasting life." It is always the tenses of present possession and assured future possession that are used, and no hint of doubt is ever given. Let us then believe Him as simply as they did, and our assurance will be as undoubting as theirs.

This sprinkling of the blood was the first step in their deliverance. The second is given us in chap. xiv. where they crossed the Red Sea, and left behind them forever their " house of bondage." The manner of this crossing was very significant. Shut up in a narrow pass, between two high mountains, with the sea in front of them and their enemies behind, it is no wonder that they seemed to their enemies and to themselves to be "entangled in the wilderness," and that they reproached Moses for having led them there. "And they said unto Moses, Because there were no graves in Egypt, hast thou taken us away to die in the wilderness? wherefore hast thou dealt thus with us, to carry us forth out of Egypt? Is not this the word that we did tell thee in Egypt, saying, Let us alone, that we may serve the Egyptians? For it had been better for us to serve the Egyptians, than that we should die in the wilderness." Exodus xiv. 11, 12. But the reply of Moses reveals God's very purpose in this entanglement, that He might compel them, because of their utter helplessness, to leave all their deliverance to Him. "And Moses said unto the people, Fear ye not, stand still, and see the salvation of the Lord, which he will shew to you to-day: for the Egyptians whom ye have seen to-day, ye shall see them again no more forever. The Lord shall fight for you, and ye shall hold your peace." Exodus xiv. 13, 14. Man wants to do something to deliver himself, but God puts him where he cannot do anything, and then says, "Stand still" and see what I will do. To stand still and see, means for us, simply to believe in God's record of what He has done. I "see" an event in history which I believe on the authority of another, as really, and often far more understandingly, than if I had been actually present at the

time; and thus by faith we may "see" the path made
for us out of our "house of bondage," as plainly as
the Israelites saw the one made for them. And having
seen it, the word comes to us, as it did to them, xiv. 15.
"And the Lord said unto Moses, Wherefore criest thou
unto me? Speak to the children of Israel, that they go
forward." Now is not the time to pray, but to act.
I have made the path, now walk on it. Leave the
house of bondage, and go forward. Take the deliverance I have provided. Or in other words, I have put
away your sins by the sacrifice of Myself. You do not
need to ask me to do it, for it is done. Believe it,
and reckon yourselves to be free. The New Testament
doctrinal counterpart to this is to be found, I think,
especially in Rom. iv. and v., where the fact is brought
out and established beyond controversy, that our salvation is a free gift, given to us out of the boundless grace
of God, and not to be worked for, nor earned, nor purchased, but to be received and rejoiced in, as one always
receives and rejoices in the gifts of love. "For if by
one man's offence death reigned by one; much more"
not they which *do* anything, but "they which *receive*
abundance of grace, and of the gift of righteousness,
shall reign in life by one, Jesus Christ." Rom. v. 17.

In Exodus xv. 1–19, the song of deliverance is sung,
answering to the song of triumph sung by every redeemed soul, when the knowledge of its redemption first
dawns upon it. It will be found very interesting to compare this song of Moses with what I have sometimes

called the triumphal song of Paul in Rom. vi., where a grander deliverance is celebrated, and a more glorious victory anticipated. But I shall speak of this again.

The feeding with manna described in Exodus xvi. is typical of the soul of the believer feeding on Christ, as is plainly shown us in John vi. 31–35. Our food is Christ, and Christ only. Not our frames, nor feelings, nor experiences, but Christ. And to feed on Him, and not on them, requires that we should turn away from them wholly, and not dwell on them, nor examine them, nor even think about them, but that we should think always and only of Him, and see nothing but His work and His love.

The giving of the law comes next in chapters xix. to xxiii. And the place this occupies, following and not preceding redemption, is very significant to me. Man's thought always is, obedience first and redemption after-wards, but God's way is, first redemption and then obedience. First the tree, then its fruits. Obedience is in fact only possible where redemption has taken place. Israel in Egypt could not have kept God's law ; and the carnal mind, we are told, is "enmity against God, for it is not subject to the law of God, neither indeed can be. So then they that are in the flesh cannot please God." (Rom. viii. 7, 8). The first event in any life must always be the birth into that life. The child obeys the father's laws only after he is born into that father's family, and also just because he is so born. The slave can begin a life of liberty, only after he has been set free. And to

5*

demand from either child or slave, the fruits and development of their lives, before the life itself is given
would be folly indeed. Let us never then say to ourselves or to one another, " You cannot be redeemed
until you obey;" but let us say instead, " You must obey
and you can obey, because you are redeemed." I use
redemption here of course in the simple sense of being
translated out of the kingdom of Satan into the kingdom
of God's dear Son, and beginning the life in that kingdom; and not in the sense of the full salvation from sin
that is to follow. The redemption out of Egypt was only
the beginning of the full and grand salvation that
awaited the children of Israel further on. But that
which followed could not come until this was accomplished. And we cannot become followers of God as
dear children, until we have first been made " children
of God by faith in Christ Jesus."

I dwell particularly on this point, because I am sure
God's order is often missed here, and we put Sinai on
the wrong side of the Red Sea, and will not permit any
deliverance from Egypt, until the law is first given and
obeyed.

The latter part of the book of Exodus is occupied
with God's directions concerning the preparation of a
place where He might dwell in the midst of His people. Not content with redeeming them out of Egypt,
He desired also to take up His abode with them, and to
give them the unspeakable blessing of His manifested
presence in their midst. " Let them make me a sanc-

tuary" He said to Moses, "that I may dwell among them." God so loves His people and longs after them, that He even stands at their door and knocks, asking for admission. "Behold," He says, "I stand at the door and knock; if any man hear my voice, and open the door, I will come in to him, and will sup with him and he with me." And again He says, "If a man love Me, he will keep my words; and my Father will love him, and we will come unto him, and make our abode with him."

This tabernacle, and its furniture, and its service was, as we are told in Heb. ix., a "figure for the time then present," of a "greater and more perfect tabernacle, not made with hands," even the person and work of our Lord Jesus Christ, who was at once our sacrifice offered for us, our High Priest interceding for us, and the dwelling-place of God in the midst of a world of sin. It was also a type of the spiritual yet invisible temple, in which we worship, the "holy place" of God's presence and of His spiritual sanctuary. But I cannot here go into the details of these blessed types.

On the day that the tabernacle was finished and reared up, we read, Exodus xl. 34, 35: "Then a cloud covered the tent of the congregation, and the glory of the Lord filled the tabernacle. And Moses was not able to enter into the tent of the congregation, because the cloud abode thereon, and the glory of the Lord filled the tabernacle." This coming of the Lord's presence to fill the place prepared for Him by His people, is to me a very blessed type of the baptism of the Holy Ghost, promised by the Lord Jesus to every believer, given first on the day of Pentcost to the waiting disciples, whose hearts were prepared for His coming, and ready, I believe, to be given now to us and to our children, and to " all that are afar off, even as many as the Lord our God shall call." And I believe that to each one of us individually, the command comes now, as it did to the children of Israel then, to prepare a place for our Lord that He may dwell in our midst. And sure I am that many have responded to this call, and have known what it was on the day when the tabernacle of the heart has been made ready, to have the glory of the Lord so to fill the house of the Lord, as to leave no room for any other inmate. May we all learn so quickly the lessons of our book, as to be brought by rapid stages to its consummating glory, and know for ourselves this wondrous indwelling!

Texts illustrating Redemption and its consequences: Rom. iii. 21-26; v. 8, 10; viii. 1-4; 1 John iv. 9, 10; Acts xiii. 37, 38; John iii. 14-18; John xi. 49-52; Gal. i. 4; Eph. i. 3-7; ii. 4-10; Gal. iv. 4, 5; Heb. ii. 9-15; vii. 25; ix. 11-14; Heb. viii. 10-12; 1 Pet. i. 3-5, 18, 19; Eph. ii. 13-22; Col. i. 12-14; 1 Pet. ii. 24; Col. i. 20; Is. liii. 4-6; xliii. 25; Ps. ciii. 11, 12; Titus iii. 4-7, &c., &c.

CHAPTER V.

THE WORSHIP AND COMMUNION OF A REDEEMED PEOPLE.

Keynote: Eph. ii. 18–22.

THE book of Leviticus is a book of worship and communion. It gives us the results of God's presence in the midst of His people, and shows us the things that help and the things that hinder communion with Him.

It is a wonderful typical representation of the truths taught us in Eph. ii. 13, 18: "But now, in Christ Jesus, ye who sometime were afar off are made nigh by the blood of Christ." For through Him we both have access by one Spirit unto the Father." And again, in Heb. x. 19-22: "Having, therefore, brethren, boldness to enter into the holiest by the blood of Jesus, by a new and living way, which He hath consecrated for us, through the veil, that is to say, His flesh; and having a high-priest over the house of God; let us draw near with a true heart in full assurance of faith, having our hearts sprinkled from an evil conscience, and our bodies washed with pure water."

In Leviticus we see God dwelling in the midst of His

57

people and making known His mind to them. The
promise to them in Ex. xxv. 22 had been, "And there
will I meet with thee, and I will commune with thee from
above the mercy seat, from between the two cherubims
which are upon the ark of the testimony, of all things
which I will give thee in commandment unto the children of Israel." And here this promise is fulfilled.
Between thirty and forty times in this book is the expression used, "And the Lord spake, saying;" and the
whole book is simply a revelation of the Lord's mind and
thoughts to a people who had been brought into the
secret of His presence. It is an illustration of our Lord's
words in John xv. 15, "Henceforth I call you not servants, for the servant knoweth not what his lord doeth;
but I have called you friends; for all things that I have
heard of the Father, I have made known unto you."
Only to the heart where Christ dwells, can His secrets be
revealed, and to them alone can He show His covenant.

It is very important to notice that this book does not
tell how they were to be delivered from bondage, but
only how they were to live and worship after they were
delivered. Its very position, following Exodus instead
of preceding it, shows us plainly God's order in these
things. First redemption, then worship and communion.
Not worship and communion in order to be saved, but
because we have been saved. Many souls seek to reverse this order, and think if they could only know real
communion with God, then they could have some hope
that He would redeem them. They think this acceptable

worship would make them more fit to be redeemed, or would make Him more willing. Whereas the truth is that the knowledge of redemption must come first, before there can be any satisfying communion. The very object of our redemption is that we may worship and serve God. If we could have done it before we were redeemed, then there would have been no need of redemption. The word of Moses to Pharaoh was, "Thus saith the Lord God of Israel, Let my people go, that they may serve me." Pharaoh had no objection to their serving God, if only they would not go out of his land to do it; and he said, Exod. viii. 25, "Go ye, sacrifice to your God *in the land*."

If Satan can only keep us in his own land, slaves to himself, he cares very little what we do there, and is even well pleased that we should attend church, and say our prayers, and seek to serve God, as long as we will do it "in the land," thinking so to blind our eyes to our slavery, and make us more willing slaves.

But Moses answered, "It is not meet so to do." "We will go three days' journey into the wilderness, and sacrifice to the Lord our God as He shall command us." He knew that the true worship of the God of Israel was simply impossible in the land of Egypt. And the soul now, that understands God's truth, knows also that "except a man be born again, he cannot see" nor "enter into the kingdom of God." We must be translated out of the kingdom of Satan into the kingdom of God's dear Son, before we can serve the King of that kingdom, and above all before we can expect to be told His secrets.

But Satan's devices do not stop here. When Pharaoh found that he could not induce Moses to remain in the land, he gave up that point, saying, "I will let you go that ye may sacrifice to the Lord your God in the wilderness; only," he added, cunningly, "ye shall not go very far away." That is, when Satan sees that he cannot keep us in his kingdom, he next tries to persuade us that it is not necessary to go very far away, and that the world and the church need not be separated by any great distance after all. He knows well, as Pharaoh knew, that it is very easy to take captive those who dwell in the border land, and that it is just because they do not go very far away, that Christians suffer so much from his assaults.

The book of Leviticus, therefore, gives us, as I have said, the worship and communion of a redeemed people, a people in whose midst God was consciously present, revealing His mind, and teaching them His will. And many very deep lessons are taught here which can, I believe, only be understood aright by the soul in whom the Holy Spirit consciously dwells as Teacher and Guide.

The first revelation God gives is concerning the offerings, in chapters i. ii. iii. iv. v. vi. vii. There were five of them, the burnt-offering, the meat-offering, the peace-offering, the sin-offering, and the trespass-offering. These offerings were types of different aspects of the work of the Lord Jesus Christ, meeting the need of His people in their daily life and walk in His kingdom. Exodus gives us the blood of the Lamb redeeming God's

people out of Egypt. And this is the aspect in which it
must always first be known, before anything else can be
learned. But after redemption has been experienced,
we then have to learn that there is much more in Christ
for us, than merely deliverance from the guilt of sin.
And it is only in the wilderness, in separation from Egypt,
that Israel is taught all the value of the offerings. It is
Christ, as He is discerned by those who already know
they are redeemed ; Christ as the Priest, the Offerer, and
the Offering, meeting the believer's every need, who is
set forth here.

Each offering is believed to present some especial aspect of His work. The burnt-offering in Chap. i., which
was all burned on the altar, an offering made by fire of
a sweet savor, unto the Lord, i. 9, was a type of Christ
as He is described in Eph. v. 2, where we read that, " He
loved us, and gave Himself for us an offering and a sacrifice to God of a sweet-smelling savor." The *whole*
burnt-offering typified the entire surrender of self to God.
It was Christ offering Himself up with a complete consecration to accomplish the purposes of God's glory ; and
His perfect spotlessness and devotedness was a sweet-
smelling savor to God, something in which He could
take unclouded joy. It was " acceptable " to God, and
was accepted for the offerer, so that it might be said of
each one of us, that we are " accepted in the Beloved."

The meat-offering in Chap. ii. represents Christ in His
perfect humanity as He lived, and walked, and served
down here on earth, presenting His life to God as an of-

6

fering of a sweet savor, and giving Himself to man as
the food provided for those who are in God's service;
as we read, " And the remnant of the meat offering shall
be Aaron's and his sons;" ii. 3. This offering was
taken from the fruit of the earth, and was of the finest
wheat, ii. 1. Setting Him forth as real man, taking upon
Him our earthly nature, tempted in all points like as we
are, and, therefore, able to succor them that are tempted.
It is the type of that which is declared to us in Heb. ii.
14, " For as much as the children are partakers of flesh
and blood, He also himself likewise took part of the
same." And the picture is full of divinest comfort for us,
since we read, that, because He that sanctifieth and they
who are sanctified are all thus of one, He, therefore, for
this cause, "is not ashamed to call us brethren." Our
God, our Brother! Can human words convey a grander
or sweeter thought?

In the peace-offering, Chap. iii., the leading thought
is the communion of the worshipper, "And the flesh of
the sacrifice of his peace offerings for thanksgiving, shall
be eaten the same day that it is offered," Lev. vii. 15.
It was not here as in the burnt-offering, Christ enjoyed
exclusively by God, but the worshipper feasting upon
Christ in communion with God. The offering was shared
between the altar, the priest, and the offerer. That is,
the picture presented to us here is of the believer coming
to God to be filled with Christ, to have his thoughts occupied with Christ, and his mouth filled with His praises.
Many souls have *access* to God who do not have *commu-*

nion. They come full of themselves, and their own needs, and all they have to say is about their feelings, or their sins, or their trials. It is all self, self, self. But communion means to dwell upon and delight in that which God dwells upon and delights in. And this can never be anything in or about ourselves, but always and only things pertaining to His well-beloved Son.

Only the clean could partake of this offering, Lev. vii. 20, 21 ; and only the Christian whose heart is purified by faith can enter into this blessed communion. "If we walk in the light, as He is in the light, we have fellowship one with another; and the blood of Jesus Christ His Son, cleanseth us from all sin," 1 John i. 7. This is, I believe, the New Testament statement of the truth typified in the Peace-Offering.

The Sin-Offering, chapters iv. and v., was for "sins of ignorance," or involuntary sins. "If a soul sin and commit any of these things which are forbidden to be done by the commandments of the Lord ; though he wist it not, yet is he guilty, and shall bear his iniquity," v. 17. The sin hidden to man is not hidden to God, and while He can forgive everything, He can let nothing pass. "The priest shall make an atonement for him concerning his ignorance, wherein he erred, and wist it not ; and it shall be forgiven him," v. 19. The sin-offering is a type of Christ bearing our sins in His own body on the tree. As we read in 2 Cor. vi. 21, "For He hath made Him to be sin for us who knew no sin, that we might be made the righteousness of God in Him." It is the especial aspect of sin in us, that is here brought out, the sin of our nature. What we *are*, rather than what we *do*. And it teaches us plainly, that it is not our own conscience, nor our measure of light, but the truth of God, that is the standard by which sin is to be measured. But it also teaches that in the atonement of the Lord Jesus Christ, perfect provision is made for it all.

The trespass-offering, chapter vi. was an offering for sins of wrong-doing, either towards God or towards man. It was not so much here what a man *was*, as what he *did* which is considered, his *acts* of sin ; and, therefore, this offering was accompanied with restitution on the part of the sinner. He was not only forgiven, but he was to " restore that which he took violently away, or the thing which he hath deceitfully gotten :" vi. 4. This signifies, I think, first, the blessed truth that "where sin abounded," and even because sin abounded, " grace did much more abound." And also teaches us that forgiveness is not the whole of salvation, but righteousness must accompany it.

Such were the offerings, each one revealing Christ and some especial aspect of His work for us ; and each one also, I believe, teaching us what we ought to be, as one with Him and walking as He walked, even living sacrifices giving ourselves to God, and to our brethren. But I cannot dwell on this now.*

*I would refer my reader to Jukes' " Law of the Offerings," for further teaching on this part of Leviticus, for sale at the Willard Tract Repository.

To me the one grand lesson of the offerings is to be found in the constant repetition of the declaration "and it shall be forgiven him." No room was left for doubt here. God said it, and the question was settled. No Israelite could look inside at his own feelings to settle this question, nor outside at his life. The one only point was, had he brought the offering, and had it been consumed on the altar? If so, then he was forgiven, whether he felt it or not; and we cannot imagine an Israelite entertaining a doubt on the subject. Had such a thing occurred, I cannot but think that the friends and neighbors of the unfortunate man, and, in fact, the whole nation, would have been horrified at such presumption. "Do you dare to doubt God's word?" they would have asked. "Are your feelings to be put in opposition to His express declaration?" But if they could be thus sure of forgiveness, who only offered a bullock, or a lamb, or a turtle dove, surely we, for whom Christ has been offered, ought to be infinitely more sure; and doubts with us should be even more summarily dealt with. May the type teach us this all important lesson!

Priesthood comes next in chapters viii. and ix. A type of the Lord Jesus Christ as our High Priest interceding for us, and giving us access to God. "Now of the things which we have spoken this is the sum: we have such an High Priest, who is set on the right hand of the throne of the majesty in the heavens; a minister of the sanctuary, and of the true tabernacle, which the Lord pitched, and not man," Heb. viii. 1, 2. "And they

truly were many priests, because they were not suffered
to continue by reason of death ; but this man, because
he continueth ever, hath an unchangeable priesthood.
Wherefore He is also able to save them to the uttermost,
that come unto God by Him, seeing He ever liveth to
make intercession for them," Heb. vii. 23–25.

I believe that Aaron as High Priest was the especial
type of Christ; and that his sons were meant to be types
of believers in their position as "priests unto God,"
built up, as Peter says, "an holy priesthood, to offer up
spiritual sacrifices acceptable to God by Jesus Christ."
The priest typifies the soul in communion with God,
dwelling in the secret of His presence, and handling the
holy things of His sanctuary. And we, as priests, are
called, as were the sons of Aaron, to a blessed separation from all the cares and burdens of the world, and
to a life of consecration to the service of our Lord.

Chapters xi. xxii. give us the discernment between
clean and unclean things, the judgment of defilements,
what was to be done with defiled persons, and directions
to preserve them from defilements. These chapters
touch on many things in the daily lives of the Israelite,
which were calculated to hinder or to help communion,
and show us how nothing is unimportant to the soul where
God dwells. The food they ate, the garments they wore,
the houses they lived in, their family relations with each
other, their treatment of one another, the sowing of their
seed, the gathering in of their harvests, their births and
death, in short all the smallest details of their every-

day life were of importance, and all were to be regulated
by the law of their God. The reason of this is told in
Lev. xx. 26, "And ye shall be holy unto me ; for I the
Lord am holy, and have separated you from other people
that ye should be mine." "Sanctify yourselves, therefore, and be ye holy: for I am the Lord your God. And
ye shall keep my statutes and do them; I am the Lord
which sanctify you." Lev. xx. 7, 8.

These chapters are to me most precious, because they
show us that our God loves us enough to care about
every little detail of our lives, and that to belong to Him
means to have each step of our way regulated by His
sweet control. To the heathen nations round about, it
might have seemed an almost intolerable thing to have
God entering so minutely into all their affairs ; beside
their bed at night, and around their board by day. But
to the soul that knew His love, nothing could have been
more blessed. The surveillance of true and unselfish
love is always most lovely, and can bring nothing but
blessing and joy. We know that we ourselves do not
care for the details of any lives but of those we love.
The majority of the people around us may live, and eat,
and wear, and act as they please, and so long as they
do not interfere with us, we are perfectly indifferent.
But the moment we begin to love, all is changed, and
the least detail in the life or ways of our loved ones becomes of deepest interest to us. It is because God
loves us therefore, that He cares what we do, and it is
one of our sweetest joys, if we only knew it, to have a

dear command of His for every day and hour of our lives.

In Chapter xvi. we have the provision made for de- filement. "For on that day shall the priest make an atonement for you to cleanse you, that ye may be clean from all your sins before the Lord," xvi. 30. This atone- ment was two-fold. One goat was killed and its blood sprinkled on the mercy-seat to "make an atonement for the holy place, because of the uncleanness of the children of Israel," xvi. 16; and of the other goat we read xvi. 21, 22, "And Aaron shall lay both hands upon the head of the live goat, and confess over him all the iniquities of the children of Israel, and all their transgressions in all their sins, putting them upon the head of the goat, and shall send him away by the hand of a fit man into the wilderness. And the goat shall bear upon him all their iniquities unto a land not inhabited: and he shall let go the goat in the wilderness."

Of all the types of the Lord Jesus, this seems to me one of the most wonderful. The way of access for the sinner into the presence of God is made by His death, and the sins of the sinner are borne away "into a land not inhabited," cast as it were into the very depths of the sea, to be no more remembered, even by the God against whom they were committed, but who has thus "laid on Him the iniquity of us all." And if that day was to be a "Sabbath of rest" to the soul of the Israel- ite, because he was thus cleansed from all his sins, how much more ought our souls to "enter into rest," when we see by faith the Lamb of God, who "taketh away the sin of the world."

The Lord's feasts come next in chapter xxiii., a wonderful picture of the stages in the soul's experience, which are each one well pleasing to the Lord, and which lead onward, one by one, from the first stage of coming to Jesus and finding rest to our souls, to the culminating stage of fulness of joy in His love.

These feasts are seven—the Sabbath, the Passover accompanied with the feast of unleavened bread, the First-fruits of the Harvest, Pentecost, the Feast of Trumpets in the seventh month, the Day of Atonement, and the Feast of Tabernacles.

The first, the Sabbath, verse 3, is a type of that rest into which we, which have believed, do enter; and it must always be the first stage in all real progress. "Come unto me," said Jesus, "all ye that labor and are heavy laden, and I will give you rest." Many other things also He has in store for us, but this must come first—rest to our souls; and without it all the others are useless.

The second, the Passover, with the feast of unleavened bread, verses 5-8, typifies the assurance of faith, and its result in a holy life. The Passover was the memorial of their deliverance in Egypt, and must have reminded them every time they celebrated it, that their deliverance was a grand fact. The feast of unleavened bread typified the separation from evil that must be the result of this; leaven always being a type of evil.

This whole feast teaches us, I think, that it is God's will and therefore pleasing to Him for the believer to *know* that his sins *are* forgiven, and that he *has* been delivered from the bondage of Satan through the redemption that is in Christ Jesus. John says: " These things have I written unto you that believe on the name of the Son of God, that ye may know that ye have eternal life." 1 John v. 13. Many have this life who do not know it, who only hope so, or perhaps fear they have not. But God would have us *know* it, and commands us to keep our Passovers by continually reminding ourselves of the grand fact of our redemption, through the blood of the Lamb. But that this assurance was intended not to encourage sin but to hinder it, is taught by the accompanying feast of unleavened bread, which is shown us in 1 Cor. v. 6–8 to be a type of that separation from all evil, required by God from every one who belongs to Him.

The third feast, the First Fruits, verses 10-14, occurring on the day after the Sabbath, the eighth day, was a type of the resurrection of Christ, who "at the end of the Sabbath, as it began to dawn toward the first day of the week," rose triumphant from the grave, and became the "first-fruits of them that slept." 1 Cor. xv. 20. And since we who believe have been "buried with Him by baptism into death; that like as Christ was raised up from the dead by the glory of the Father, even so we also should walk in newness of life," this feast typifies also our resurrection life as one with Him, and the soul by faith entering into the apprehension of it. And until this is done, v. 14, we cannot feed on the glorious harvest, nor even taste the bread and the corn which are the only food of the resurrection life.

The fourth feast, Pentecost, verses 15–21, typifies the outpouring of the Spirit upon the soul that has thus died with Christ and risen with Him to newness of life. A " *new* meat offering " was presented then, " baken with leaven," a type of the union of Christ with His people, who, being still upon earth, have in them the taint of evil. All the different sacrifices were offered on this day, showing how, when our Pentecost comes, Christ in all His fulness will be apprehended and rejoiced in.

The fifth feast, the Feast of Trumpets, verses 24, 25, is a type of the believer bearing testimony. " Endued with power from on high," on the Day of Pentecost, we can now be witnesses unto Christ.

The sixth feast, the Day of Atonement, verses 27-32, a day when they were to " afflict their souls," was a type, I think, of the death of self, the final and complete self-sacrifice, when all of self is surrendered and crucified with Christ. " Afflict your souls," that is, mortify, reckon dead, " take up the cross," " forsake all."

And this ushered in the seventh feast, the feast of joy. " These things have I spoken unto you, that my joy might remain in you, and your joy might be full," John xv. 11.

This seventh feast, the Feast of Tabernacles, verses 24-43, is the foreshadowing of the Christian's highest joy, when the soul fully realizes its deliverance and its victory, and is so cut loose from earth as to be able to see things as God sees them, and to enter into His joy. It is more than the joy of faith, as at the first-fruits, that is realized here; it is the joy of possession, all is gathered in at last, verse 39.

It is very striking to observe the continual recurrence of the expression throughout all of these feasts, " ye shall do no servile work therein," illustrating wonderfully the truth that, from beginning to end, our salvation is not of works, lest any man should boast.

Another expression is also to me very suggestive, and that is that these feasts were called " the feasts of the Lord." Not our feasts, but His. That is, the joy of the Lord in our progress is far greater than ever our own joy could be. " The Lord thy God in the midst of thee is mighty; He will save, He will rejoice over thee with joy; He will rest in His love ; He will joy over thee with singing," Zeph. iii. 17.

Chapter xxv. gives us the Jubilee, a beautiful type of the Millennium, the final " restitution of all things," when " righteousness shall cover the earth as the waters cover the sea." " And ye shall hallow the fiftieth year, and proclaim liberty throughout all the land unto all the inhabitants thereof: it shall be a jubilee unto you ; and ye shall return every man unto his possession, and ye shall return every man unto his family." This year was reached by an ascending scale of Sabbaths, one Sabbath day each seven days, one Sabbath year

each seven years, and finally the Jubilee, a Sabbath
year each seven times seven years. All these Sabbaths,
with the rest they brought, being each one foretastes
of the final Sabbath, when the whole earth shall be at
rest and quiet, and shall break forth into singing, Ps.
xiv. 7.

In chapter xxvi. we have given to us the blessings
that follow obedience, and the miseries that will follow
disobedience, striking pictures of the joy of the obedient
Christian life, and the loss and sorrow of the disobedient.

Our book closes with chapter xxvii. which treats of
God's rights in those things devoted to Him, and shows
us that every such thing becomes "most holy," because
it is thus set apart for Him. His possession of it makes
it holy, whatever it may have been before. "Every
devoted thing is most holy to the Lord," verse 28. A
blessed truth to the poor soul that feels its unholiness,
and yet longs to be all the Lord's, "sanctified and meet
for the Master's use, and prepared unto every good work."

Satan continually tempts such to think that they are
too unholy for the Lord to accept, and what he suggests
as to their unworthiness is so true, that it seems impossible to gainsay his conclusions. But the answer here
is simply this, that the altar sanctifies the gift, that anything given to the Lord is made holy by the very fact
of being so given. And that even our bodies, if presented unto Him a living sacrifice, are thereby rendered
"holy and acceptable." Just as we have sometimes
read in our childish tales of a water that changed every-

7

thing put into it into gold, so here we read of a God so
infinite in holiness that everything devoted to Him becomes holy by His simple possession of it. Take comfort then, dear humble soul, and transfer at once thyself
and all that thou hast into this grand possession, that it
may all become " most holy unto the Lord."

Such is the book of Leviticus, a book concerning the
worship and communion of a redeemed people, among
whom God dwells. A book that more than any other
seems to show in type what it is to have the blessed gift
of the abiding presence of the Holy Spirit in our hearts;
that gift which is " the promise of the Father" to all
who believe in the Lord Jesus Christ, and which alone
brings us nigh to God, and makes it possible for us to
commune with Him. It is therefore especially full of
deep teaching for Christians, and contains many blessed
lessons concerning the interior life of spiritual communion, that are worthy of most careful study.

Texts illustrating the life of communion with God:
John xv. 15, 26; xvi. 13, 14; xiv. 16, 17, 20, 21, 23, 25;
Ez. xxxvi. 26, 27; Rom. viii. 9, 10: 1 Cor. iii. 16; 1 John
iii. 24; ii. 27; i. 7; iv. 12, 15, 16; v. 14, 15; Ez. xi. 19,
20; Gal. v. 16–18; Col. i. 9–11; Phil. i. 9–11; ii. 13;
Eph. v. 9, 18, 19; iii. 14–19; i. 16–19; ii. 18; Heb. viii.
10, 11; x. 19–23.

CHAPTER VI.

THE WILDERNESS WANDERING OF THOSE WHO ARE REDEEMED.

Keynote: Rom. vii. 9-24.

THE book of Numbers gives us the wilderness wandering of a redeemed people, and answers to the experience of the Christian who knows that he is redeemed out of the world and brought nigh to God, but who fails to enter into possession of the fulness of his salvation. In this book we see the children of Israel brought to the borders of the promised land, and failing to go in "because of unbelief"; and we see them, on account of this failure, condemned to wander for forty years in the wilderness. The seventh chapter of Romans is the New Testament counterpart of this book. Paul gives us in that chapter the experience of a redeemed soul, who knows what it is to delight in the law of God after the inward man, but who finds another law in his members warring against the law of his mind, and bringing him into continual captivity. It is too common an experience to need any

75

description; for we all, I doubt not, know it for ourselves
only too well, either in the past or the present.   It is, in
short, that experience in the church which has produced, and is best expressed by such hymns as the following:

> "Look how we grovel here below,
>   Fond of these earthly toys;
> Our souls, how heavily they go
>   To reach eternal joys!
> In vain we tune our formal songs,
>   In vain we strive to rise;
> Hosannas languish on our tongues,
>   And our devotion dies."

That Christians could ever be willing to *sing* such experiences as these, seems a strange phenomenon.   One
would think, if it were unfortunately true, that it would
be buried with shame in the deepest recesses of the heart,
or spoken of only with the greatest sorrow.   It is as
though wives should put into verse, and sing to one
another, their want of love and devotedness to their
husbands.   Or as though the children of Israel should
have sung instead of weeping, when they found themselves turned back to wander in the wilderness.

The wilderness wandering, however, does not fill up
the whole book of Numbers.   The first twelve chapters
give us the details of God's provision for His people's
need, as to service and warfare.   And it is a provision
so ample and complete, as to seem to leave no possible

room for failure to come. As we read also concerning the Christian in Phil. iv. 19, "My God shall supply all your need, according to His riches in glory by Christ Jesus." Neither they nor we can find any excuse for our failure in the insufficiency of His supplies.

In chapters i. and ii. God numbers His people, and arranges them around His dwelling-place, assigning to each one his rightful position, and calling them by their names; a blessed illustration of the Good Shepherd's individual care of His flock, who "calleth His own sheep by name and leadeth them out." The numbering here was especially for warfare, "from twenty years old and upward, all that are able to go forth to war;' and typifies the especial aspect of Christians, as engaged in spiritual conflicts with their enemies, the world, the flesh, and the devil. Only those who were able, were called into this warfare. The young, and weak and aged were to be spared; showing that only a vigorous Christian life can really fight the fight of faith. And all were to "declare their pedigrees," i. 18, that it might be known beyond a shadow of doubt whether they really belonged to Israel. Souls who doubt whether they belong to God or not, can scarcely fight His battles, for their very doubts are a siding with the enemy against Him.

In chapters iii. and iv. we have the Levites set apart for service: "Bring the tribe of Levi near, and present them before Aaron the priest, that they may minister unto him. And they shall keep his charge,

7*

and the charge of the whole congregation before the tabernacle of the congregation, to do the service of the tabernacle" (iii. 6, 7). We may consider the Levites as a type of the church in service, doing the Lord's work, and having in charge His truth. The priest was a type of a soul in communion, and the Levite of the same soul in service. The Levites waited on the priests, and performed their service only "at the appointment" (iv. 19) of the priests. It is the soul in communion that finds out what the soul in service ought to do; and service is valuable only as it waits on, or "ministers unto" communion. The Levites carried the tabernacle, and its furniture, and its vessels in all the journeyings of the children of Israel, and set it up in every new encampment: a striking type of the fulfilment of Christ's command to His disciples, "Go ye into all the world and preach the gospel." The service of each Levite was marked out for him by the "commandment of the Lord," as we read concerning the service of the church in 1 Cor. xii. 11, "But all these worketh that one and the selfsame Spirit, dividing to every man severally as He will."

In chapter v. we have provision made for the purity of the camp: "Command the children of Israel, that they put out of the camp every leper, and every one that hath an issue, and whosoever is defiled by the dead: both male and female shall ye put out, without the camp shall ye put them; that they defile not their camps, in the midst whereof I dwell," v. 2, 3. God's presence requires perfect purity on the part of those

among whom He dwells. He takes knowledge of every
wrong, even of that which may be hidden from those
nearest us, and brings it to judgment. This is very
blessed to the soul that really loves holiness and hates
sin. Knowing the deceitfulness of our own hearts, and
how easily grave and serious defects may be hidden
from us, and knowing, as we do, the grievous and sometimes fatal results that flow from our secret and often
scarcely recognized faults, we may well rejoice that we
have to do with a God who is of purer eyes than to
behold iniquity without recognizing it, and who is a
" discerner of the thoughts and intents of the heart."

In chapter vi. we have given us God's mind respecting those whose hearts stir them up to a life of peculiar
devotedness to the Lord, either for a particular work, or
for an especial season : "When either man or woman
shall separate themselves to vow a vow of a Nazarite, to
separate themselves unto the Lord," vi. 2. Such a one
may be called for a time to deny himself from things
not evil in themselves, and to which it may be he can
one day return, (compare ver. 3 with ver. 20). But if the
Lord has thus called us into separation for an especial
purpose, either of service or of training, let us beware
lest "our separation be defiled" by any lack of obedience to the divine command, or any want of watchfulness against the divine forbiddings. This separateness
and this self-denial will bring us to a place of joyful
communion "when the days of our separation are fulfilled," and Christ in all His manifold fulness will be

revealed to our souls, (see vi. 13-20). And the Lord can then pronounce over us without any hindrance His richest blessings, as He did upon Israel at the close of this chapter.

"The Lord bless thee and keep thee;
The Lord make His face shine upon thee,
and be gracious unto thee;
The Lord lift up His countenance upon thee,
and give thee peace!"

In chapter vii. we have the offerings of the princes of Israel. Willing offering is always the result of bless ing. "Freely ye have *received*, freely *give*," is always the Lord's way with us. These offerings are a type of the willing offerings of God's children now, who may be princes in giving, even though poor in this world's riches. And He notes it all; every bowl and every spoon, and even every cup of cold water given in the name of the Lord is written in His book of remembrance, and not one shall lose its reward.

Chapter viii. gives us further details as to the Levitical service and the cleansing necessary for it, teaching us in type the absolute necessity for purity of heart, as the basis for any effectual and acceptable service to God.

Chapter ix. gives us the provision for keeping the Passover in the wilderness, and for the guidance of the children of Israel in their journeys. The passover was the memorial of their redemption out of Egypt, and was to be kept by the people, even in the wilderness. A type, I think, of the continual remembrance on our part of the fact that we *have* been redeemed, even though we may know ourselves to be wandering in wilderness places. Neither defilement nor distance was to hinder from the keeping of the passover: "Speak unto the children of Israel, saying, If any man of you or your posterity shall be unclean by reason of a dead body, or be in a journey afar off, yet he shall keep the passover unto the Lord," ix. 10. But it was to be kept in the second month, instead of the first, see ix. 11, teaching that defilement hinders or delays assurance, although it does not deprive the soul of its right to it. A child may be naughty, but it will be still a child, and no parent would be pleased to have it begin to consider itself no longer a child.

The presence of the pillar of cloud and fire guiding and protecting the children of Israel in all their journeys, (ix. 15–23), seems to me a very beautiful type of the presence of the Holy Spirit in the hearts of God's people, guiding them day by day in all the journey of life. "And when the cloud was taken up from the tabernacle, then after that the children of Israel journeyed: and in the place where the cloud abode, there the children of Israel pitched their tents. At the commandment of the Lord the children of Israel journeyed, and at the commandment of the Lord they pitched," ix. 17, 18. There were no roads nor guide-posts in that " great and terrible wilderness," and none of whom they could inquire their way. Yet they journeyed "without carefulness," because the Lord led them at every step. They had

none of the care nor responsibility of the journey.
They had no need to meet and consult as to the best
paths to take, nor to send out scouts to choose their
route.   They had only to watch the pillar of fire and of
cloud and follow its movements, and all was well.   A
beautiful picture of the believer's absolute dependence
upon the blessed guidance of the Holy Spirit, and of
what ought to be his complete subjection to it.

And now that all had been arranged in God's order,
the journey began.   "And it came to pass on the
twentieth day of the second month, in the second year,
that the cloud was taken up from off the tabernacle of
the testimony.   And the children of Israel took their
journeys out of the wilderness of Sinai ; and the cloud
rested in the wilderness of Paran.   And they departed
from the mount of the Lord three days' journey : and
the ark of the covenant of the Lord went before them in
the three days' journey, to search out a resting place for
them " (x. 11, 12 and 33).   It is thus that the Lord, when
He putteth forth His own sheep goeth before them.
And how little cause for fear or anxiety can there be in
a journey so guided, by such a Leader.

Yet almost at once the evil heart of unbelief showed
itself, and the people "complained" (xi. 1) ; and,
seduced by the mixed multitude who accompanied them,
they began to look back longingly to Egypt.   "We remember," they said, "the fish, which we did eat in
Egypt freely ; the cucumbers, and the melons, and the
leeks, and the onions, and the garlic : but now our soul

is dried away: there is nothing at all, besides this manna, before our eyes" (xi. 5, 6). The soul that begins by complaining, soon ends by something worse. It loses its relish for heavenly food, and looks back with longing to that which the world gives. And the end is sadly typified in the closing verses of our chapter, xi. 33, 34. "He gave them their request; but sent leanness into their soul," Ps. cvi. 15.

The spirit of criticism follows swift upon spiritual leanness, as we see in chapter xii. : "And Miriam and Aaron spake against Moses because of the Ethiopian woman he had married." The soul filled with the love of Christ has lost the spirit of judging. The divine charity spread abroad in the heart "thinketh no evil." But an inward want of union with Christ always leads the soul to climb up on the judgment seat, and to take upon itself the task of removing the mote out of its brother's eye, regardless of the beam in its own. God deals with all such, however, sooner or later, and sounds in the inmost ear the solemn question, "Wherefore then were ye not afraid to speak against my servant Moses?" And in mercy He reproves and chastens until the sin is acknowledged and the soul restored, 10–15.

In chapter xiii. we enter upon one of the saddest epochs of the history of the children of Israel. They are here brought to the very borders of the land which the Lord had given them for an inheritance, and for the very purpose of possessing which He had brought them out of Egypt. In Ex. iii. 8 He had said, "I am come down to deliver them out of the hand of the Egyptians, and to bring them out of that land unto"—what?—the wilderness? No; "unto a good land and a large, unto a land flowing with milk and honey." And now that they had reached the borders of this land, the word to them was, "Behold the Lord thy God hath set the land before thee: go up and possess it, as the Lord God of thy fathers hath said unto thee; fear not, neither be discouraged," Deut. i. 21.

But the previous rebellion had weakened the heart of the people, and when they heard from their spies of "giants," and "cities walled and very great," they were afraid and refused to go up. "Whither should we go up?" they said, "our brethren have discouraged our heart, saying, The people is greater and taller than we; the cities are great and walled up to heaven: and moreover, we have seen the sons of the Anakims there," Deut. i. 28. In vain Caleb and Joshua "stilled the people saying, Let us go up at once and possess it; for we are well able to overcome it." The remaining ten spies persisted in declaring, "We be not able to go up against the people; for they are stronger than we." And the children of Israel were finally so incensed at the faithful report of Caleb and Joshua that they "bade stone them with stones," xiv. 10.

This whole scene is a picture, I think, of a stage of Christian experience, which is, alas! only too common. The soul, which has been translated out of the kingdom of darkness into the kingdom of God's dear Son, is brought face to face with the wonderful promises and blessings of the gospel, and longs to go up and possess them. The glorious liberty and triumphs, for instance of the eighth chapter of Romans confront us, and we ask, "Is it not our privilege to enter into these things now?" But we are met on every hand by "spies," who tell us of the giants in our way, and of the difficulties that we shall not be able to overcome; and thus our brethren so " discourage our hearts" that we finally give up in despair, as Israel did, and turn back to wander in the wilderness of the seventh of Romans, afraid to take possession of the very land of promise which the Lord our God declares He has given us, and into which it was the very purpose of our redemption that we should be brought.

I know what it is to have been discouraged in the early part of my Christian course by the story of these " spies," and to have become in turn a spy myself, bringing up a bad report of the land. When I was first converted I never dreamed of anything but of taking possession, of course, of all the rich and glorious things which I saw promised in the Bible to believers in the Lord Jesus Christ. I had never been used to hearing Christians talk much about their spiritual experience, and I supposed in my simplicity that to be in the king dom of Heaven meant really to be in a kingdom of righteousness, peace, and joy in the Holy Ghost. And when in the course of a few weeks the "giants" began to appear in my land, and I found myself surrounded

8

and overcome by a "people greater and taller" than I
was, I at once concluded this must be because I had not
learned the whole gospel, and that it only needed for me
to be taught something more in order to get the victory.

I had found in the Lord Jesus a deliverer from the
guilt of sin, but now I wanted to find in Him a deliverer
from the *power* of sin, and I did not know how to set
about it. I went therefore to a "spy" to find out. He
was a beloved Christian teacher who had been many
years in the way, and must know, I supposed, all about
it. But never shall I forget my disappointment! After
I had stated my case and told my need, saying that I
knew it was because of my ignorance, and because I
had not taken in the fulness of the gospel that I was in
so sad a case, my friend said, "Oh, no! You are all
right. You cannot expect such a deliverance as you are
seeking. We all of us are more or less under the power
of sin all our lives, and we must not expect the early
joy of our conversion to last for ever. The seventh of
Romans is the experience of the Christian throughout his
whole life." I thought my friend knew, and I received
his report as final, and at once settled down to my condition as being inevitable, and therefore to be endured
with the best grace I could ; but my heart sank as I left
the house, and, like the children of Israel, I could have
"lifted up my voice and cried," so great was my disappointment. And many a time in the years that followed
would I recall with saddest longing the blessedness I
had felt when first I knew the Lord.

But, so ignorant was I of God's ways, that I in turn became a spy, bringing a bad report of the land to the Christians who came to me for counsel, telling them it was indeed a good land and a large, but adding the fatal "nevertheless" of unbelief, that the people who dwelt in the land were too strong for them, and the cities were walled and very great. Many a one did I thus turn back, causing them to wander with me in the wilderness for many years.

I am sure I but relate the experience of others of my readers in thus giving my own. In prayer-meetings, in sermons, in private converse, and in books, this report of the spies is declared to us over and over; until at last if any faithful Caleb or Joshua, who have " wholly followed the Lord," comes forward with the assertion that, " We are well able to overcome," the church is ready, in a figurative sense, even to stone them with stones. And I think if we are, many of us, honest with ourselves, we shall be forced to confess that some of these stones have been at one time or another cast by our own hands. Let us thank God if we have learned better, and if now we also can say of the people of the land, " they are bread for us; their defence is departed from them, and the Lord is with us; fear them not."

The New Testament tells us that the cause of this sad failure of the Israelites was unbelief. " So we see that they could not enter in because of unbelief," (see Heb. iii. 15-19, and iv. 1-10). It was not their own weakness nor the strength of their enemies that hindered their entrance. They were, it is true, "grasshoppers," and their enemies were "giants," and it was indeed manifest that they were not able to overcome. But the Lord was able. And He it was who was to fight for them and to bring them in. They had recognized this when they sang that triumphant song in Ex. xv., just after they had crossed the Red Sea: "The Lord is a man of war," they sang, "the Lord is His Name." "Thy right hand, O Lord, is become glorious in power; thy right hand, O Lord, hath dashed in pieces the enemy." "The people shall hear and be afraid: sorrow shall take hold upon the inhabitants of Palestina." "Fear and dread shall fall upon them; by the greatness of thine arm they shall be as still as a stone; till thy people pass over, O Lord, till the people pass over, which thou hast purchased. Thou shalt bring them in and plant them in the mountain of thine inheritance, in the place, O Lord, which thou hast made for thee to dwell in."

Their enemies were as great and they themselves were as weak when this song was sung, as when the borders of the land were reached. But the people, fresh from the Red Sea victories, had no fear on account of this. The Lord was to do it all; and what mattered to the Lord, the giants' strength or the weakness of the children of Israel? It is nothing to Him to work with many or with few, and no giants or walled cities can successfully oppose Him. It was unbelief, therefore, and unbelief alone that prevented their going

in. It may have sounded like humility to themselves
to talk thus of their own weakness, and the strength of
their enemies, but it was really unbelief. See Ps. cvi. 24–
27. And while to us also it may seem very humble to
dwell on our own weakness, and the strength of sin, and
to be thereby hindered from realizing the gospel's
richest blessings, yet it is as really unbelief in our case as
in theirs. For the Lord our God which goeth before us,
He it is who is to fight for us, and is to bring us in, and
plant us in the land of our inheritance, as actually as He
was to do it for them. Without Him we can do nothing
literally. With Him we can do all things, and depend-
ing on Him we are always "more than conquerors"
over every enemy. He hath blessed us, He declares,
"with all spiritual blessings in heavenly places in
Christ," and it only remains for us by faith to go up
and possess them. If we do not, it will not be because
of our weakness or the strength of our enemies, but because of unbelief. It will be because we measure our
enemies with ourselves, instead of measuring them with
the Lord. We may be, and indeed are "grasshoppers"
in their sight, but what are they in the sight of God?
Truly by the greatness of His arm they shall all be as
"still as a stone," before the soul that dares to step out
on His promises and trust all to Him.

The consequence of this failure on the part of the
children of Israel was a forty years' wandering in the
wilderness. See Num. xiv. 33, 34. The Lord did not
forsake them because of it, but went with them in all

8*

their journeys, and still protected and guided them with
His presence. And they might perhaps have been
tempted, because of this, to think they must after all be
about right, or He would not favor them so. But His
estimate of this wilderness wandering is to be found in
this, that in speaking of it He called it "the time of
provocation," or "the provocation" See Heb. iii. 8–15,
Ps. xcv. 8, Ps. lxxviii. 40. The Lord does not forsake
the soul that fails to enter into the possession of the
fulness of His salvation. In all our wanderings He
accompanies us, and we may have many precious
seasons when He delivers us from our enemies, or
supplies our needs. In fact in the sacrifice of the
Red Heifer, in Num. xix., we see an especial provision made for the uncleannesses sure to be contracted
in the wilderness journey; answering, I believe, to the
declaration in 1 John ii. 1, where the apostle, after
having told us that he has written these things unto us
that we sin not, adds, "And if any man sin we have an
Advocate with the Father, Jesus Christ the righteous."
It is not that He sanctions the sin by His forgiveness,
any more than He sanctioned the wilderness journey by
His presence. But, like a loving parent, if His children
will wander, He must keep with them through it all.

Other rebellions followed this failure to go in and possess the land. They broke God's rest, chap. xv. 32–36.
They rebelled against Moses and Aaron, chap. xvi., and
sought to assume to themselves the place. which could
only be received as the gift of God. They complained

at having been brought into such an " evil place," chap.
xx., and " chode with Moses" because of it. And in
chap. xxi. 4, 5 we read, "And the soul of the people was
much discouraged because of the way. And the people
spake against God and against Moses, Wherefore have
ye brought us up out of Egypt to die in the wilderness?"
And thus brought upon themselves the scourge of the
fiery serpents, xxi. 6–9. And finally, in chap. xxv.,
" Israel joined himself unto Baal-peor : and the anger
of the Lord was kindled against Israel." Until the
Divine comment on it all is, " How oft did they provoke
Him in the wilderness, and grieve Him in the desert,"
Ps. lxxviii. 40.

Each sin was no doubt the occasion of fresh displays
of grace, but no one surely would argue from this
that because grace abounded therefore sin might also
abound. Rather would we cry with Paul, " God forbid !
How shall we that are dead to sin live any longer
therein?" I would refer my readers to the seventy-
eighth Psalm for the Lord's thoughts about this whole
wilderness wandering.

And yet at the close of it, when the children of Israel
took up their final encampment in the " plains of Moab
on this side Jordan by Jericho," xxii. 1, we have those wonderful chapters concerning Balaam and Balak, xxii., xxiii.,
xxiv., where God's richest blessings are pronounced
upon this very people, who had so often provoked and
grieved Him ; and where we even read these remark-
able words, xxiii. 21 : " He hath not beheld iniquity in

Jacob, neither hath He seen perverseness in Israel : t_e
Lord his God is with him, and the shout of a king is
among them." What can this mean but that He has so
completely put all our sins behind His back, and cast
them so utterly into the depths of the sea, that He remembers them no more forever?

From this time the wilderness wandering was over.
The camp was not removed from the plains of Moab
until in the book of Joshua they crossed the Jordan into
the promised land. In the remaining chapters of Numbers we have given to us the final arrangements that
had to be made before this could be done.

In chapter xxvi. God numbers the people afresh, as
heirs ready to take possession of their inheritance.

In chapter xxvii. a new leader is appointed in the place
of Moses to lead them out and bring them in, " that the
congregation of the Lord be not as sheep without a
shepherd."

In chapters xxviii. and xxix. we have details as to worship and sacrifices.

Chapter xxx. is concerning the vows of women, showing us God's provision for folly and weakness, that those
who are not responsible (as women were not among
them) may have their foolish plans set aside by Christ,
the heavenly Bridegroom.

Chapter xxxi. gives us the story of a war which resulted from the sin of chap. xxv. The conflicts in the
wilderness experience are not like the conflicts in the
land of promise where actual spiritual ground is ac-

quired as the result. They are always the result of sin, and are fruitless in results, as far as the acquisition of territory is concerned, although no conflict can be without immediate fruit in present spoils from the enemy.

In chapter xxxi. we have the account of the children of Reuben and the children of Gad who took up their abode on the wilderness side of Jordan. They had a "very great multitude of cattle," and behold, "the place was a place for cattle." Therefore they said to Moses, "Bring us not over Jordan." And many Christians are likewise tempted to take up their abode this side of Jordan, by the multitude of their cattle and because the place is a place for cattle. But such dwellers in the border-land are the first to fall a prey to the enemy, and are continually harassed by his attacks.

Chapter xxxiii. reviews the way by which they had come, and commands the utter destruction of all the enemies in the land of their inheritance.

Chapter xxxiv. marks the limits of the country they were to possess.

Chapter xxxv. appoints the portion of the Levites, and the cities of refuge; the last being wonderful types of Christ as the Refuge of sinners.

Chapter xxxvi. taken in connection with the first part of chap. xxvii. shows us the blessedness of a bold claim of faith, when regulated by the divine limitations. These daughters of Zelophehad would not forego the privileges which belonged to them by inheritance, although to the eye of man they had no rightful claim.

But this boldness of faith must be limited by the commandments of the Lord.　See xxxvi. 1-12.

The book closes with the children of Israel still encamped "in the plains of Moab, by Jordan near Jericho," waiting for the rehearsing of the law which was to precede their final entrance into the promised land. This rehearsal we have given to us in Deuteronomy.

The practical lesson taught us in the story contained in this book of Numbers is summarized in Heb. iv. 1, 2: "Let us, therefore, fear, lest, a promise being left us of entering into His rest, any of you should seem to come short of it.　For unto us was the Gospel preached, as well as unto them ; but the word preached did not profit them, not being mixed with faith in them that heard it." A wonderful "land of promise" is opened out before every believer, and we are commanded to go in and possess it.　But except this "good news" is "mixed with faith" in those who hear it, it will be of no avail, and they will find themselves among the number "who could not enter in because of unbelief."　The great thing necessary therefore is that we should believe.　But believe what, some may ask ?　Believe that the land *is* ours, that the Lord is able to bring us in and give us our inheritance there, and that not an enemy shall be able to stand before us all the days of our life.　And then, believing this, we shall have the courage of faith to "apprehend that for which also we are apprehended of Christ Jesus," and shall realize that we which have believed do, even now and here, "enter into rest."

CHAPTER VII.

DEUTERONOMY.

CONSECRATION.

Keynote: Rom. xii. 1, 2.

HE book of Deuteronomy is a book of consecration. It shows us God's redeemed
people standing a second time on the borders of the land of promise, and consecra-
ting themselves afresh to Him, as a preparation for
going in and possessing it. "Now therefore hearken,
O Israel, unto the statutes and unto the judgments
which I teach you, for to do them, that ye may live, and
go in and possess the land which the Lord God of your
fathers giveth you," iv. 1.

It is the consecration of a redeemed people that is
prefigured here. It is not the surrender which the sinner
is required to make before he can know the forgiveness
of his sins; but it is the surrender required from the Christian, who already knows this, and who is seeking to
enter into the full possession of the gifts and privileges
of the Christian life. It answers to Rom. xii. 1: "I be-

seech you, therefore, brethren, by the mercies of God, that ye present your bodies a living sacrifice, holy, acceptable unto God, which is your reasonable service. And be not conformed to this world : but be ye transformed by the renewing of your mind, that ye may prove what is that good, and acceptable, and perfect will of God."

No such scene as this took place when the Israelites stood on the borders of the Red Sea. The only point then was deliverance out of Egypt in the quickest way possible. And the surrender called for was only that they should consent to turn their backs on Egypt with its " fish, and cucumbers, and melons, and leeks, and onions, and garlic," and should follow the Lord their God as He led them out into a land they knew not. " Repent and believe the Gospel," turn your backs on the old life of sin and begin the new life of faith, is the New Testament expression of this stage in their experience.

As long as the Israelites were in Egypt they could not keep God's law, because they were Pharaoh's slaves; and they had to be delivered in order that they might be able to keep it. But being delivered, and having been made God's people, they were then ready to hear the law and to consecrate themselves to obey it. And with us likewise, the first step in our experience must be, deliverance out of Satan's kingdom, and the new birth into the kingdom of God's dear Son ; for the carnal mind, we are told, " is not subject to the law of God, neither indeed can be." The consecration, therefore, which is set before us in this book, can never precede the new birth, but must always follow it.

And, in fact, as a general thing, many points exercise our hearts before we come to this consecration,—how to be safe from the destroying angel; how to be delivered out of Egypt; how to have access to God; how to be led through the wilderness; how to overcome the enemies there. Until at last we come in our experience, as Israel did, a second time to the borders of the land of promise, and our souls begin to long to know something of the power of Christ's resurrection, and to live, even now and here, in "heavenly places." And at this point the need for consecration presents itself before us. We realize that unless we are in very truth wholly the Lord's, He cannot lead us into the land of our inheritance. Not that there has been no consecration of ourselves previously. There may have been one or many; there must be, in fact, a measure of consecration in the heart of every believer in the Lord Jesus Christ. The law had been given to Israel just after their deliverance out of Egypt, and they had promised to obey it (see Ex. xix. 5–8). But now that they were about to enter Canaan, it was necessary that a deeper consecration should be made, which should have especial reference to their conduct in the land, and the conditions of their relationship with the Lord there. "These are the statutes and judgments which ye shall observe to do *in* the land which the Lord God of thy fathers giveth thee to possess

9

it, all the days that ye live upon the earth," xii. 1.   And
however it may have been as regards former consecra-
tions in our own experience, I am sure we shall find
that, when we seek to enter into the " land of promise," a
renewed surrender will be necessary, and that it must
be of a far deeper and more heart-searching character
than any former one has ever been.

It is necessary to keep all this clearly in mind in order
to understand the conditional character of the book of
Deuteronomy. We meet here continually with the word
" if." "All these blessings shall come upon thee and
overtake thee, *if* thou shalt hearken unto the voice of
the Lord thy God," xxviii. 2. " But it shall come to
pass, *if* thou wilt not hearken unto the voice of the Lord
thy God, to observe to do all His commandments that
all these curses shall come upon thee and overtake
thee," xxviii. 15. The blessings of the gospel of the Lord
Jesus Christ are so unconditional, and His gifts are so
free, that we are apt to think there are no " ifs " to be
found in it any where, and that the introduction of any
conditions are always a mistake of legality. But while
it is true that forgiveness is a free gift, bestowed without
money and without price upon all who need it and will
take it, it is also equally true that holiness of heart is a
gift with conditions   No sick man *can* be healed by
a physician, be he ever so skilful, unless he will submit himself to that physician's prescriptions and obey
his orders. And no soul *can* be cured of the dreadful malady of sin, until it is willing to surrender every

sin, and submit itself to the Lord's commands against it. Conditions do necessarily come in here. Obedience to law has its inevitable blessings, and disobedience its inevitable curses. And the consecration set forth in Deuteronomy is no legal demand of so much surrender for so much blessing, but is simply the necessary state in which blessing can be bestowed. And it remains to be as true now as it was then, that, "if thou shalt keep the commandments of the Lord thy God, and walk in His ways," the Lord "shall establish thee an holy people unto Himself as He hath sworn unto thee," xxviii. 9. "But it shall come to pass, *if* thou wilt not hearken unto the voice of the Lord thy God to observe to do all His commandments, " that "the Lord shall send upon thee cursing, vexation and rebuke in all that thou settest thine hand unto for to do," and "thou shalt grope at noonday as the blind gropeth in darkness, and thou shalt not prosper in thy ways : and thou shalt be only oppressed and spoiled evermore, and no man shall save thee," xxviii. 29.

Consecration is therefore, if we only understood it, not a sacrifice demanded, but a privilege bestowed. It is the only pathway there is to the unspeakable and inestimable blessings promised to the believer; and the Lord who calls us into this pathway knows that He is calling us to something that will make for us almost a Heaven upon earth. I speak strongly, but none too much so I am sure. To be wholly the Lord's, does bring to the soul spiritual blessings that answer, step by step, to the temporal blessings which followed obedience with the children of Israel. Read the book of Deuteronomy with this thought in mind, and see how wonderful are the similitudes. First of all the land into which obedience was to bring them: "For the Lord thy God bringeth thee into a good land, a land of brooks of water, of fountains and depths that spring out of valleys and hills ; a land of wheat, and barley, and vines, and fig trees, and pomegranates ; a land of oil olive, and honey; a land wherein thou shalt eat bread without scarceness, thou shalt not lack anything in it; a land whose stones are iron, and out of whose hills thou mayest dig brass," viii. 7–9. And again, the Lord thy God will give thee " great and goodly cities which thou buildedst not, and houses full of all good things, which thou filledst not, and wells digged, which thou diggedst not, vineyards and olive trees, which thou plantedst not," vi. 10, 11.

How exactly these descriptions answer to those rich spiritual possessions, and that blessed land of spiritual rest and joy, into which the obedient soul enters now.

Take also the blessings that "follow and overtake" the obedient in vii. 12–16 and xxviii. 1–13 : "The Lord shall command the blessing upon thee in thy storehouses, and in all that thou settest thy hand unto." "Blessed shalt thou be when thou comest in, and blessed shalt thou be when thou goest out." Thy enemies shall be conquered, vii. 16; thy diseases shall be healed, vii. 15; thou shalt have riches in abundance to bestow on all who need, xxviii. 11, 12; the Lord shall love thee with a peculiar love, vii. 13; and shall fulfil His promises to thee, vii. 12; and finally, and best of all, He shall "establish thee an holy people unto Himself as He hath sworn unto thee," *if* only thou wilt keep the commandments of the Lord thy God, and walk in His ways, xxviii. 9.

Take on the other hand the curses which it is declared in xxviii. 15–68 will surely "come upon and overtake" those who "will not hearken" unto the voice of the Lord; and notice the marvellous similitude there is between them, and the spiritual loss and suffering which we all know invariably comes upon and overtakes the disobedient soul now. When such pray, the heaven seems to have become as brass, xxviii. 23; their spiritual enemies smite them and cause them to flee, v. 25; spiritual diseases of all kinds prostrate and afflict them, and even the old "diseases of Egypt" from which they had hoped to have been delivered, return upon them, and the old temptations of their unconverted days again overcome them, verses 27, 60; spiritual blindness overtakes them, and they "grope at noonday" and cannot find their way, verses 28, 29; their strength fails, v. 32; their work is fruitless, and they have no stores to give to others who are in need, verses 38–44; and, in short, the Lord's word to such a one is the same as to disobedient Israel of old, that thou shalt "find no ease, neither shall the sole of thy foot have rest: but the Lord shall give thee there a trembling heart, and failing of eyes, and

9*

sorrow of mind ; and thy life shall hang in doubt before thee; and thou shalt fear day and night, and shalt have none assurance of thy life."

But that this consecration was not to be looked upon as a painful demand ; can be seen from the continual exhortations to rejoice throughout this book, see xii. 7, xiv. 26, xvi. 14, 15, xxvi. 11, and from the word of warning in xxviii. 47, 48, "Because thou servedst not the Lord thy God with joyfulness, and with gladness of heart, for the abundance of all things ; therefore shalt thou serve thine enemies, which the Lord shall send against thee, in hunger, and in thirst, and in nakedness, and in want of all things : and He shall put a yoke of iron upon thy neck, until He have destroyed thee."

Faber says,—

> " God's will on earth is always joy,
>   Always tranquillity."

And the soul that has learned to know God can say, Amen, to this with eager gladness. For the will of God is the will of love, and the will of love can never be anything but richest blessing to the loved one. We all know this, even in our poor meagre human experience of love. We know that where we love, our will towards the object of our affections embraces and demands only their blessing and their happiness. Our own happiness is as nothing in comparison, and our only trouble is that we cannot find ways enough in which to express and pour out our love. We know that the one question of our hearts is not, "What can they do for me?" but, "What can I do for them?" Their good is our good, their sufferings are ours, and every joy that lights up their faces lights ours as well. Would they submit themselves utterly to our will, and let us have our way with them in all things, how infinitely happy we would make them if we could, along what smooth pathways we would lead them, and how tenderly we would guard them from danger or pain. And if this is true of our paltry human love, what must it be with the infinite, unspeakable and unknowable love of God? If therefore, we have ever been able to trust ourselves gladly to an earthly lover, or to surrender our wills to the call of human affection, surely we might with a fearless devotion abandon ourselves to the dear disposal of our Lord and Saviour and might say to Him with the gladdest joy, "Thy will be done, Thy will be done, Thy will be done on earth as it is done in Heaven."

I confess that to me these words are among the sweetest ever put into mortal lips—"Thy will be done on earth as it is done in Heaven." It is the perfect doing of God's will that makes Heaven what it is, and to have His will done perfectly here would turn this earth into a Heaven also. And in so far as it is done in any individual life or by any individual heart it does bring Heaven down into that heart and life, and makes that man dwell in a perpetual kingdom. For he does indeed " always reign who sides with God," since God's way is his way, and God's will is his.

Alas! how grievous it is that any one should ever

have a different thought from this. And yet we all know how common it is, even for Christians, to look upon consecration as a stern demand, and to shrink from the will of God as from the worst evil that could befall them. I knew of a Christian teacher once who was asked by one of his friends to speak on the subject of consecration. " Oh do not ask me to do that," was his shuddering reply ! " Do you know what consecration means ?" he continued. " It means that all that is bright and pleasant in your life will be taken out of it, and that every hard and sad thing you can conceive of will come into it. It means that you will have to do impossible things, and that your ease and comfort will be gone forever." How little could such a soul have known about the Lord whom he was trying to serve ! Sometimes children misjudge their parents in this way, and expect from them only harshness and stern demands. But where such is the case, it argues, either a very cruel parent, or a very naughty child, and the universal instincts of the human heart condemn it. How is it then that we can so calmly misunderstand and misjudge our Lord, whose will *can* be nothing but goodness and love, since He Himself is these and these only ?

Oh, dear friends, if this has been the thought of any one of you, if your heart has been afraid of your Father's will, and has hesitated to consent to it, confess your sin now with shame and sorrow, and begin from this time forward to say to Him a continual, "Yes," throughout all the range of your being.

        " Thy wonderful grand will, my God,
            With triumph now I make it mine,
            And faith shall cry a joyful, Yes !
            To every dear command of Thine."

The book of Deuteronomy may be divided into three
parts. The first eleven chapters contain mostly exhortations to obedience, with the motives of love and gratitude that should urge to it. Moses here beseeches the
people, as Paul did the Romans, " by the mercies of
God," to present themselves a living sacrifice, holy and
acceptable unto God, which he proves is but their " reasonable service." He begins with a narrative of their
past experiences, chaps. i., ii., iii., and on the ground of
the Lord's gracious dealing with them and their own
unfaithfulness, he urges them in chap. iv. to take heed
to themselves and keep their souls diligently, "lest," he
says, " thou forget the things which thine eyes have seen,
and lest they depart from thy heart all the days of thy
life ; but teach them thy sons, and thy sons' sons," v. 9.
In chaps. v. and vi. he reminds them of the ten commandments, and shows them that they are still binding,
and still full of infinite blessing. " Ye shall walk in all
the ways which the Lord your God hath commanded
you, that ye may live, and that it may be well with you,
and that ye may prolong your days in the land which ye
shall possess," v. 33. In chaps. vii.–xi. he reiterates
over and over, in the most touching language, God's
love and care for them, declaring to them how He had
chosen them to be " a special people unto Himself

above all the people that are upon the face of the earth,' vii. 6. And showing them that this was not because of their own greatness or goodness, but because the Lord loved them, and because He " would keep the oath which He had sworn," vii. 7, 8. He exhorts them to " remember all the way" by which the Lord had led them, viii. 2, and sets before them the blessings to which He was bringing them, viii. 7–9.

In chapters xii. to xxix. are given the new commandments which were made necessary by the new position they were about to occupy as God's peculiar people, dwelling in a land of enemies. These had especial reference to their worship, chapters xii., xvi., xvii., xxvi. ; their utter separation from all evil, either of idols, chap. xiii. ; or of unclean food, chap. xiv. ; or of moral sin, chaps. xxi., xxii. ; or of natural defilement, chap. xxiii. ; and their dealings in love and grace with one another, chaps. xv., xxiv., xxv. Chap. xxviii. sets before them the blessings that follow obedience, and the curses that follow disobedience. Chapter xxix. is the personal application to the consciences of the people of all that has preceded. Chapters xxx. and xxxi. are prophetic of their backsliding, and contain a blessed message of God's restoring love. Chapter xxxii. is Moses' song, which was to be taught to the children of Israel, to be in their remembrances as a continual witness against them when the days of their failure should come, see xxxi. 19– 22. Chapter xxxiii. contains the revelation of the wondrous blessings the Lord had still for His people, although

He knew their weakness and their foolishness, and foresaw their wanderings ; blessings sure to come at last,
though they may have to tarry long because of the
hardness of their hearts. "Happy art thou, O Israel ;
who is like unto thee, O people saved by the Lord, the
shield of thy help, and who is the sword of thy excel
lency ! And thine enemies shall be found liars unto
thee; and thou shalt tread upon their high places,"
xxxiii. 29.

Chapter xxxiv. gives us the death of Moses, preceded
by his view into the promised land from Pisgah's height ;
and closes with God's testimony concerning him, that
"there arose not a prophet since in Israel like unto
Moses, whom the Lord knew face to face."

That Moses could not enter the promised land seems
to me significant of the fact that the law can have
nothing to do with the soul that is "seated in heavenly
places in Christ Jesus." Moses was in a very especial
way the representative of the law, as we are told "the
law was given by Moses, but grace and truth came by
Jesus Christ," John i. 17. And to make the picture complete, we may well believe that Moses must die before
Joshua could lead the people in. The very opening of
the book of Joshua implies this, for we read there that
the Lord spake unto Joshua, saying, "Moses my servant
is dead : now *therefore* arise, go over this Jordan, thou
and all this people, unto the land which I do give to
them."

It may seem strange to insist upon a perfect obedience

to the law, and then to talk about the law being dead.
But it is a fact in experience that complete surrender to
any law, always makes the soul free from that law. The
law-abiding citizen who has no thought of breaking the
laws of his country, is as free from those laws as though
there were none. The law is dead as far as he is concerned, because it demands only that which he himself
thinks is best and right, and which therefore he *wants*
to give; and for him in effect there is no law. But he is
made free by obeying the law, not by disobeying it.
And so also it is said of the Christian who has submitted
himself fully to the law of God and who walks in the
Spirit, "that against such there is no law," Gal. v. 23.
If the law is written in our hearts, we shall not need it in
outward code; and we shall "walk at liberty" as the
Psalmist says, just because we seek God's precepts, and
keep His law continually, Ps. cxix. 44, 45.

In chap. xxvi. we have given us what might be called
the *process* of consecration. The believer comes here
before the Lord bringing the first-fruits of his land as a
free will offering, and confessing his standing and his
possessions, " I profess this day unto the Lord thy God,
that I am come unto the country which the Lord sware
unto our fathers for to give us." See also verses 5–10.
No doubts are here. " I *am* come;" "He *hath*
brought;" "He *hath* given." Doubts are fatal to
consecration. The soul must be assured that it belongs
to the Lord, before it can consecrate itself to His service.
But being thus assured, and acknowledging it, the path

is simple, and is clearly laid down in verses 16–19   In
verse 16 we have the command.   In verse 17 the surrender to obedience.   And in verses 18, 19 the Lord's
acceptance.   We avouch the Lord to be our God, and
that we will walk in His ways and keep His commandments ; and He at once avouches us to be His peculiar
people, and declares that we *shall* keep His commandments, and that He will make us an holy people.   Our
part is to surrender ourselves to Him, and His part is to
accomplish the work.

To pass through the experience of Deuteronomy
therefore, brings the soul out into a large place, into a
land of liberty and rest, and joy, and blessings innumer-
able ; and I would entreat every one of my readers, before turning to another chapter of this book, to surrender
themselves, gladly and unconditionally to the sweet will
of God, to be its captive forever !

> " Thy beautiful sweet will, my God,
>   Holds fast in its sublime embrace
> My captive will, a gladsome bird
>   Prisoned in such a realm of grace.
> O lightest burden, sweetest yoke,
>   It lifts, it bears my happy soul ;
> It giveth wings to this poor heart
>   My freedom is Thy grand control.
> Upon God's will I lay me down
>   As child upon its mother's breast,
> No silken couch, nor softest bed
>   Could ever give me such sweet rest.'

10

It may be that you have not hitherto looked upon
God's will in this light, and have shrunk from abandoning yourselves to its control. What words can I use,
dear friends, to make you see that it is the one only desirable thing in earth or Heaven; and that to be all the
Lord's, and entirely at His dear disposal is Heaven
begun below? No human words can tell this story, for
it hath not entered into the heart of man to conceive the
things which God hath prepared for them that love Him.
But to every surrendered soul He will reveal them by
His Spirit, and you shall know the fulfilment of that wondrous promise of our Lord's, " He that hath My commandments and keepeth them, he it is that loveth Me ;
and he that loveth me shall be loved of my Father, and
I will love him, and manifest myself to him. * * *
If a man love me he will keep my words, and my
Father will love him, and we will come unto him, and
make our abode with him." John xiv. 21–23.

Joseph Cook in one of his scientific statements concerning conscience says, " It is fact of experience that
whenever we submit utterly, affectionately, irreversibly
to the best we know, that is to the Innermost Holiest of
conscience, at that instant, and never before, there
flashes through us with quick, splendid, interior, unex-
pected illumination, a Power and a Presence not ourselves ; and we know by the inner light that God is
with us in a sense utterly unknown before."

Surely for such an end as this any surrender could be
nothing but joy. Try it, dear reader, and see if all I

say is not true and infinitely more that I cannot say. And thus going step by step with the children of Israel through the book of Deuteronomy, let us be prepared in Joshua with them to cross the Jordan and go in and take possession of the promised land.

Texts on the consecration of the Redeemed soul: Rom. xii. 1, 2 ; Ex. xix. 5; xxii. 22; 1 Sam. xv. 22; Jer. vii. 23; Rom. vi. 13; 2 Cor. vii. 1; 1 John iii. 3; Heb. vi. i; 1 Thess. iv. 1-4; Col. iii. 1-5; 2 Cor. vi. 14–18; 1 Cor. vi. 20; Matt. x. 37-39; xvi. 24, 25; Luke xiv. 26-33; Mark viii. 34, 35; Neh. viii.; ix. 38; x. 1, 28, 29; 2 Kings xxiii. 3; Num. vi.; Matt. vii. 21.

CHAPTER VIII.

JOSHUA.

THE REDEEMED IN HEAVENLY PLACES.

Keynote Rom. viii. 1-4.

THE book of Joshua gives us the redeemed in heavenly places. It is the story of the entrance of God's chosen people into the land of their possession, and their victories and rest there. It answers to the book of Ephesians, where we are shown the believer as " blessed with all spiritual blessings in heavenly places," made to " sit together in heavenly places in Christ Jesus," and wrestling there against spiritual wickedness, or as the margin has it "against wicked spirits in heavenly places." Eph. i. 3 ; ii. 6 ; vi. 12.

God's redeemed people in this book come out of the wilderness, and enter at last into possession of the land which He had promised them, the land from which they had been turned back forty years before by their unbelief. They conquer the very cities, great and walled up to heaven, which had frightened them so then, and overcome the giants of whom they had said, "We were in our own sight as grasshoppers, and so we were in their sight." In this book the Christian, in type, comes out of the wilderness of the seventh chapter of Romans, where his language is, "Oh wretched man that I am! who shall deliver me from the body of this death," into the promised land of the eighth chapter, where he can triumphantly exclaim, "Nay, in all these things we are more than conquerors through Him that loved us."

The land of Canaan is often taken as being intended for a type of heaven, and crossing the Jordan as a type of death. But this can hardly be, since in heaven we shall have no foes to conquer, and there will be no danger of failure there, while in Canaan there were enemies on every hand, and many instances of grievous defeat. In Hebrews iii. and iv. the Holy Ghost takes up the story of Israel's failure to enter into the land of Canaan, and applies it to the consciences of Christians, as a warning to them not to make a similar failure. "Let us therefore fear," he says, "lest a promise being left us of entering into his rest, any of you should seem to come short of it. For unto us was the gospel preached as well as unto them: but the word preached did not profit them, not being mixed with faith in them that heard it. For we which have believed do enter into rest." This rest is plainly a present possession of the trusting soul; something that can be enjoyed in this life; for we are told that those who believe do now and here "enter into rest. And I think there-

10*

fore that we must look upon the land of promise then, as a type of the land of promise now and the victories and rest there, as pictures of the victories and rest the soul finds in the present day, when it has fully taken possession of God's promises, and is dwelling in the enjoyment of them.

I was once taught a very striking lesson on this point by a dear old colored saint, who was attending a Bible class of which I was the teacher. The portion of Scripture we were considering was the book of Romans, and I was expounding especially the seventh and eighth chapters. I thought the dear old sister seemed rather puzzled by my explanations, but put this down to her want of intelligence, when suddenly she burst out with, "Why, honey, it 'pears like you don't understand dem chapters. You talk just as if you thought we was to live all de time in de seventh of Romans, and only pay little visits now and then to de eighth." "Certainly," I replied, "that is just what I do think, do not you?" "Oh honey," she said with infinite pity and surprise in her tone, "I'se afeard you don't know much. Why I *lives* in de eighth!" And the old face shone through all its blackness with what Joseph Cook calls the "solar light," as she said the words, and I felt they were true; but I was actually so ignorant as to think that it must be because she was colored and poor, that God had given her such peculiar blessings, in order to make up to her for these misfortunes! And I almost wished I too was colored and poor, that I might have a chance for similar blessing ! But I could never forget the impression made upon me, and from that time onward sought continually for the secret of her joy. Until at last the path across from the seventh to the eighth of Romans was revealed to me, and I saw that people who were not old, nor poor, nor colored, might yet also take up their abode in the blessed land of promise there revealed.

The book of Joshua opens on the children of Israel encamped in the plains of Moab "on this side Jordan, in the wilderness." Their long weary wanderings, since they had refused to enter the land forty years before, had not brought them any nearer Canaan than they were when they set out. They were on the borders then, and they were only on the borders now. They had been moving, certainly, during all these forty years, but like a great deal of what is called "religious growth," their course had not been "upward and onward." They had gone round and round in that dreary wilderness, doubling on their track continually, and journeying onward, only to journey back again. And now a river lay between them and the land of their possession. Had they gone in at first, at Kadesh-barnea, they would have had only an unseen boundary to cross, and the transition would not have been so strongly marked. And so I believe that in the experience of the Christian, there need not be that definite step, to which so many object, in entering into the more full enjoyment of the promises of the gospel, if only at our conversion we were taught that we were well able to overcome the land, and were urged to go in at once and possess it. Doubtless some do thus enter in at Kadesh-barnea. But the majority of Christians, like the Israelites, fail to enter in at first, because of unbelief, and are turned back like them to wander in the wilderness of the seventh of Romans.

But there comes a time to all such, sooner or later, I believe, when they are brought a second time to the borders of the land ; and to them this book is full of most blessed teaching.

It opens with the Lord's command to His people. "Now therefore, arise, go over this Jordan, thou and all this people, unto the land which I do give to them." (i. 2.) It was not only a privilege He offered them, but a command He made. His object in redeeming them out of Egypt had been to bring them into this land. " I am come down," He said in Exodus, "to deliver them out of the hand of the Egyptians, and to bring them up out of that land unto,"—what ? the wilderness, to wander there forty years ?—no,—"unto a good land and a large, unto a land flowing with milk and honey ; unto the place of the Canaanites, and the Hittites, and the Amorites, and the Perizzites, and the Hivites, and the Jebusites." And unless they should actually be brought into this land, the nations round about, who knew of their going out of Egypt, and who had heard that the Lord was among them and " was seen face to face," and that He went " before them, by day time in a pillar of cloud, and in a pillar of fire by night," might well say, as Moses feared they would, that it was " because the Lord was not able to bring this people into the land which He sware unto them. '' Numbers xiv. 14–16. Therefore, for His own glory's sake, it was necessary that His people should go in and be planted in the land of their inheritance. And with us also it is not a privilege only, but the commandment of our Lord, that we shall enter into possession of the promises, into that land of blessing and of rest which corresponds spiritually to the Canaan of the Israelites. "Abide in me." " Be filled with the Spirit." " Reckon yourselves to be dead indeed unto sin." "Be careful for nothing." "Let not your heart be troubled, neither let it be afraid." All these are glorious privileges, but they are positive commands also. And unless Christians do as a fact enter into this blessed fullness of their salvation, they will surely give occasion to the world to say ; that it is because God is not able to bring them into the land which He sware unto them. For as we read in Luke i. 69-75, the declaration concerning the Lord Jesus by the Holy Ghost was, " Blessed be the Lord God of Israel; for he hath visited and redeemed His people, and hath raised up an horn of salvation for us, in the house of his servant David : As he spake by the mouth of his holy prophets, which have been since the world began : that we should be saved from our enemies, and from the hand of all that hate us; to perform the mercy promised to our fathers, and to remember His holy covenant; the oath which He sware to our father Abraham, that He would grant unto us, that we, being delivered out of the hand of our enemies, might serve Him without fear, in holiness and righteousness before Him, all the days of our life." If we then as Christians, say this is impossible, we in effect declare that what God has promised, He is *not* able to perform; and thus bring dishonor on His great name.

It is the Lord's command to us, therefore, that we go in and possess the land of our inheritance. And to me God's commands are even more comforting than His promises; for if He commands me to do a thing, I am sure He will give me the power of His Spirit to do it. His commands are not grievous, we are told, but surely they would be grievous, if we were utterly unable to obey them. It would have been a grievous thing indeed had He commanded the children of Israel to go in and possess the land of Canaan, and yet, knowing that they were utterly unable to do it, had not Himself intended to supply them with the power. And, in fact, He uses His very command as the reason why they should have no fear. "Have not I commanded thee?" He asks. "Be strong and of a good courage; be not afraid, neither be thou dismayed; for the Lord thy God is with thee whithersoever thou goest," i. 9. As much as to say, "Thou needst have no fear in undertaking to do what I have commanded thee to do, for I am in every command I give, and will always bestow the necessary power to obey it."

Another thing is to be noticed in this opening proclamation of the Lord to His people. "Every place that the soles of your feet shall tread upon that have I given unto you," i. 3. Not "that *will* I give," but "that *have* I given." It was all theirs in the purpose and mind of God, but unless they actually *went* there and set their feet upon it, it did not become theirs practically and ex- perimentally. This is necessarily true of any gift. The giver may give it with all the sincerity and good-will pos- sible, but unless the one to whom he gives it, actually re- ceives it, and appropriates it, and calls it his own, it never comes really into his possession at all. Even though a gift should be laid on the table, or put in the pocket of a friend, unless that friend closes the hand of acceptance over it, and says mentally, " It is mine," he will not after all possess it.

The children of Israel were going in to take possession of their own land. The Lord had given it to them centuries before, and it was theirs all the while, only waiting for their coming. And so of ourselves we read that God " *hath* blessed us with all spiritual blessings in heavenly places in Christ;" although we very well know that until the hand of faith really closes over and appropriates these blessings, and we begin to say " they are mine," we do not actually and experimentally come into their enjoyment at all.

This land of promise seems to me to typify, as I have said, that experience in the Christian life which is called variously sanctification, perfect love, the rest of faith, the interior life, full salvation, the higher Christian life, and many other names, which all however I believe mean one and the same thing. And what they mean is

according to my understanding of it, that at some certain
time in its experience the soul finds in the Lord Jesus
Christ not only a deliverer from the *guilt* of sin, but also
a deliverer from its *power;* and comes into a life of victory, and rest, and liberty, and peace, and joy in the
Holy Ghost. The Christian who has entered into this
experience finds himself in possession of the promises
at which he has hitherto looked with longing but hopeless eyes. His will is in harmony with God's will.
Obedience becomes a delight, and service sweet. Cares,
and fears, and anxieties are all lost in the infiniteness of
God's love. And the law of the Spirit of life in Christ Jesus
is found experimentally to set the soul free from the law
of sin and death. Romans vi. and viii. are perhaps the
best expressions of this life ; though the whole New Testament is one long declaration and description of it.

The way into it is like the way out of the wilderness
into the promised land. It is by the pathway of
consecration and faith. Entire surrender to the will of
God and perfect trust in His love, will take thee there
dear seeker, whether thou clearly understandest the doctrines concerning it or not ; and once in, thou wilt know
more about it, than I could tell thee if I should write a
book full concerning it. Let me earnestly beg of thee,
therefore, to be strong and of a good courage, for has not
the Lord commanded thee? Arise then, this very day,
and, with Israel, go in to possess the land which the
Lord thy God giveth thee, to possess it. Step the foot
of thy faith upon each one of His promises, and stand

there steadfastly, sure that they shall be every one thine.
Thy part is to step, His it is to give thee possession. And
His blessed Spirit, who abides in every promise, will
make thee mighty through God to the pulling down of
every stronghold, and the overcoming of every enemy.

In chapter second we have given us the history of Rahab, a wonderful picture of how acceptable faith is to the
Lord, even when exercised in the midst of great ignorance
and distance from Himself. The comment of the Holy
Ghost is given us in Heb. xi. 31: "By faith the harlot
Rahab perished not with them that believed not." And
her faith so strengthened the faith of the spies that they
returned to Joshua with the triumphant language, " Truly
the Lord hath delivered into our hands all the land: for
even all the inhabitants of the country do faint because
of us," ii. 24. How different the report of these spies
from that of the spies sent out forty years before. The
giants were as mighty now as then, and the cities as
great, and they themselves were as weak. But *then*
they had left out the Lord, and had measured their enemies
with themselves ; and *now* Rahab had brought Him in
for she had said, "I know that THE LORD hath given
you the land," ii. 9. When God is brought into the
scene and our enemies are measured with Him, there
can no longer be any doubt or fear remaining. And I
believe, dear reader, that if we could send out spies into
the land of our possession, as Israel did, we would find
also, that our enemy faints because of us, and that he
knows, whether we do or not, that the Lord hath delivered

11

into our hands all the land.   He is an already conquered foe, and the courage of faith will soon discover this, let him bluster as he may.

In chapter third we have the wonderful scene of the crossing of Jordan,—a crossing which, while in many respects it is similar to, was yet very different from the crossing of the Red Sea.   At the Red Sea no preparation was needed to make them ready, but they crossed in haste to escape from a pursuing enemy.   Here the command was, " Prepare you victuals, for within three days ye shall pass over this Jordan to go in to possess the land which the Lord your God giveth you to possess it," i. 11.   And again we read in iii. 5 that Joshua said unto the people, "Sanctify yourselves; for to-morrow the Lord will do wonders among you."   There was no pursuing enemy now behind them, but instead, a glorious land lay before them, and a preparation was necessary before they could enter it.   This preparation was one of consecration.   The word sanctify means set apart, separate yourselves from all evil.   It means just what Paul says in 2 Cor. vii. 1. " Having therefore these promises, dearly beloved, let us cleanse ourselves from all filthiness of the flesh and spirit, perfecting holiness in the fear of God."   All that consciously defiles must be laid aside, before the soul can expect to enter into the fulness of God's promises.

Again, at the Red Sea the path was made, before the Israelites were called upon to take a single step.   But here the path was only made *when* they stepped, " And it shall come to pass, as soon as the soles of the feet of the priests that bear the ark of the LORD, the Lord of all the earth, shall rest in the waters of Jordan, that the waters of Jordan shall be cut off from the waters that come down from above; and they shall stand upon an heap." Joshua iii. 13. The priests who are types of Christians in communion with God, were to step into the brimming river, for at this time Jordan was overflowing all its banks; and as they thus stepped in, the waters stood and rose up on an heap and the path was made. iii. 15–17. And so in realizing the forgiveness of our sins, we believe in an already accomplished fact, and enter into the enjoyment of a finished work. While in sanctification we believe in a fact that is accomplished *when* we believe, and enter into the enjoyment of a work that is going on *as* we trust.

It required a far stronger faith to cross the Jordan than to cross the Red Sea; and the faith which can trust for the forgiveness of sins, needs to be greatly strengthened, in order to believe in victory over sin. To me, this stepping into a brimming river, when as yet there was no sign of a path, is one of the grandest pictures of faith on record. I can fancy the heathen nations around, if they witnessed the scene, sneering at the folly and presumption of a people who could thus act. They must have known only too well that they could not trust their gods after such a fashion. But I think their cry afterwards must have been, "Surely no people have a god like unto these people!" And could the world but see more of this sublime sort of faith among Christians now, I feel sure they would be won to yield allegiance to a God who can thus be trusted, and who never fails His people's confidence.

But as this was an untrodden path to Israel, the Ark of the Covenant, which in one aspect typifies Christ, was to precede them in this journey, "that ye may know the way by which ye must go; for ye have not passed this way heretofore," ii. 4. The path of faith is always a new and untrodden way to the soul, and it is only by "looking unto Jesus" that we can ever "know the way by which we must go."

The crossing of the Jordan, it seems to me, is a type of death and resurrection; not the death of the body, but the death to sin spoken of in Rom. vi. and else-where, and the resurrection to newness of life now; as declared in Rom. vi. 4. "Therefore we are buried with him by baptism into death: that like as Christ was raised up from the dead by the glory of the Father, even so we also should walk in newness of life." It is the believer by faith reckoning himself to be "dead indeed unto sin, but alive unto God in Jesus Christ our Lord." At the Red Sea, death also was the type, but our share there was more that of entering into the accomplished results of the death and resurrection of Christ, by know-ing our sins to be forgiven, and by realizing our transla-tion out of the kingdom of Satan into the kingdom of God's dear Son. While here the type is our being crucified with Christ, and realizing our resurrection life of holiness and separation in Him. As Paul says, "knowing this, that our old man is crucified with Him, that the body of sin might be destroyed, that henceforth we should not serve sin," Rom. vi. 6. Here in type, it seems to me, we do what Paul exhorts us to do in Eph. iv. 22-24, "That ye put off concerning the former conversation the old man, which is corrupt according to the deceitful lusts; and be renewed in the spirit of your mind. And that ye put on the new man, which after God is created in righteousness and true holiness."

To look at it practically and experimentally, I mean that this crossing of the Jordan typifies the crossing of the soul out of the experience of the seventh chapter of Romans into the experience of the eighth. It is the step by which the believer who has been justified, comes to know what it is to be sanctified also. It is in short the obeying of the command, "Reckon ye also yourselves to be dead indeed unto sin, and alive unto God through Jesus Christ our Lord." It is dying with Christ by faith, in order to be raised with Him into newness of life.

In experience this is an intensely practical thing. For nothing so gives victory over sin as to reckon one's self to be *dead* to it, and nothing so enables the soul to walk in righteousness as to realize its resurrection life in Christ. It may be difficult to explain this theologically or doctrinally; but to my mind the great point in studying the Bible is to get at its truths experimentally; and thousands of witnesses can testify to the blessed reality of being dead to sin and alive to God in Jesus Christ. I have known life-long besetments conquered in this

11*

way, that had not yielded one iota to all the struggles
and efforts of years. I knew a lady with such an irritable temper that it was almost intolerable to live with
her. She was a Christian, and she grieved over it with
bitter sorrow, but seemed to find it impossible to get
the victory by years of struggling and agonizing.
Finally when she was almost in despair, she was told by
one who knew the way of faith, to reckon herself dead to
it, and that if she did, God would make it real by the
power of His Spirit. In her despair she grasped at the
hope, and. kneeling before her open Bible with her
finger on Rom. vi. 11, she dared to obey the divine command and reckoned herself, on the authority of God's
own word, to be dead indeed unto sin, but alive unto God
through Jesus Christ. It seemed like a step off from a
fearful precipice into a sheer abyss. But the step of
faith, found, as it always does, the rock beneath, and
according to her faith it was unto her. She met every
temptation to irritability by saying, " I am dead to sin.
I am crucified with Christ. I am alive in Him," and
from that hour, now for many years, not even an inward
ruffle has disturbed her peace.

Take the step of faith then, dear friends, into the
brimming flood, and in obedience to God, apprehend
your position as dead and risen with Christ and in
Christ; and henceforth walk as those ought to walk who
are indeed alive from the dead.

The twelve stones left in Jordan's bed, and the twelve
brought out and set up as memorials, in chapter iv.

both show the twelve tribes of Israel as being actual
sharers in the death and resurrection, iv. 21, 22, and
are a symbol of our union with Christ in these.

Chapter v. gives us the circumcision at Gilgal. "For
ye are dead, and your life is hid with Christ in God.* *
Mortify therefore your members which are upon the
earth." Col. iii. 3, 5.

If we are indeed dead to sin, it is necessary that we
should practically realize it. Col. iii. 10–12 expresses this.
Self must be mortified before victories can be won. The
reproach of Egypt must be rolled away, ver. 9, before we
can take possession of Jericho. We must always bear
about in the body the dying of the Lord Jesus, if we
would have the life of Jesus manifested in our mortal
flesh. 2 Cor. vi. 10, 11. And until this is done we cannot eat of the "old corn of the land," vers. 11, 12 ; which
means, I think, a feeding on Christ in a far deeper sense,
than was typified by the manna, even that which is set
forth in John vi. 48–56, "He that eateth my flesh and
drinketh my blood, dwelleth in me and I in him."
Furthermore, when we have passed through the circumcision of Gilgal, we find ourselves in a place where we
can have a revelation of our Captain, and can roll upon
Him all the burden and the responsibility of our warfare. Vers. 13–15.

Chapter vi. gives us the taking of Jericho, one of those
very cities "great, and walled up to Heaven," which
had discouraged the heart of the people forty years before. The Lord Himself arranged the plan of the cap-

ture, and in it, I believe, gave us a sample of the "fight of faith." The people of Israel had no weapons of warfare with which to meet their enemies, nor any battering rams for those mighty walls. They had nothing but their God and their faith. Their part was simply to march and to shout. The Lord's part was to make the walls fall down, and to conquer their enemies. 2 Cor. x. 4. "For the weapons of our warfare are not carnal, but mighty through God to the pulling down of strong holds." And therefore we read in Heb. xi. 30: "By faith the walls of Jericho fell down, after they were compassed about seven days." Prudence would have said, "Do not shout until the walls show some signs of tottering,' but faith said, while yet the walls seemed as firm as ever, "Shout, for the Lord hath given you the city." vi. 16. "So the people shouted when the priests blew with the trumpets: and it came to pass, when the people heard the sound of the trumpet, and the people shouted with a great shout, that the wall fell down flat, so that the people went up into the city, every man straight before him, and they took the city." vi. 20.

And so likewise I believe the Christian is called to shout the shout of victory over his foes, even at the moment perhaps when they seem stronger than ever. I mean just this, that if we meet our enemy as an already conquered foe, and claim by faith our victory over him in Christ, we shall overcome far more quickly, than if we look upon him as an enemy who has yet to be conquered by our vigorous conflict against him.

"This is the victory that overcometh the world, even our faith." 1 John, v. 4. And I have found experimentally that the little words, "Jesus saves me, Jesus saves me *now*," repeated over and over, in any great stress of temptation, will bring a far more speedy victory than I can gain in any other way. For our Lord Himself says, "That whosoever shall say unto this mountain, Be thou removed and be thou cast into the sea; and shall not doubt in his heart, but shall believe that those things that he saith shall come to pass, he shall have whatsoever he saith. Therefore I say unto you, What things soever ye desire when ye pray, believe that you receive them, and ye shall have them." Mark xi. 23, 24.

This victory at Jericho was followed by a disastrous defeat at Ai, in chapter vii., caused by a hidden sin. In the life of faith, our only strength is in the Lord, and if any indulged evil shall cause Him to withdraw His strength, we find ourselves utterly unable to "stand before our enemies," vii. 11-13. Nothing but perfect integrity of heart before the Lord can ensure a continuous victory. This whole story of the taking of Ai contains most striking teaching, concerning the causes of failure and the way to deal with it, in this life of faith, but I cannot here enlarge on it.

From chapters ix.—xii. we have an account of the further conquest of the land, full of many deeply interesting lessons of the overcoming by faith. "So Joshua took the whole land, according to all that the Lord said

unto Moses, and Joshua gave it for an inheritance unto
Israel according to their divisions by their tribes.   And
the land rested from war."   xi. 23.

In chapters xiii.–xxii. we have the story of the parti-
tion of the land among the tribes of Israel, with the ap-
pointing of the cities of refuge, and the assigning of their
inheritance to the Levites.   All being, I doubt not, typical of that which is set before us in 1 Cor. xii., and else-
where, " Now there are diversities of gifts, but the same
Spirit."   * * *   " But all these worketh that one and
the self-same Spirit, dividing to every man severally as
He will."

Chapters xxiii. and xxiv. give us Joshua's closing
words to the people he was about to leave ; an address
which in many things reminds us forcibly of Paul's fare-
well address to the elders of the Ephesian church, Acts
xx. Both Joshua and Paul foresaw evil days for the flocks
over whom they had so faithfully watched, both warned
them against the corruption of evil association and companionship, and both also assured them of the power
of the Lord to deliver, if they would but trust Him. And in
the case of both, I doubt not that there was already cause
for much sorrow of heart.   The Israelites had lost the
freshness of their early zeal, and had become " slack to go
up" and possess the land of their inheritance.   Large
portions of it remained still in possession of their
enemies, and the leaven of these associations was working
among them. Therefore Joshua, gathering the elders and
judges and officers of the people around him in Shechem,

xxiv. 1, seeks to stir them up to a fresh consecration of themselves to God, before he should be called to leave them. He reminds them of all the way by which the Lord had led them, of the deliverances He had wrought, and the victories He had granted, and closes with an enumeration of the gifts He had bestowed as an incentive to a whole-hearted surrender of themselves to Him. "I have given you a land for which ye did not labor, and cities which ye built not, and ye dwell in them ; of the vineyards and oliveyards which ye planted not do ye eat. Now therefore fear the Lord and serve Him in sincerity and in truth ; and put away the gods which your fathers served on the other side of the flood, and in Egypt ; and serve ye the Lord. And if it seem evil unto you to serve the Lord, choose you this day whom ye will serve." Won by Joshua's eloquence, and convinced in their hearts that no service could make them so happy as the service of the Lord their God, the people answered and said, " God forbid that we should forsake the Lord to serve other gods." And when Joshua tried to show them the danger there was of failure, they but reiterated their promises over and over, "Nay ; but we will serve the Lord." "The Lord our God will we serve, and His voice will we obey." * * * " And Joshua wrote these words in the book of the law of God, and took a great stone, and set it up there under an oak, that was by the sanctuary of the Lord. And Joshua said unto all the people, Behold, this stone shall be a witness unto us." xxiv. 14–25.

Beloved, have we not come also to a Shechem in our own experience, when with full purpose of heart we have given ourselves to the Lord our God to serve Him and Him only? And shall we not seek for a stone of witness to be raised up before our Lord, that in days to come when our enemies shall try to entice us from our allegiance, will hold us to our covenant in better fashion than Israel was held, even the witness and the seal of the indwelling Spirit, who comes to fill and possess every fully consecrated soul?

"And it came to pass after these things that Joshua died." And the significant announcement is made that Israel served the Lord " all the days of Joshua, and all the days of the elders that overlived Joshua, which had known all the works of the Lord, that He had done for Israel;" thus preparing us somewhat for the sad story of failure that is to follow in the book of Judges.

Their Joshua died. But our Joshua never dies; and we, if we serve the Lord all our days, will serve Him forever, and need never in our experience go out of this book of triumph, nor know the sorrows and bondage of the book of failures that here succeeds it.

A chain of texts illustrating the lesson of Joshua :—
Ex. iii. 7, 8. vi. 6-8. Deut i. 20, 21. Luke i. 68-75. Acts iii. 26. Titus ii. 14. Rom. vi. 4, 6. viii. 1-4, 35-39. 2 Cor. ii. 14. ix. 8. Eph. i. 3. ii. 6. iii. 14-21. 1 Thess. iv. 3, 4. v. 23.

CHAPTER IX.

JUDGES.

THE FAILURE OF THE REDEEMED IN HEAVENLY PLACES.

Keynote, 1 Cor. iii. 1--4.

THE book of Judges is a book of failure. We see God's redeemed people here, living in the land of their inheritance, with all their enemies subdued before them, and yet continually overcome and enslaved by the inhabitants of the land. It seems to me to be in type the story of the dangers and temptations which beset the soul that is seated in heavenly places in Christ, and the enemies they are likely to meet there; and is a book of warning written for our admonition " to the intent that we should not lust after evil things, as they also lusted."

The whole story of this book may be given in a few verses out of the second chapter. " And the children of Israel did evil in the sight of the Lord, and served Baalim : and they forsook the Lord God of their fathers, which brought them out of the land of Egypt, and followed other gods, of the gods of the people that were round about them, and bowed themselves unto them, and provoked the Lord to anger. And they forsook the Lord, and served Baal and Ashtaroth. And the anger of the Lord was hot against Israel, and He delivered them into the hands of spoilers that spoiled them, and He sold them into the hands of their enemies round about, so that they could not any longer stand before their enemies. Whithersoever they went out, the hand of the Lord was against them for evil, as the Lord had said, and as the Lord had sworn unto them : and they were greatly distressed. Nevertheless the Lord raised up judges, which delivered them out of the hand of those that spoiled them. And yet they would not hearken unto their judges, but they went a whoring after other gods, and bowed themselves unto them : they turned quickly out of the way which their fathers walked in, obeying the commandments of the Lord; but they did not so. And when the Lord raised them up judges, then the Lord was with the judge, and delivered them out of the hand of their enemies all the days of the judge: for it repented the Lord because of their groanings by reason of them that oppressed them and vexed them."

This state of things went on from bad to worse. Each restoration was followed by a long season of backsliding, until finally we find nothing but confusion and failure on every hand, with no hope of deliverance, and the book closes with this sad record of the utter absence of rule or control. " In those days there was no king in Israel : every man did that which was right in his own eyes." xxi. 25.

And this history of Israel is too often found to be the history of the Church, or of individual souls. The failures and the restorations correspond to the times of deadness and wandering in the church, or in the Christian, and the seasons of revival which for a little while deliver them from this backsliding. The church, or the individual Christian, is carried captive by the world, the flesh, or the devil; old and apparently conquered forms of evil are continually reappearing on the scene, which mightily oppress the children of God, as Israel was oppressed under their enemies; and they cry unto the Lord, as Israel did, and the Lord raises up a deliverer in the form of some great leader, such as Luther, or some fresh revelation of a neglected and forgotten truth; such as justification by faith, or the second coming of Christ, and for a time the land has rest again and is in quietness, until the enemies afresh rise up to enslave and overcome.

Two causes lay at the root of Israel's backsliding, and I believe they are the very causes that lie at the root of all Christian backsliding also. They compromised with evil, and they worshipped idols. The whole land of Canaan had been given to the children of Israel, "from the wilderness and this Lebanon, even unto the great river, the river Euphrates, all the land of the Hittites, and unto the great sea, toward the going down of the sun." And the command of the Lord to them concerning it was, "When ye are passed over Jordan, into the land of Canaan, then ye shall drive out all the inhabi tants of the land from before you, and destroy all their pictures, and destroy all their molten images, and quite pluck down all their high places: and ye shall dispossess the inhabitants of the land, and dwell therein : for I have given you the land to possess it. * * * But if ye will not drive out the inhabitants of the land from before you; then it shall come to pass, that those which yet remain of them shall be pricks in your eyes, and thorns in your sides, and shall vex you in the land wherein ye dwell." Num. xxxiii. 51–56. "They shall not dwell in thy land, lest they make thee sin against me : for if thou serve their gods, it will surely be a snare unto thee." Ex. xxiii. 33.

Moreover He also promised them a sure possession of it, saying, " Every place that the sole of your foot shall tread upon, that have I given unto you. * * * There shall not any man be able to stand before thee all the days of thy life : as I was with Moses, so will I be with thee. I will not fail thee nor forsake thee." Josh. i. 3, 5.

The land of promise was therefore all theirs in the purpose of God, and all they had to do was to step upon it and claim it for their own. But we see, even in Joshua, that in spite of all this there yet remained very much land to be possessed, and the people were "slack to go up and possess it." xiii. 1, and xviii. 3. And here in the first chapter of Judges we find, that they seem to have given up entirely all hope or expectation of driving out the inhabitants of the land, or even in many cases of dispossessing them from their dwelling-places. We read over and over, "And the children of Benjamin did not drive out the Jebusites that inhabited Jerusalem." i. 21. "Neither did Manasseh drive out the inhabitants of Beth-shean and her towns, nor Taanach and her towns ; * * * but the Canaanites *would* dwell in that land. * * Neither did Ephraim drive out the Canaanites that dwelt in Gezer. * * Neither did Zebulun drive out the inhabitants of Kitron. * * * Neither did Asher drive out the inhabitants of Accho, * * but the Asherites dwelt among the Canaanites, the inhabitants of the land ; for they did not drive them out." And it is all summed up in this, "And it came to pass when Israel was strong that they put the Canaanites to tribute, and did not utterly drive them out," i. 28. They might have done it, but they did not. And as a consequence we find in the second chapter that the triumphant experience of Gilgal is exchanged for the weeping of Bochim. Comp. Josh. v. 9–12 with Judges ii. 1--5. And the Lord who had said concerning their enemies in Joshua, " and the Lord your God, He shall expel them from before you and drive them out of your sight ; and ye shall possess their land, as the Lord your God hath promised unto you ;" now says, "I will not drive them out from before you, but they shall be as thorns in your sides, and their gods shall be a snare unto you."

Because they would not drive out their enemies when they were strong and could have done it, the Lord now refuses to enable them to do it any more ; and from henceforth throughout the whole story of the book of

12*

Judges, although we have many records of victories over their enemies, we read of no more being driven out ; but find instead, that, as they had been warned, so it resulted, and these ve y enemies who had been made tribute in the days of tl ir strength, rose up in the days of their weakness ano enslaved and oppressed them.

The lesson f all this for us is, that since the command of our Lord to s as Christians is that we should drive out every enemy from our hearts and lives, and should permit none to dwell among us, if we refuse to do this, and, instead of utterly driving them out, seek merely to make them tribute to us, we shall find ourselves continually enslaved and oppressed by those very enemies whom we have suffered to remain. The promise to Israel was that not a man should be able to stand before them all the days of their life, because the Lord would be with them and His strength would always give them the victory. And the promise to us is that we shall be delivered by the power of our Lord from the hands of all our enemies, and shall be enabled always to triumph in every contest with our foe. But if we, as they, refuse to avail ourselves fully of this promised strength, and use it only to make our enemies tribute, instead of driving them out utterly, we shall suffer the same results. This accounts for the condition of so many Christians, who find themselves enslaved and oppressed continually by their inward ene- mies, and whose victories, even when they cry to the Lord and are victorious, are yet followed by ever re- curring defeats. They groan under it and cannot understand it. But the secret lies in this, that they have not utterly driven out their enemies. They have thought perhaps that they could not. They have said, it may be, " My circumstances are so peculiar, or my temperament is so sensitive, or my temptations are so great ;" and excusing themselves on these accounts, they have not even *expected* to be entirely delivered from their irritable tempers, or their roots of bitterness, or their seasons of discouragement, or their sharp tongues, but have felt themselves very successful if they have been able to make these things tributary, as it were, and have managed to keep them under by constant watchfulness and prayer. And so they compromise with the enemy, instead of utterly driving him out. In this way many Christians compromise with doubt, or with the disobedience of timidity, or with a shrinking from saying " Thy will be done," or with anxiety, or with a hundred other forms of evil, against which God's commands of utter renunciation and death have plainly gone forth. And as a consequence *He* no longer drives out the enemies *we* have consented shall remain, and they are indeed snares and traps unto us, and scourges in our sides, and thorns in our eyes.

Dear reader, this is exceedingly practical to thee. Hast thou permitted any of thy enemies to dwell in thy midst ? Art thou seeking only to put them to tribute, and hesitating to utterly drive them out ? If so, do not wonder at the enslavement and misery that oppress thee. Be sure that in the Lord's order it could not be otherwise, and that he alone who reckons himself dead, not to a few only of his sins, but to every sin, can gain the continual victories, and live the life of uniform triumph. And I think it is just in this that the great difference arises in the experiences of those who enter into the land of promise now. With some, self seems to be swallowed up at once by the revelation of Christ, and to lift up its head no more; while with others the death of self is accomplished only by slow degrees and through great conflicts. The triumphant experience under Joshua is a type of the first, and the failing experience of Judges is a type of the second. Through death to life is always God's way, and there is no other. If we would live, we must first die. We must lose our own life, if we would find the life that is hid with Christ in God. We must reckon ourselves dead before we can reckon ourselves to be alive. And the more thorough and wide-reaching is the death, the more all-pervading and victorious will be the life. Is it not a grand proposal of the gospel then that we should put off at once and always the old man, and put on forever the new man? And shall we hesitate to do it?

For to us the declaration is as sure as to them, that every place that the foot of our faith shall tread upon, that shall be ours. "What things soever ye desire when ye pray, believe that ye receive them, and ye shall have them." Mark xi. 22–24. "Believing" is to us what "stepping the foot upon" was to them. The land of promise lies spread out before us, and in the purpose of the Lord is already ours. We are responsible therefore for actually taking possession of it. And our Lord has promised that He will be with us all the days of our life, and that we shall be made more than conquerors through Him. Let us then, in the power of the Holy Ghost, step out on each promise as it is made known to us, and confidently claim it as ours. And let us drive out every inhabitant of the land and make no league with any, but "cleansing ourselves from all filthiness of the flesh and spirit," let us "perfect holiness in the fear of the Lord."

I knew a poor Christian woman whose life was made bitter to her through the sufferings and remorse caused by the combination of an exceedingly irritable temper and circumstances of peculiar trial. She had struggled against it, and sought to keep it tributary with all her might during many years, but was continually finding it rising up and oppressing her, until she was almost in despair. Among other things she was obliged every morning to have a late breakfast for a son whose work kept him out late at night, and who therefore slept long in the morning. She was a tidy woman who liked to get her work done and things cleaned up, and this daily recurrence of a late and uncertain breakfast hour, which kept her pots and pans standing around, and her stove uncleaned, was a source of continual provocation. She knew it was not only unchristian, but unreasonable as well, and each day she resolved that the next morning she *would* control herself and be sweet, but the fresh provocation always overcame her, and her life was a burden to her. She even longed for death to set her free. But she heard at last of another sort of death that would deliver her. She was told of the glorious possibilities of being made dead to sin by faith in Christ, and the command was brought home to her to "reckon herself dead." In great weakness, but in simple faith, she obeyed this command, and began thus to reckon. Peace and rest flowed into her heart, and when the temptations came next she found herself possessed of an inward sweetness that made all the old annoyances matters of perfect indifference to her. Her son who had been used to cross looks and words during his late breakfasts watched her in amazement the first morning, and at last said, " Why, mother, what *is* the matter with you? Has anything happened to you?" " Yes, Albert," she replied, "something has happened. Your mother is dead." " Dead!" he exclaimed, " Why mother what do you mean?" The mother explained it to him as well as she could ; and he listened in amazement. Morning after morning he watched her, and finally he said "Well, mother, if you are going to be dead every morning, it makes you so lovely, that I am going to try to get to bed earlier, so as to come down early in the morning and see you."

Let us die then. " He that is dead is freed from sin," the Bible tells us, and we know it must be so. And I believe it is the only freedom that is really effectual or lasting.

But a worse evil than enslavement came from these

enemies left in the land. Idolatry swiftly followed in
the train. As we read in chapter ii. 7–10, iii. 7, "And
the people served the Lord all the days of Joshua, and
all the days of the elders that outlived Joshua, who had
seen all the great works of the Lord that He did for
Israel. And Joshua, the son of Nun, the servant of the
Lord, died, * * * also all that generation were gathered
unto their fathers : and there aıose another generation
after them which knew not the Lord, nor yet the works
which He had done for Israel. And the children of
Israel did evil in the sight of the Lord, and forgat the
Lord their God, and served Baalim and the groves."

The typical teaching of this sin of idolatry, is, I think,
very much misunderstood. Many think it means only
loving some dear one too much, or being too fond of
some earthly comfort or pleasure. But to my mind
idolatry means a far graver sin. It meant among the
Israelites worshipping a false god, and it means the same
now among Christians. And it matters little whether
this god is one carved out of wood or stone, or carved
out of our own imaginings. If our thought or idea of
Him is in any way different from the Lord whom the
Bible reveals, we are as really in so far worshipping an
idol, as though we had built up for ourselves a god of
wood. And in this sense idolatry is a far more common
sin in these days than some of you have been used to
think. Let me illustrate what I mean by a most common
occurrence. How many people say to their children
continually all through their childhood, "the Lord

does not love naughty children, and now that you are
naughty, He does not love you." Nothing more directly
contrary to the Bible, nor more untrue of the God of the
Bible, could be taught; for there we are told that " God
so *loved* the world that He gave His only begotten Son"
to die for it; and that on account of "His great *love* wherewith He *loved* us; even when we were dead in trespasses and sins," He quickened us; and that He
"commendeth His love toward us, in that even while we
were yet *sinners* Christ died for us." Surely then to
teach the innocent little children such a sad untruth as
this, is to set up an idol for them to worship. And when
they grow older and are compelled to learn that the God
of the Bible is other and different from what they have
been taught; that He hates only the sin but loves the
sinner, and that even when they are naughty, His for-
giving love is calling upon them to come to Him and
be saved, is it to be wondered at that they are so wedded
to their false idea of Him, as to find it very difficult and
often almost impossible to believe that He can really be
what the Bible declares Him to be, and to worship Him
as He is there revealed ? My heart aches at the thought
of the idols being fashioned in so many nurseries at this
very day for the little ones to worship ; and I feel that
the heathen mother who leads her child to the heathen
temple and makes it bow down before the image of wood
or of stone, is hardly so responsible as these Christian
mothers, who, with the Bible in their hands, can yet
fashion such a false God for the imaginings of their chil-

dren. I speak strongly for I feel strongly. I believe
many a soul has thus been burdened, even in the nursery, with such false ideas of God, as never to be able
in this life to shake off the doubts and discouragements
they have caused. And I am convinced that the amount
of this sort of idolatry in the Church to-day would be ap-
palling, if we could but see it in all its magnitude and de-
formity.

And for each of us personally, dear friends, it is a
solemn question, as to how far we are guilty of this sin.
Are we sure we are worshipping, and trusting, and
loving, *just* the God whom Christ reveals, or have we
let in some false notions concerning Him, which have
made Him appear to us other than He really is? Do
we for instance really believe that He loves us individually? Do we believe that He has blessed us with all
spiritual blessings in Christ, and that He will freely give
us all things? Do we believe that He has actually
made with every temptation a way of escape, that we
may be able to bear it? Do we believe that He does
truly care for us in all the little affairs of our lives, even
to the very numbering of the hairs of our heads, and
that He will carry every burden and bear every sorrow
for us, if we will but let Him? Or does He seem to us
like a hard task master, too far off and too grand to take
much note of our petty personal trials or needs, and
giving us impossible commands which He knows we are
not able to obey?

I entreat of you, dear friends, to search and see how

13

it is with you in this matter. For sure I am that idolatry of any sort, whether of outward fashioning or inward, is most grievous to our Lord, and most disastrous to us.

The children of Israel it appears served the true God as long as any were alive who remembered the wonderful deliverance out of Egypt, but when Joshua died and all the elders that outlived Joshua, who had seen all the great works of the Lord that He did for Israel, then they soon forgot Him and served other gods And I think this is significant of one form of idolatry which perhaps is peculiar to the higher stages of Christian experience. The soul, becoming absorbed in the deeper truths of our religion, is apt to lose sight of the fundamental doctrine of coming out of Egypt, or of justification by faith, and to speak and to think so exclusively of the fruits of the Spirit, and the life and walk of the believer, as almost or even quite to forget the necessity of pressing the foundation truths of salvation, and the way of entrance into the spiritual life. This leads to a onesided statement of truth, that may become very dangerous, especially to the soul which has had no clear teaching on the other side ; and may end in very false views of God. May the lessons of warning contained in our book save us each one from such mistakes.

Chapter iii. gives us the story of the three first captivities, and the deliverers who were raised up in answer to the people's cry. iii. 9, 15, 31. Whenever they cried the Lord delivered them. Let their sin against Him

have been ever so great, or their slavery to their enemies ever so hopeless, still we always read that *when*
they cried, *then* He delivered them. A beautiful type
of the truth taught in 1 John i. 9, "If we confess our sins,
He is faithful and just to forgive us our sins, and to
cleanse us from all unrighteousness." *When* we confess, *then* He forgives and cleanses. At once, without
any delay. And we must believe that He does, and rejoice in our deliverance.

Chapters iv. and v. give us the story of Deborah, and
her song of victory. I cannot but think that all these deliverers are types of some especial forms of the revivals
the Lord sends when His people cry. But I do not feel
prepared to enter upon this. To me however Deborah
seems to set forth most strikingly the lesson of God's
strength made perfect in our weakness. A woman here
leads the armies of the Lord against a captain who had
nine hundred chariots of iron, and who for twenty years
mightily oppressed the children of Israel; and even
Barak, whose name means thunder, the strong captain
in Israel, dared not go without her. "If thou wilt go
with me," he said, "then I will go; but if thou wilt not
go with me then I will not go." iv. 8. A picture it
seems to me of Paul's teaching in 2 Cor. xii. 7-10, "when
I am weak then I am strong." And a striking illustration of the truth that God hath chosen the weak things
of the world to confound the mighty, that no flesh might
glory in his presence. For Deborah said, "I will surely
go with thee: notwithstanding the journey that thou

takest shall not be for thine honor ; for the Lord shall
sell Sisera into the hand of a woman." iv. 9.

Chapters vi., vii. and viii. give us the story of the
captivity under Midian, and the deliverance wrought out
for them by Gideon. So low had the Israelites fallen by
their repeated failures, that at first one man only is found
faithful enough to be called into the work. Gideon's
first thought is of his own weakness, vi. 15, and he said,
" O my Lord, wherewith shall I save Israel ? behold my
family is poor in Manasseh, and I am the least in my
father's house ?" But the Lord's answer shows him the
secret of strength, " Surely I will be with thee." And
the whole story reveals to us this one grand fact that it
was the Lord who worked, and He alone. "And the
Lord said unto Gideon, The people that are with thee
are too many for me to give the Midianites into their
hands, lest Israel vaunt themselves against me, saying,
Mine own hand hath saved me." And Gideon finally
learns the lesson the Lord was seeking to teach by means
of all His dealings with him, and is willing to trust Him
with entire confidence, so that with only three hundred
men armed with trumpets, and empty pitchers, with
lamps within the pitchers, he was not afraid to attack the
mighty host that "lay all along in the valley like grasshoppers for multitude ;" and whose camels were "without number as the sand by the sea side for multitude."
vii. 12, 16. And so mighty was the influence of this display of overcoming faith upon the children of Israel, and
so complete was the rout of their enemies, that for forty

years afterward their country was in quietness, and they served the Lord. viii. 28.

But no sooner was Gideon dead, than we read that the " children of Israel turned again and went a whoring after Baalim, and made Baalberith the r god." viii. 33. And in chapter ix. we have a sad scene of confusion and sin caused by divisions among themselves. Faith had failed, and contention and strife entered.

Chapter x. shows us the increasingly sad result of Israel's repeated failures. When they cried to the Lord here He could not at once grant them the deliverance they sought. He had first to deal with their consciences to make them know the depth of their backsliding and of their need. " Ye have forsaken me," He said, " and served other gods ; wherefore I will deliver you no more. Go and cry unto the gods which ye have chosen : let them deliver you in the time of your tribulation." x. 13, 14. But he could not long delay His goodness, for " His soul was grieved for the misery of Israel." And in chapter xi. He raised up another deliverer, Jephthah, who again subdued their enemies and set them free. But although this was a real deliverance, yet the instrument used, the captain of a band of vain men, and the results in Jephthah's own sorrow, and the quarrel with Ephraim, chap. xii., show how low Israel had fallen, that even their recovery was of so poor a sort.

Chapter xiii. opens with the sad and oft repeated words, " And the children of Israel did evil again in the sight of the Lord." And now, so repeated had been their failures

13*

and so weakening had been the effect, that none but a Nazarite can be used as the deliverer. xiii. 5. Nazariteship is a type of entire separation to God. See Num. iv. And in this case the enemy who had assumed dominion over Israel were the Philistines, who were not a scourge sent from without, but a plague dwelling within their own territory; and against an evil within, nothing but the spirit of entire separation to God can give victory. xiii. 24-25. Therefore to Samson, the one Nazarite in all Israel, as far as appears, it is given to plague and harass the Philistines continually, and to keep them in check. But he alone could not entirely conquer them, much less extirpate them; and from this time forward, until the time of David, they remained to be Israel's bitterest foes. And even Samson himself, Nazarite though he was, had a walk of only intermittent faithfulness, and brought himself into great trouble, by disobedience to the Lord's express command against inter-marriages with the nations who dwelt in the land, in taking one of the daughters of the Philistines for his wife, xiv. 1-2. The Lord, however, who can and does, make all things, even our mishaps, work together for good to them who love Him, used this connection to punish the Philistines. xiv. 4.

Again, after the death of his wife, another connection with the Philistines brought him into even greater trouble, leading him to betray the Lord's secret, xvi. 5-20, and is the occasion in the end of his losing his life; although this too God used to punish the Philistines, and help Israel, xvi. 30.

From this time forward no deliverer was raised up for Israel, nor does it appear that they even cried for one. So hardened had they become by the long course of sin and idolatry, that they no longer felt the yoke of their enemy. Mind and conscience had become defiled, and to them was fulfilled what Paul described as being characteristic of the latter times, in 1 Tim. iv. 1–2, " Now the Spirit speaketh expressly, that in the latter times some shall depart from the faith, giving heed to seducing spirits, and doctrines of devils; speaking lies in hypocrisy; having their conscience seared with a hot iron." And the remaining chapters of our book lift the veil from the inner life of the Israelites, and show us to what length this apostasy had really gone. Heretofore they had forsaken the Lord and worshipped idols, but now they turn the very worship of God Himself into idolatry; chapter xvii. and xviii., " every man doing that which was right in his own eyes," xvii. 6. " And the children of Dan set up the graven image ; and Jonathan the son of Gershon, the son of Manasseh, he and his sons were priests to the tribe of Dan until the day of the captivity of the land. And they set them up Micah's graven image, which he had made, all the time that the house of God was in Shiloh." xviii. 30–31.

The book closes in the final chapters on a scene of sin and confusion, and strife, almost unparalleled in the history of Israel. Their continual backsliding of heart had at last produced its legitimate outward results in the lives of the people, and self-will and license seemed to have nothing to restrain them, and the book ends, as I have remarked before, with the ominous words, "In those days there was no king in Israel: every man did that which was right in his own eyes." xxi. 25.

The lessons of this book are sad and painful, but deeply needed, I am sure. No position in grace, no height of Christian attainment can keep the soul from failing. Only the present power of an indwelling Holy Ghost can do this, and nothing but continual faithfulness to the Lord can secure His abiding presence. We never, at any stage of our experience reach a place where we may relax in our obedience, or become indifferent in our trust. Obedience must keep pace with knowledge, and our trust must be daily and hourly fixed on our keeping Saviour, or all will go wrong. Sanctification is not a state so much as a walk, and every moment of that walk we need the Spirit's power and the Spirit's presence as much as we did at first. Not even after dwelling in the land of promise for many years, are we strong enough to do without this. Always from the beginning to the end of our Christian life, obedience and trust are the two essential conditions of our triumph. We must make no more compromise with evil at the end than at the be-ginning. And failure, if it comes, will always arise from one or the other of these two causes, either want of consecration or want of trust. It is never the strength of our enemies, nor our own weakness that causes us to fall. While the Lord continues to be with us, no man can stand before us all the days of our life ; and if we will only steadfastly abide in Him, we need not be in the least discouraged at the thought of the temptations that surround us on every hand.

But, let me repeat it, there must be no compromise with sin. By faith we must put to death every one of our enemies, every day of our lives. And this death is a real thing. Our faith reckons it, and the Lord makes it real. The faith is our part, but the process is His. And the faith is a very different thing from the process. As the Rev. Andrew Jukes of England once wrote to a friend here, " The faith that you can come to Europe in ten days, and that if you take a ticket all is done for you, is a very different thing from the voyage itself, and the actual experience of crossing the Atlantic ; and just so the joy of faith that in Christ you are already perfect, is not the same thing as the experience of being made perfect through suffering, even as He was. But this and this only is the royal road."

I mean therefore, a reality in all that I say. And realities are what we want. We cannot put up with any thing merely judicial here. We must have our enemies actually to die, and our souls to be actually delivered from them, or there is no peace or security. Always " bearing about in the body the dying of the Lord Jesus," is the sole pathway to having His divine life of sweetness and power, manifested in our mortal flesh. But who would shrink with such an end in view ? Who would not gladly cut off hand or foot or eye, if by so doing the death to self and the life in Christ could be practically reached ?

Consent then to die. Let the Lord send crosses or afflictions or pain, if only by these He will but rid us of pride, and self-will, and anger, and all others of our inward enemies, and will conform us in every thing to the image of Christ. Let us, if Israel did not, obey the command of our Lord to drive out *every* enemy from our land, and then we need have no fear that the sad and God dishonoring experience of the book of Judges will be ours.

———

A chain of texts illustrating the lesson of Judges :—

OLD TESTAMENT.

Ex. xxiii. 27–33; xxxiv. 11–16. Num. xxxiii. 51–56. Deut. vii. 1–6; xii. 1–3. xx. 16–18. Deut. vii. 16-24; ix. 1–4; xx. 1--4. xxxi. 3--8. Josh. i. 2–9; vi. 2; x. 8 -10, 24, 25, 42. xi. 6--8, 16, 23. xiii. 1; xviii. 1--9. xxiii. 5--13.

NEW TESTAMENT.

Rom. vi. 6, 11, 12, 13. Eph. iv. 21-24. Gal. ii. 20. Col. ii. 12. iii. 1-4. Gal. v. 24. 2 Cor. iv. 10-11. Col ii. 20. 2 Cor. vi. 16-18. vii. 1. Rom. vii. 1-6. Rom. viii. 2–4, 10.

CHAPTER X.

RUTH.

Keynote: Eph. vi. 22–32.

THE book of Ruth is considered by many students of the typical teaching of Scripture, to be a type of the union of Christ and the Church. It is the story of the marriage of a Gentile bride to an Israelitish bridegroom, a thing forbidden in the Jewish law, and yet here approved of God, and made an especial blessing to those concerned in it. As we have seen in Judges, the Israelites had grievously failed, and had forsaken the God of their fathers to worship Baalim and Ashtaroth. All was confusion and sin in Israel. In the midst of this confusion, where Israel had so failed, a Gentile is brought in and exalted to a place of especial honor. And in all this we seem to see a type of that which Paul declares in Acts xiii. 46. "It was necessary that the word of God should first have been spoken to you; but seeing you put it from you, and judge yourselves unworthy of everlasting life,

155

lo, we turn to the Gentiles." It is a typical foreshadowing of the truth set forth in Rom. xi. Some of the
branches are here "broken off," and the "wild olive"
is "graffed in among them, and with them par-
takest of the root and fatness of the olive tree." "For
I would not, brethren, that ye should be ignorant of this
mystery, . . that blindness in part is happened to
Israel, until the fulness of the Gentiles be come in." I
believe this picture was meant to be hung up in the
great picture gallery of the Old Testament, as a type of
the "mystery," which, Paul says, "in other ages was
not made known unto the sons of men, as it is now revealed unto His holy apostles and prophets by the
Spirit; that the Gentiles should be fellow-heirs, and of
the same body, and partakers of His promise in Christ
by the gospel," Eph. iii. 3–6.

It was, as we have seen, a sin for the Israelites to
make any inter-marriages with the Gentile nations round
about. And yet here a Moabitish woman is married to
one of the chief men among the Jews, and is raised to a
place of especial honor; teaching, as I think, in type,
the lesson, that "by one Spirit we are all baptized into
one body, whether we be Jews or Gentiles, whether we
be bond or free; and have all been made to drink into
one Spirit," 1 Cor. xii. 13.

No doubt this interpretation of the book of Ruth will
seem fanciful to some. But to me it is full of very
blessed teaching. It expresses to my mind in a beautiful story of domestic life, the oneness of Christ and the

Church, the blessed union, of which we are told in Eph.
v. 32 : " This is a great mystery ; but I speak concerning
Christ and the Church." Our Lord has chosen us to be
His in a very near and tender sense. He says to us :
"As the Father hath loved Me, so have I loved you,"
John xv. 9. He loves us with so deep a love that He
gave Himself for us; and He is continually seeking to
win us to His side. He is the Bridegroom, and He tells
us that " as the Bridegroom rejoices over the bride, so
shall thy God rejoice over thee." . . . " For thy
Maker is thine Husband: the Lord of Hosts is His
name," Is. lxii. 5 and liv. 5.

And I believe all this is intended to set before us a
blessed experience of the love of Christ, which is far
beyond our ordinary apprehensions, and which would
indeed satisfy the hungriest heart ; a love which would
lift the soul out of the servant's place into the place of
the bride, would change drudgery into delight, and cause
us to rise, as one has said, " from law to love, from
penance to purity, from poverty to power, from fainting
to fulness, from sadness to sunlight, from indwelling sin
to an indwelling Saviour, from widowhood to wedlock,
from sorrowful mourning to a heavenly marriage."

The story in this little book is concerning the time in
the history of Israel to which we have been brought in
Judges, when all was in confusion, and the Lord seemed to be left almost without a witness, even among His
own chosen people.

It opens with a famine, i. 1 ; natural result of such a

14

state of affairs. In consequence of this famine, an Israelite went to sojourn in the land of the Lord's enemies, doubtless in the hope of bettering his condition for a time, but probably with no thought of living and dying there. But we read in verse second that he "continued there." And it generally happens to any believer who goes among the Lord's enemies to seek for the food which his own spiritual famine has made to seem a necessity, that, although it may have been his purpose merely to sojourn for a while, he also ends by "continuing there." The result of this long sojourn is that all Mahlon's household die but Naomi, who finds herself left a desolate widow with two widowed daughters. Then in her sorrow she hears "how that the Lord had visited His people in giving them bread." And she sets out to return unto her own land. But she had evidently so little faith in the God of Israel, whom yet she recognized as her God, that she urged her daughters not to go with her, afraid, doubtless, that it would involve them in new troubles and losses. Christians who have had only an experience of spiritual famine, can never be very earnest in urging others to come to dwell in their land, i. 8–15. Orpah yielded to her mother's entreaties, and returned "unto her people, and unto her gods." But Ruth clave unto her mother. I think that Ruth must have seen in this mother-in-law something of goodness or sweetness that had won her heart, and had made her believe that her mother's God must be better worth serving than her own gods. At all

events she said to her those beautiful words of loving
allegiance, " Entreat me not to leave thee, or to return
from following after thee: for whither thou goest, I will
go ; and where thou lodgest, I will lodge : thy people
shall be my people, and thy God my God : where thou
diest, I will die, and there will I be buried : the Lord do
so to me, and more also, if aught but death part thee
and me," i. 16, 17.

And when her mother saw that she was " steadfastly
minded to go with her, she left off speaking unto her,"
i. 18. " So they two went until they came to Bethlehem
. . . and they came to Bethlehem in the beginning
of barley harvest," i. 19–22. What grace was here !
Naomi left in a famine, but she returned in the time of
harvest. And every backsliding soul that returns to the
Lord always finds, as the prodigal did, a feast prepared
for him.

But better blessings even than the barley harvest were
awaiting these returning wanderers, and blessings it had
not entered into their hearts to conceive of. Ruth had
not thought of finding a bridegroom and a home of her
own in the land of Judah. She had gone there because
her heart was desolate and lonely in her own land, and
the religion of Naomi had attracted her. But almost at
once upon her arrival, she went out to glean, and her
" hap was to light on a part of the field belonging unto
Boaz," her " near kinsman," ii. 1–3.

And so the souls, who turn their backs on the world to
seek the Lord, even although very ignorant of all the

blessings in store for them, find themselves soon gleaning in the field of Christ, who is our near Kinsman, and who, as Boaz did, "takes knowledge" of them, although they are strangers; and causes His servants to "let fall some handfuls of purpose" for them, that they may not go "to glean in another field," but may "abide fast" by His people, ii. 8-13. Ruth had come to trust under the wings of the God of Israel; and no one ever yet trusted in Him and was confounded.

This it seems to me is the first experience of the returning sinner. He leaves, figuratively speaking, his father, and his mother, and the land of his nativity, as Ruth did, and comes unto a people which he has not heretofore known, ii. 11. Then he begins to glean, and gathers in from the Lord's harvest fields spiritual food to supply his daily needs. And for a while the soul is satisfied with this.

But a time comes when a deeper want is felt. "Then Naomi her mother-in-law said unto her, My daughter, shall I not seek rest for thee, that it may be well with thee?" iii. 1. This expression, "seeking rest," meant among the Hebrews all that is contained in the sweet tie of married life, a home, and a care-taker, and all the joys of wedded union. And the soul of the believer begins sooner or later to hunger and thirst after this rest in a realized union with Christ, of which the marriage union is so precious a type.

Very often some older Christian first urges the soul to press its claim for this, as Naomi did to Ruth. And where, as in Ruth's case, there is the true spirit of teachableness and submission on the part of the Christian, who has comparatively lately begun his course, towards those who are further advanced, he will learn his privileges far more quickly, than if left to his own crude conceptions and limited knowledge.

In submission to the advice of Naomi, Ruth made her claim, using as her plea, "for thou art a near kinsman," iii. 9. The kinsman's plea was an unanswerable one among the Jews; and our Lord, in assuming the place of a kinsman, meant that we should have all the benefit of this plea. And His answer to us is always, like that of Boaz to Ruth, "And now, my daughter, fear not; I will do to thee all that thou requirest," iii. 11.

Even the very boldness of her claim pleased Boaz. "And he said, Blessed be thou of the Lord, my daughter, for thou hast showed more kindness in the latter end than in the beginning." At first she sought his gifts only, now she sought himself. The gleaner would be the wife. And just so it is with us. The work of Christ is our first knowledge; the person of Christ is our last. At first we are occupied with our needs, and come to the Lord simply to have them supplied. But at last we lose sight of the gifts in the Giver, and can be satisfied with nothing short of Himself. Our souls cry out for a personal Saviour. We want not only something to enjoy, and be thankful for, and use; but we want some One to love, and trust, and serve. His manifested presence comes to be far more to us than His

14*

mercies, and nothing but a realized union with Himself
can meet the craving of our heart's hunger. Having
Him, we realize that we shall have all things, and without Him nothing is valuable to us. We say, in the
language of the hymn—

> "Thy gifts, alas! cannot suffice,
> Unless Thyself be given;
> Thy presence makes my paradise,
> And where Thou art 'tis Heaven."

Ruth's claim looked like presumption, but Boaz called
it "showing kindness." And our Lord also delights in
every claim we make upon Him for this realized oneness with Himself, however bold it may seem to us.
It is indeed His own prayer for us, "That they all may
be one; as thou Father art in me, and I in thee, that
they also may be one in us: that the world may believe
that thou hast sent me. And the glory which thou
gavest me, I have given them; that they may be one,
even as we are one; I in them and thou in me, that they
may be made perfect in one; and that the world may
know that thou hast sent me, and hast loved them as thou
hast loved me." I believe indeed, that, far dearer to Him
than the greatest activities of service, is the longing of
the heart to know this oneness, and the claim of faith
that comes boldly to His feet to receive it. "Having
therefore, brethren, *boldness* to enter into the holiest by the
blood of Jesus, by a new and living way which He hath
consecrated for us, through the veil, that is to say, His
flesh; and having a high priest over the house of God,

let us draw near with a true heart, in full assurance of faith," Heb. x. 19-22.

> " God loves to be longed for, He loves to be sought,
>   For He sought us Himself with such longing and love;
>   He died for desire of us, marvellous thought!
>   And He yearns for us now to be with Him above."

Having made her claim, Ruth then was simply to wait until she should see what Boaz would do, for Naomi said to her, " Sit still, my daughter, until thou know how the matter will fall; for the man will not be in rest until he have finished the thing this day," iii. 18. And to those souls who have been stirred up by the blessed Holy Spirit to see their need of a realized oneness with their Lord, and to make their claim for it, the same command comes to-day, " Sit still, my daughter, until thou know how the matter will fall." For the Lord Himself has declared, " For Zion's sake will I not hold my peace, and for Jerusalem's sake I will not rest, until the righteousness thereof go forth as brightness, and the salvation thereof as a lamp that burneth," Isa. lxii. 1. This " sitting still" means faith. When there is anything to be done, none who are interested *can* sit still, unless they are sure that some one else has undertaken the matter, who is both able and trustworthy, and in whose hands they can feel that it is as safe as in their own. The soul that " sits still," therefore, is the soul that trusts. It has made its request known to the Lord, and it knows that He has taken the matter in hand and will surely " finish it " in His own time and way. And therefore it waits in patient faith, sure that it already *has* the petition it desired of Him, even before the realization of the fulfilment has come.

I cannot but feel that we need more of this "sitting still" in Christian experience. There is too much restless anxiety about our prayers, too much of a feeling that unless we help in some way, or at least unless we wrestle and agonize over it, the matter cannot be finished satisfactorily at all. I saw an illustration of this not long ago which will explain what I mean. I was visiting a mother in her nursery, where her little boy was playing. We were talking on the subject of prayer, and asking each other the question as to what sort of praying was right—the trusting kind, or the agonizing kind, when we were interrupted by the child's asking for some biscuit. His mother said "Yes" at once, and went to the closet for them, but found the biscuit can empty. She told the child the state of the case, but said she would send for some, and the child saw the nurse put on her bonnet, and take the money, and start out to make the purchase. A good child, upon this, would have gone to playing again, and would have waited quietly and trustingly until the biscuit came. But this child stood at his mother's elbow, saying over and over, first in a plaintive tone, which however rapidly rose to an agony of entreaty —"Mother, give me biscuit. I want biscuit. Please let me have some biscuit. Do give me biscuit. I *must* have biscuit!" Until finally our conversation was drowned in the noise of his wailing, and we could do

nothing but sit still in the best patience we could muster.
My question about prayer was answered; and never
from that time have I dared to agonize over any request
I have made of the Lord. I do not mean, however, that
we are to forget our prayers, or be indifferent to their
results, but simply that, having made our request known,
we must then wait in a quiet and patient faith, sure that
our Lord will not rest until He has finished the matter we
have put into His hands. We are not always prepared
ourselves to receive an immediate answer to our prayers. We do not give the best things in our possession
to our youngest children, even though they ask, lest they
should hurt themselves, or spoil the things. We wait
until they grow old enough to take the proper care of
them, and to understand their use. A delicate watch
would be only a burden to a five year old boy, and
would be sure to come to grief. And our Father is too
wise in His love, to give us what we are not yet prepared
to receive. But when we ask Him, He will first make
us ready for the gift, and will then bestow it, when we
can receive and use it, without injury to the gift or loss
to ourselves, for He "knows *how* to give good gifts"
unto His children."

In the case of Ruth something had to be done, before
the request which she had made to Boaz could be fulfilled. And this was typical, I think, of that which must
take place in our own case, when our souls come to the
Lord, and ask for a more fully realized union with Himself. The claims of a kinsman nearer than Boaz had

to be disposed of. "And now it is true that I am thy near kinsman : howbeit there is a kinsman nearer than I. . . . If he will perform unto thee the part of a kinsman, well: let him do the kinsman's part: but if he will not do the part of a kinsman to thee, then will I do the part of a kinsman to thee," iii. 12, 13.

This nearer kinsman may be taken as a type of the law, which is declared in Rom. vii. 1–4 to be, as it were, our first husband, having dominion over us until we are released from him by death. As we read there, "Wherefore, my brethren, ye also are become dead to the law by the body of Christ, that ye should be married to another, even to Him who is raised from the dead, that we should bring forth fruit unto God." Legality is the one great hindrance to a realized and conscious soul union with Christ. Just as it is in the earthly marriage relation, any thought of law as controlling the conduct of one to the other, or any service that springs only from a fear of consequences, in so far as it is allowed, destroys the soul union between husband and wife, so it is here. Love must be the motive, or the service is valueless, and the oneness is marred. There must be, as Cook says, "similarity of feeling" between souls that would be one. Each must desire what the other desires, and each must hate what the other hates. And the mutual service must spring, not from "I ought to," but "I want to." The little word *ought*, which is grand in other relationships, is fatal here. For this relationship is of so

tender and subtle a nature, that it cannot admit of any
bondage but the bondage of love. What wife could
endure to have her husband say to her in the morning
as he left home for business, "Well, I suppose it is my
duty to work for you, and I mean to do it faithfully, but
it is a very great cross I can assure you, and I only do it
because I must." Would not a support so legally given
be rejected with indignation, and would not all hope of
any real union between that husband and wife be utterly
gone?

But if legality would be fatal in an earthly union, how
much more in the heavenly. And therefore, before the
soul can be " married to another, even to Him who is
raised from the dead," it must be fully " delivered from
the law," by being " dead to that wherein it was held,"
in order that it may " serve in newness of spirit, and not
in the oldness of the letter." And this is brought about,
as was Ruth's deliverance from her nearer kinsman, by
purchase. Boaz purchased Ruth from Mahlon to be his
wife, iv. 9, 10; and Christ " hath redeemed us from the
curse of the law," having " purchased us with His own
precious blood" that we may be united to Him in a
blessed oneness, far nearer and dearer than any earthly
union could be, but which the earthly one most blessedly
symbolizes.

At last of Ruth we read, iv. 13, " So Boaz took Ruth,
and she was his wife." And of the Church we read, that,
" Christ loved the Church and gave Himself for it; that
He might sanctify and cleanse it with the washing of

water by the Word, that He might present it to Himself
a glorious Church, not having spot or wrinkle, or any
such thing, but that it should be holy and without blemish," Eph. v. 25–27.

In the divine order, the son born of this marriage was
one in the line of the ancestors of our Lord. "And
Salmon begat Boaz of Rachab; and Boaz begat Obed
of Ruth; and Obed begat Jesse; and Jesse begat David
the king," Matt. i. 5. And thus the poor Gentile widow,
who had gone to put her trust under the wings of the
God of Israel, ii. 12, found rest there, and a bridegroom,
and a home, and was exalted to a place of especial honor.
Surely before she went, it had not entered into her heart
to conceive of the things God had in store for her, any
more than it has entered into our hearts. And if we,
who like Ruth, are a "wild olive tree," find ourselves
grafted in among the branches and with them partaking
of the "root and fatness of the olive tree," there is
surely no room for boasting on our part, except as our
souls shall "make their boast in the Lord," and shall
say with Ruth, "Why have I found grace in thine eyes,
that thou shouldst take knowledge of me, seeing that I
am a stranger?"

The practical lesson to be drawn from this little book
would seem to be this, that, should there be in the experience of any the sad failure typified in Judges, the
remedy for it is to be found, not in going back into the
wilderness, nor, much less, in going back into Egypt, but
in coming into a nearer and deeper union with Christ,

such a union as is set before us in the words of our
Lord in John xvii. 22, 23 : " And the glory which Thou
gavest me I have given them; that they may be one
even as we are one : I in them and Thou in me, that
they may be made perfect in one : and that the world may
know that Thou hast sent me, and hast loved them as
Thou hast loved me."

The promise is ours. Let us boldly make our claim,
and then " sit still " until we know " how the matter will
fall ; " for we may rest assured our Lord will not be in
rest, until He has perfected that which concerns us. He
has made our souls capable of a marvelous oneness with
Himself, and has removed every barrier. But He will
not force it upon us. A compelled marriage can never
be other than a wretched one ; and the glory of our destiny is, that, on our part, it is to be a voluntary and glad
surrender to a love that woos and wins our hearts by its
sweet constraint. We love Him because He first loved
us, and we can come to Him with unshrinking faith to
claim that which He Himself has already told us is His
own purpose and prayer. " That they may be one "—
it is all shut up in this. One with the Father *as* the Son
is one ! Similarity of thought, of feeling, of desire, of
loves, of hates ! We may have it all, dear Christian, if
we are but willing. We may walk through this world, so
united to Christ, that our cares and our interests, our
sorrows and our joys, our purposes and our wishes will
be the same. One will alone to govern us, one mind to
control us. He in us and we in Him ; until so intermin-

15

gled and conjoined will be our lives, that we can say at last in very truth, always and everywhere, "Not I, but Christ." For self will vanish in such a union as this, and this great "I" of ours, which so fills up the present horizon, will wilt down into nothing before the glory of His overcoming presence.

Seek after this oneness then, with all thy heart, dear reader. Thy Lord intends it for thee, and will grant it, as soon as He has prepared thy soul to enter into it. Let nothing discourage thee. Though He tarry, wait for Him, for He will surely come and will not tarry ; and if thou wilt but persevere, the blessed day must and will come, sooner or later, when thy soul shall be satisfied with the fullness of His love, and thou shalt abide continually in His conscious presence. He will come and take up His abode with thee, and, like Ruth, thou shalt "find rest" at last in the heart of thy Heavenly Bridegroom.

Texts illustrating union with Christ:—John xvii. 21-23. Rom. xii. 5. 1 Cor. xii. 12, 13. Gal. ii. 20. Eph. v. 23–33. 2 Cor. xi. 2. Is. lxii. 5. Hosea ii. 16–20. Is. lxi. 10. Rev. xxi. 2, 9. Is. liv. 5. 1 Cor. vi: 17; x. 17. Eph. i. 10. Rev. xix. 7, 8. John xv. 4, 5. Matt. ix. 15. John iii. 28, 29. Matt. xxv. 1–13.

CHAPTER XI.

I SAMUEL.

THE REIGN OF SAUL.

THAT KINGDOM WHICH IS AFTER THE COMMANDMENTS AND TRADITIONS
OF MEN.

Keynote: Mark vii. 9.

THE six books of Samuel, Kings, and Chronicles may all be considered as only different chapters of one book, for they all give us the story of Israel during the period of its being a kingdom. They are, I think, typical of that "kingdom of heaven" which exists now upon the earth, outwardly in the Church in all its branches, and inwardly in the heart of every child of God.

The keynote to these books is to be found in the New Testament passages concerning the "kingdom of God" or the "kingdom of Heaven;" which occur over one hundred times there. And the title I would suggest would be, "The kingdom of God both inward and outward." In these books we have given to us, as it seems to me, types or pictures of different forms under which His kingdom is set up in the Church outwardly, and in-

wardly in the hearts of believers. We are shown here
the sorts of rule which are acceptable to Him, and those
which displease Him. We are shown the privileges and
glory of the kingdom, when rightly governed by the
Prince of Peace, and the dangers and disgrace that
result from a divided rule.

There are four of these pictures. The first gives us
the kingdom under Saul, with the causes that led to it;
the second the kingdom under David; the third the
kingdom under Solomon ; and the fourth the failure
and division of the kingdom, and its gradual declension
down to the Babylonish captivity.

The story of Saul is to be found in the first book of
Samuel, and the character of rule which he seems to represent, is that rule which is according to the commandments and traditions of men. The Divine comment on
his character was simply this, " He inquired not of the
Lord : *therefore* He slew him, and turned the kingdom
unto David the son of Jesse," 1 Chron. x. 14. During
all his reign the Ark of God, which was the only Divine
dwelling-place in all the land of Israel, remained in
obscurity at Kirjath-jearim, and David declares in 1
Chron. xiii. 3.that they "inquired not at it in the days
of Saul." Saul preferred his own thoughts and his own
ways, to the thoughts and ways of the Lord ; and therefore
we read in 1 Chron. x. 13; " So Saul died for his transgression which he committed against the Lord, even
against the word of the Lord, which he kept not, and
also for asking counsel of one that had a familiar spirit,

to inquire of it." In all this he was a striking type of that rule which obtains in so many Christian churches and Christian lives, where man, rather than God, is consulted and obeyed.

The causes which led Israel to desire a king are given to us in the first eight chapters of I Samuel. The first cause was the failure of the priests; see ii. 22-36. I have stated previously that the priests seem to me to be a type of a soul in communion; and the failure of the priesthood, therefore, would represent the failure of the soul's communion with the Lord. The result of this failure was the loss of the Ark of God, which was taken by the Philistines and carried away to their own country, and set up in the house of their god Dagon, iv. 17, v. 1, 2. The Ark was the Lord's dwelling place in the midst of His people, where He continually manifested His presence and revealed His will. "For there," He had said in Ex. xxv. 22, "I will meet with thee, and I will commune with thee from above the mercy-seat, between the two cherubim which are upon the ark of the testimony, of all things which I will give thee in commandment unto the children of Israel." Nowhere else in Israel was this communion possible; and when the Ark was gone from their midst, Israel was shut out from their Lord. The loss of the Ark therefore was a striking type of the soul's loss of communion.

The conscious indwelling of the Holy Spirit, and His blessed teaching and guiding are no longer realized by the soul that, through unfaithfulness, has suffered this

15*

saddest of all losses; and Ichabod, or "there is no glory," is the grievous realization of such now, as truly as it was of Israel then, as we read in chap. iv. 22: "And she said, The glory is departed from Israel; for the Ark of God is taken."

The priesthood having failed, and the Ark being thus carried captive, the Lord raised up a prophet to supply their place. "And the word of the Lord was precious in those days; there was no open vision." "And all Israel, from Dan to Beersheba, knew that Samuel was established to be a prophet of the Lord. And the Lord appeared again in Shiloh: for the Lord revealed Himself to Samuel in Shiloh, by the word of the Lord," 1 Sam. iii. 1, 20, 21.

For a while this was partially effectual. The Ark was restored, not indeed to its rightful place in Shiloh, but to Kirjath-jearim, a place within the borders of Israel, 1 Sam. vi., vii.; and the Philistines, who had oppressed the Israelites, were subdued, and "came no more into the coast of Israel; and the hand of the Lord was against the Philistines all the days of Samuel. And the cities which the Philistines had taken from Israel were restored to Israel, from Ekron even unto Gath; and the coasts thereof did Israel deliver out of the hands of the Philistines. And there was peace between Israel and the Amorites," 1 Sam. vii. 13, 14. But in Samuel's old age the prophets also failed, for we read that " His sons walked not in his ways, but turned aside after lucre and perverted judgment." And this was the second cause of Israel's desire for a king. Immediately they gathered themselves to Samuel and said, " Behold, thou art old, and thy sons walk not in thy ways: now make us a king to judge us like all the nations," viii. 5.

When *communion* fails, *teaching* comes in to supply its place. Doctrines are looked to as the remedy for spiritual coldness and wandering ; and lost or forgotten truths are revived. The effect at first seems blessed, communion seems partially restored, and the soul's enemies are for a time subdued. But this communion is only after all on the surface or borders of our natures, for truth alone, without the Spirit, can not reach the central home of the soul ; and sooner or later, therefore, teaching also fails.

I remember a time in my own experience when just this thing happened to me. It was before I knew the secret of the life hid with Christ in God, and when my soul was crying out continually, " Oh my leanness, my leanness !" I found, experimentally, that the learning of new truth helped me for a time into greater warmth and earnestness of Christian life, and I sought eagerly for every opportunity of being taught. But continually I was disappointed by finding that, in a little while, the freshness of the new discovery in truth would wear off, and with its freshness, its power would seem to go, and my soul would be left drier than ever ; and yet the only remedy of which I then knew, was to go on learning more new truth, hoping that at last I should discover something whose effects would be permanent, and from which there would be no reaction. But this can never be. It takes an experience far deeper than the learning of new truth alone to keep the soul alive; and the result of repeated disappointments, unless a more vital experience is known, is to drive the soul into seeking by some outward rule to supply the empty place from which the Lord is lost. The "commandments and traditions of men" take the place of the "commandment of God;" and the soul endeavors by the "law of a carnal commandment" to remedy the state, into which it has been brought by the loss of inward communion, and by the consequent lack of spiritual power to restore, in even the clearest teaching of truth.

This desire of Israel for a king was displeasing to the Lord, because it was a token that they had rejected Him, that He "should not reign over them." And He warned them faithfully of the results that would certainly follow any rule but his own: "This will be the manner of the king that shall reign over you: he will take your sons, and appoint them for himself, for his chariots, and to be his horsemen; and some shall run before his chariots. And he will appoint him captains over thousands, and captains over fifties; and will set them to ear his ground, and to reap his harvest, and to make his instruments of war, and instruments of his chariots. And he will take your daughters to be confectionaries, and to be cooks, and to be bakers. And he will take your fields, and your vineyards, and your olive-yards, even the best of them, and give them to his servants. And he will take the tenth of your seed, and of your vineyards, and give to his officers, and to his servants. And he will take your men-servants, and your maid-servants, and your goodliest young men, and your asses, and put them to his work. He will take the tenth of your sheep: and ye shall be his servants," I Sam. viii. 11-17; see also xii. 17-19.

This whole passage seems to me a striking picture of that which happens to every soul that yields itself up to be governed by the "commandments and traditions of men." The best of its strength is taken in this service, and all its powers are in bondage to its control. Time, and talents, and money, and influence are all used to establish and support some system of doctrine, or some form of worship, and the "goodliest" of our powers are put to their work. And all the while the Lord is saying to such a soul, as He did to the Pharisees of old, "In vain do they worship me, teaching for doctrines the commandments of men," Matt. xv. 2-9.

The Israelites were not influenced by Samuel's warning, for we read: "Nevertheless, the people refused to obey the voice of Samuel; and they said, Nay ; but we will have a king over us; that we also may be like all the nations; and that our king may judge us, and go out before us, and fight our battles," I Sam. viii. 19, 20.

"Like all the nations;" these words contain the secret of the power of the "commandments and traditions of men." The soul shrinks from the thought of a walk alone with an unseen God, guided only by His

Spirit, and prefers to follow in the footsteps of the fore-
fathers, and to walk "according to the tradition of the
elders." And I would that, just here, the solemn question should come home to each one of us, as to whether
in our own experience there is anything similar to this
failure of the children of Israel. Are there any of my
readers who are seeking, by an outward rule of the
commandments and traditions of men, to remedy a
state into which they have been brought by the loss of
their inward communion, and the failure of outward
teaching to supply its place? Are there any whose first
and ruling thought is not, What has the Lord commanded? but, What does my church say? or, What do my
friends believe? or, What has been the custom of my fore-
fathers? For if this is a faithful description of any, the
Lord's rebuke to such is like His rebuke to Israel, "Full
well ye reject the commandment of God, that ye may
keep your own tradition," Mark. vii. 9.

The Lord's warning having failed, He consents that
they shall have a king according to their request, but
His comment upon it all is to be found in Hos. xiii. 10,
11, "Thou saidst, Give me a king and princes. I gave
thee a king in mine anger, and took him away in my
wrath;" see xii. 16–22. As it was in the wilderness, so
it was now, "He gave them their request, but sent leanness into their souls," Ps. cvi. 15.

The first king, Saul, was chosen because of his
strength. To the eye of flesh he looked like a king
upon whom they could lean with confidence; "from his

shoulders and upwards he was higher than any of the people," x. 2. But he had one sad weakness, which yet however *looked* like strength. He depended upon his own resources and his own understanding, rather than upon a present though unseen God. "When Saul saw any strong man, or any valiant man, he took him unto him," xiv. 52. And he "gathered an host" whenever he went out to battle. Moreover, he "inquired not of the Lord" concerning his course of action, nor did he even obey the Lord's voice when it had been made known to him. When the coming of the prophet was delayed, for whom he had been commanded to wait, he "forced himself" and offered sacrifices, which he had no right to offer, from motives of expediency, lest, as he said, "the Philistines should come down upon me to Gilgal, and I have not made supplication unto the Lord," xiii. 8-12. His own apprehensions of what was expedient were always his guide. The command of the Lord concerning the Amalekites was, "Now go and smite Amalek, and utterly destroy all that they have, and spare them not; but slay both man and woman, infant and suckling, ox and sheep, camel and ass," xv. 1-3. Nothing could have been plainer. But it seemed best to Saul that some of them should be spared, and we read in verse 9, "But Saul and the people spared Agag, and the best of the sheep, and of the oxen, and of the fatlings, and the lambs, and all that was good, and would not utterly destroy them: but everything that was vile and refuse, that they destroyed utterly." It also

seemed best to him to destroy the Gibeonites, although
Israel had given them a pledge for their preservation,
for "the children of Israel had sworn unto them, and
Saul sought to slay them in his zeal." Comp. Joshua
ix. and 2 Sam. xxi. 1–14. His "zeal" seemed ever to
lead him in opposition to the will of the Lord, as we too
often see among Christians now, who, from motives of
expediency, spare what the Lord has condemned to destruction, or destroy what He would keep alive. Or they
outrun their Guide, as Saul did at Gilgal; and often from
the same motive, because they "fear the people and
obey their voice" rather than the voice of the Lord, xv.
3–22. And yet, though Saul could so disregard the commandments of the Lord, whenever it seemed best for
him to do so, he was very rigorous in insisting upon
obedience to his own commands. As we see in chap.
xiv., when he "troubled the land" by an unreasonable
requirement that they should not taste food on the day
when they were pursuing their enemies; and thus caused
them to sin in eating meat with the blood, at the day's
end, when "very faint with hunger." Moreover, he was
ready to kill Jonathan, his son, for having in utter ignorance disobeyed his unreasonable command, xiv. 24, 45.

Such was Saul, the king after man's own heart, whom
Israel had put in God's place. And he stands, I believe, as a type of all rule which is purely *vicarial;* that
is, a rule which does not act *for* the Lord, but *instead* of
Him. Such a rule involves the idea of an absent and
forgetful Lord.

Andrew Jukes, in his book called the "Mystery of the Kingdom," says concerning this: "Of such rule we have the most perfect expression in the Church of Rome. . . . But in principle it exists wherever ministerial rule of any kind is claimed or recognized as vicarial. . . . Such rule may be known by its acts and fruits, not by its words. Like Saul, standing in the strength of gift, rather than in the strength of God the Giver, it will ever choose seen things and strong things to serve Israel. It can see and own God's gifts; it cannot own Himself. . . . Zealous for gift, it denies grace; it denies God, that which He most asks for, a place among men, as Himself, beyond and above all His gifts, their one sufficient portion. And vicarial rule, as it puts God out of, so it puts man into His place. Under it the Church, as Israel in Saul's case, is brought into bondage. Indeed, it has become a proverb that spiritual dominion, or what is commonly recognized as such, is generally a spirit of domination; that it has a disposition to enslave, and imposes a heavy yoke, not only on men's bodies, but on their minds. The Church of Rome, in which the fullest manifestation of vicarial rule has as yet been seen, is proof enough of this. Like Saul, it makes rules far beyond the word of God; and then, as Saul, judges those like Jonathan, whose faith leads them, beyond or without rule, to deliver Israel. . . . One word more respecting vicarial rule. Saul did not assume his place. It was given him according to Israel's wish. So has it been with Antichristian rule in the place of Christ.

I 2

Ministers do not seize this place; it is ever yielded them by the people. Pastors have not so much arrogated it, as the flock have sought it. It is but the old story over again of Moses in the mount. The mediator is out of sight, in God's presence for Israel. Then the cry is, 'Give us gods to go before us.' Out of communion, man wants and will have something seen and tangible, to put in the place of an unseen and distrusted God."

The result of all this in Saul's case was, that God's sentence was pronounced against him, first in chap. xiii. 13, 14. "But now thy kingdom shall not continue: the Lord hath sought a man after His own heart, and the Lord hath commanded him to be captain over His people, because thou hast not kept that which the Lord commanded thee," 1 Sam. xiii. 14. And again, in chap. xv. 21, 23, 28, "And Samuel said, Hath the Lord as great delight in burnt-offerings and sacrifices, as in obeying the voice of the Lord? Behold, to obey is better than sacrifice, and to hearken than the fat of rams. For rebellion is as the sin of witchcraft, and stubbornness is as iniquity and idolatry. Because thou hast rejected the word of the Lord, He hath also rejected thee from being king." "The Lord hath rent the kingdom of Israel from thee this day, and hath given it to a neighbor of thine who is better than thou."

And similarly will the Lord deal with the Church, or the individual soul now, when the rule to which they have submitted themselves leads them contrary to His will. The government must be rent from all such, and be laid upon the shoulders of the true David, who is indeed a king "after God's own heart." And that rule, which is after the commandments and traditions of men must, sooner or later, by an immediate surrender, or by slow degrees, and through many conflicts, pass out of our lives, or Christ alone can never reign the victorious Lord of all.

Texts illustrating the kingdom of man's traditions :— Matt. xv. 1–9. Mark vii. 1–13. Col. ii. 20–23. Is. xxix. 13. Gal. i. 13, 14. Acts xxii. 3, 4. Acts xv. 1–29. Gal. ii. 11–16. Matt. xxiii. 2–4. Luke xi. 46. Acts v. 28, 29. Acts iv. 18, 19. Phil. iii. 4–9.

CHAPTER XII.

II SAMUEL AND I CHRONICLES.

THE REIGN OF DAVID.

THE KINGDOM OF GOD BOTH INWARD AND OUTWARD.

Keynote : Luke xvii. 20, 21.

AND the Lord said unto Samuel, how long wilt thou mourn for Saul, seeing that I have rejected him from reigning over Israel? fill thine horn with oil, and go, I will send thee to Jesse the Bethlehemite; for I have provided me a king among his sons."

Immediately following the rejection of Saul in I Sam. xv., we come in chap. xvi. to the anointing of David. The desired king had failed to deliver, and the Lord, who is rich in grace, now meets Israel on their own ground, and out of evil brings forth good. They had asked for a king in their folly and wickedness, and the Lord, having administered the needed reproof and chastisement turns this very sinful desire into a means of richest blessing. He chooses a king for them who

184

shall be after His own heart, and who shall lead them on to hitherto undreamed of triumphs. For we must not suppose that rule in itself is opposed to God. On the contrary, we are taught everywhere throughout the Scriptures the lesson of submission to the Lord, and to that which is according to His mind. Even if we submit to earthly authorities, it must always be "in the Lord." And while there must not be vicarial rules governing instead of the Lord, there must always be that rule which witnesses to His presence in the midst of His people, guiding and controlling them Himself personally, even though He may make known His will through the mouths of His servants.

David is an exemplification of this sort of rule. He governed Israel only as a witness of the Lord's abiding presence. He was not the Lord's vicar, but the Lord's instrument. And therefore his language always was: "For the kingdom is the Lord's; and He is the governor among the nations."

To my mind this bestowal upon Israel of a king after the Lord's own heart, is a most blessed illustration of the truth of that word that "all things work together for good to them that love God." All things—even our very mistakes and failures. Earthly parents seek to do this in their limited measures, striving always to make every failure of their children a stepping-stone to the acquirement of some greater good or some deeper lesson, which could not have come perhaps in any other way; and surely far more will our Heavenly Father, whose wis-

16*

dom and power are limitless, do the same. Therefore
we may come to Him in happy confidence, with all our
tangled skeins and ruined lives, and trust Him to pick
them up just where we give them to Him, and to make
all things work together for our final good.

The king after God's own heart did not, however, at
once upon his anointing, gain the supremacy. For many
years he was a fugitive in the very country of which he
was the rightful king, hunted, as he himself says, like
"a partridge in the mountains," xxvi. 20. And in this
he is a wonderful type of the true David, our Lord Jesus
Christ, who lived in the world which belonged to Him,
as a fugitive and an outcast, with no place even
"wherein to lay His head." In fact, all through the
Bible, David is used continually as a type of our Lord,
and even as His mouth-piece, as we see in the Psalms;
and we are warranted therefore in expecting to learn
from the story of his life many wonderful lessons concerning his great Antitype. I cannot go into all the details of these. But the one especial lesson I desire to
bring out here, is, that in reference to Christ as Head
over His kingdom, and His ways as our King, both in
the inward and the outward kingdom. We see Him
in type here as the "Captain of our salvation," leading
us on to victory, and "delivering us out of the hand of
our enemies," and causing us to be "more than conquerors" through His mighty power.

David reigned to conquer Israel's enemies. In 2 Sam.
iii, 18 we read, "For the Lord hath spoken of David,

saying, By the hand of my servant David I will save my people Israel out of the hand of the Philistines, and out of the hand of all their enemies." And Jesus also became our King "that we should be saved from our enemies, and from the hand of all that hate us," Luke i. 71. At the close of his reign David could say, " Is not the Lord your God with you? and hath He not given you rest on every side? For He hath given the inhabitants of the land into mine hand; and the land is subdued before the Lord and His people," 1 Chron. xxii. 18. And Jesus also said, "Be of good cheer: I have overcome the world." " Peace I leave with you, My peace I give unto you: not as the world giveth, give I unto you. Let not your heart be troubled, neither let it be afraid."

The very followers David had during this time of his rejection, are wonderfully typical of the followers of the Lord Jesus now. "Every one that was in distress, and every one that was in debt, and every one that was discontented gathered themselves unto him," xxii. 1, 2. And of our Lord we read, that " He came unto His own, but His own received Him not;" and that those who did receive Him were, like David's followers, the poor, and the unhappy, and the sinful. For we read that the "common people heard him gladly," and that "the publicans and the harlots went into the kingdom of God" before the religious men of that day. Moreover, the Pharisees and the Scribes murmured concerning Him, saying, "This man receiveth sinners and eateth with them," Luke xv. 2.

Throughout the whole book of 1 Samuel from chap. xvi. onward, the conflict between Saul and David went on, a striking picture of the conflict between the two sorts of rule in the heart of the believer, on the one side the commandments of men, and on the other God's anointed King. And well will it be for us, if, during this conflict, whether it be long or short, the language can be used concerning us, as was used in this case, "Now there was long war between the house of Saul, and the house of David; but David waxed stronger and stronger, and the house of Saul waxed weaker and weaker," 2 Sam. iii. 1. In such a conflict as this, the end, even though long delayed through our unfaithfulness, is sure to come, and the day will at last dawn for us as for Israel, when every power in our nature will acknowledge the supremacy of our King, and when with our whole being we will crown Him Lord of all. This blessed consummation came to Israel in 2 Samuel after the death of Saul. "Then came all the tribes of Israel to David unto Hebron, and spake, saying, Behold, we are thy bone and thy flesh. Also in time past, when Saul was king over us, thou wast he that leddest out and broughtest in Israel: and the Lord said to thee, Thou shalt feed my people Israel, and thou shalt be a captain over Israel. So all the elders of Israel came to the king to Hebron; and king David made a league with them in Hebron before the Lord: and they anointed David king over Israel," 2 Sam. v. 1-3.

The books of 2 Samuel and 1 Chronicles are taken up

with the story of David's reign. They are full of deeply interesting incidents bringing out much valuable typical teaching, but it is not within the scope of these lessons to go into the details of this. It is enough for my purpose to consider the grand outlines of David's kingship over his people, and the blessings he brought them. His first introduction to us in 1 Sam. xvi. 1, and xvii. 34, 35, as a shepherd keeping his sheep, and risking his own life to rescue one little helpless lamb that had been seized by a lion, show us the sort of king he was likely to be; caring for his people more than for himself, and fulfilling at any cost to himself the duties of ownership and control. And surely in this he sets forth, though but faintly indeed, the character of our King, the Lord Jesus, who is also the " Good Shepherd giving His life for the sheep;" and who leaves the ninety and nine that have never gone astray, in order to rescue and save the one that was lost. "And I will set up one Shepherd over them, and he shall feed them, even my servant David; he shall feed them, and he shall be their shepherd," Ezek. xxxiv. 23.

A shepherd and a king seem widely separated in rank, and yet, if we but understand it, their duties are the same, and their responsibilities are alike. Each is bound to care for, and protect, and bless to the utmost limit of his ability, those who are under his control; and no man is fit to be a king who is not a shepherd as well. Christians are accustomed to looking so exclusively on their side of the question, their duties and their

responsibilities, that they lose sight almost altogether of
God's side, and thus miss a vast amount of comfort.
The responsibilities of an owner, and much more of a
Creator, are greater than can be expressed.   Parents
feel something of this, and by a universal instinct, which
is inalienable in our natures, all parents are held responsible within certain limitations, to their own consciences and to their fellow-men, for the well doing and
prosperity of their children.   In the same way owners
of animals, or owners of property, or owners of anything,
are bound to care for, and protect, and watch over that
which they own, and are held responsible to repair if
possible the damages which come to their possessions.
Even children feel this sense of responsibility, and will
go, perhaps reluctantly, to feed a bird because it is theirs,
and rejoice in being released from that duty, because their
property has been transferred to another owner.   The
position of authority and ownership, therefore, brings
responsibility, and a king is bound to care for his subjects.   Surely the subjects may take the comfort of this,
and may rest their souls, in a glad deliverance from
every anxiety, when under the care of a wise and loving
Ruler.   To my own mind there is immense comfort to
be found in this thought.   Our King is also our Owner.
For, says the apostle, "Ye are not your own, but ye are
bought with a price."   Therefore we may safely leave
the care and management of everything that concerns
us, to Him, who has Himself enunciated as an inexorable law that "if any man provide not for his own, he

hath denied the faith and is worse than an infidel." I feel
sure, therefore, that it was not without significance that
the Lord took David "from the sheepfolds, and brought
him to feed His people and Israel his inheritance."
He surely meant, I doubt not, to make him a type of that
future King, whose control is and can be nothing but
blessing to His people, because He is also their Shepherd and "careth for His sheep." I would that every
one could realize the blessedness of this thought. For I
feel sure that if they did, there would be no longer any
delay in their surrender to this glorious Shepherd King;
but like it was in Israel's case as related in I Chron.
xii., there would come to our David "day by day to
help Him," until there would be "a great host, like the
host of God," saying, "Thine are we, David, and on thy
side, thou son of Jesse." And there would be then
indeed among us, as among them of old, "joy in Israel."
For there are but few joys like the joy of entire surrender to the Lord Jesus Christ. The soul that has tried
it knows this, and to the soul that has not, I can only say
that the control of unselfish love is always lovely, even
when that love is earthly, because in the nature of things
love *can* choose only the best for its beloved one, and
must pour out itself to the last drop to help and to bless
that one; and that therefore the control of God, who is
love; who is not merely loving, but is Love itself, must
be and can be nothing but infinite and fathomless blessing.

I shall never forget a scene in my past life when I first

fully realized this blessed kingship of the Lord Jesus
Christ. It was in a great open air meeting, which, accounting for the difference in time, was held just at the hour
when the infallibility of the pope was being proclaimed
in Rome; and one of the preachers present stepped forward on the platform and proposed, that, while this was
going on in Rome, and the pope was being crowned
with a new and blasphemous honor, we there should rise
and crown Jesus Lord of all, by singing the well-known
hymn beginning, "All Hail the Power of Jesus' Name."
In an instant, the thousands present were on their feet,
singing it with a burst of loyalty and enthusiasm that
seemed almost to carry us away. And over and over
we sang that hymn, with a meaning it never had to
us before, while hundreds of hearts did then and there
crown "Jesus Lord of all" in their whole being, as they
had not until this moment dreamed it could be done.
It was a never-to-be-forgotten hour, and many have
been the testimonies that have come to me since, of the
lasting and blessed results that have come into the lives
that at that moment took Jesus to be their King. Come
then, dear readers, as Israel did, "with a perfect heart,"
and make the Lord Jesus King over all that you are and
all that you have. Let the "government be upon His
shoulders," and rejoice in the blessed promise that
"of the increase of His government and peace there
shall be no end, upon the throne of David, and upon
His kingdom, to order it, and to establish it with judgment and with justice from henceforth even for ever."

As far as appears, David led his people on to continuous victory, and the secret of it was his childlike dependence upon the Lord. Every step of the way he testified continually to his own weakness, and to God's strength. Over and over we have the expression used concerning him, "and the Lord was with him." When confronted with the giant he said to Saul, who told him he was not able to fight the Philistine, "The Lord that delivered me out of the paw of the lion and out of the paw of the bear, He will deliver me out of the hand of this Philistine." And to the giant himself he said, "Thou comest to me with a sword, and with a spear, and with a shield: but I come to thee in the name of the Lord of hosts, the God of the armies of Israel whom thou hast defied. This day will the Lord deliver thee into mine hand; and I will smite thee and take thine head from thee; and I will give the carcasses of the host of the Philistines this day unto the fowls of the air, and to the wild beasts of the earth: that all the earth may know that there is a God in Israel. And all this assembly shall know that the Lord saveth not with sword and spear; for the battle is the Lord's, and He will give you into our hands," 1 Sam. xvii. 45–47.

In everything David saw a present God. Unlike Saul, of whom it was said that he "inquired not of the Lord," we find David continually in every time of need going to the Lord for advice and guidance. "And David inquired of the Lord, saying, "Shall I go up and smite these Philistines?" "Will the men of

17

Keilah deliver me up?"   "Wilt thou deliver the Philistines into mine hand?"   "Shall I pursue after this
troop?"   "Shall I overtake them?"   And the Lord
always answered these inquiries as simply as they were
asked, "Go, and smite these Philistines."   "The men
of Keilah will deliver thee up."   "I will doubtless deliver the Philistines into thine hand." "Pursue: for thou
shalt surely overtake them, and without fail recover all."
See 1 Sam. xxiii. 2, 4, 10, 11, 12 ; xxx. 8 ; 2 Sam. ii. 1 ;
v. 19, 23 ; xxi. 1 ; 1 Chron. xiv. 10, 14.   The simplicity
and directness of this intercourse and communion between David and the Lord his God, is very striking, and
reveals a most blessed oneness.   In a faint way it pre-
figures the human life of dependence and obedience of
our Lord Jesus Christ, and teaches us our own privileges of a direct and personal intercourse with our
Father, who has told us "in everything to make our requests known unto Him" ; and who surely must mean to
grant us as sure a response as He did to David.   Let us
then in everything "inquire of the Lord" with childlike
confidence, believing that He hears us, and expecting a
certain reply.

Even when David failed, he "encouraged Himself in
the Lord his God," 1 Sam xxx. 6, and at once looked to
Him for a deliverance from the consequences of his
failure.   Everywhere and always, he seems to have been
on terms of such blessed intimacy and oneness with the
Lord, that nothing could come between to break it.   No
wonder that God called him a man after His own heart;

for such utter confidence in His love, and submission to His will, could not but please Him.

One of David's first acts after his establishment upon the throne of the kingdom, was to bring up the Ark of God from Kirjath-jearim into its rightful place in Jerusalem, Israel's central city; the "city of David" as it was called, because it was his presence there that made it the "throne of the Lord" for Israel. During Samuel's rule, the Ark of the Lord had been rescued from the hands of the Philistines, and had been brought as far as Kirjath-jearim, 1 Sam. vii. 1, 2, but had been left there, with no tabernacle for it to dwell in, and had been brought into "the house of Abinadab in the hill," the only man who seems not to have been afraid of its presence; and who is therefore surely a type of some hidden faithful Christians now, who, in a time of general coldness, yet retain in their own hearts the Lord's conscious presence. The ark remained in the house of Abinadab twenty years, and during all the reign of Saul it seems to have been utterly neglected, for we see no mention made of it, and are told in 1 Chron. xiii. 3 that they "inquired not at it in the days of Saul." As soon, however, as David was firmly established on his throne, the story of which is given us in 1 Chron. xii., we read in chapter xiii. that he "consulted with the captains of thousands and hundreds and with every leader," and said "unto all the congregation of Israel, If it seem good unto you and that it be of the Lord our God," . . . "let us bring again the ark of our God to us: for we inquired not at it in the days of

Saul; and all the congregation said that they would do
so : for the thing was right in the eyes of all the people,"
1-4. Chaps. xiii., xv., xvi. give us the account of this
restoration. Because of ignorance of the Lord's ways,
some difficulties were experienced in the restoration,
and there was a delay of three months, during which
the ark again found refuge in the house of one faithful Israelite, Obed-edom the Gittite, whom the Lord
"blessed with all his household, because of the Ark
of God," 2 Sam. vi. 11, 12. 1 Chron. xiii. 9-14,
But David finally "prepared a place, and pitched
for it a tent," and having learned how to seek the Lord
after the due order, he "gathered all Israel together"
and said, "None ought to carry the ark of God but
the Levites; for them hath the Lord chosen to carry
the ark of God, and to minister unto Him forever."
And he said unto the priests and Levites, "Ye are the
chief of the fathers of the Levites; sanctify yourselves,
both ye and your brethren, that ye may bring up the ark
of the Lord God of Israel unto the place that I have
prepared for it. For because ye did it not at the first,
the Lord our God made a breach upon us, for that we
sought him not after the due order. So the priests
and the Levites sanctified themselves to bring up the
ark of the Lord God of Israel. . . . So David, and the
elders of Israel, and the captains over thousands, went to
bring up the ark of the covenant of the Lord out of the
house of Obed-edom with joy. So they brought the ark
of God, and set it in the midst of the tent that David

had pitched for it: and they offered burnt sacrifices and peace offerings before God. And when David had made an end of offering the burnt offerings and the peace offerings, he blessed the people in the name of the Lord. And he dealt to every one of Israel, both men and women, to every one a loaf of bread, and a great piece of flesh and a flagon of wine." And we read that there was joy and gladness, and that " on that day David delivered first this psalm to thank the Lord into the hand of Asaph and his brethren. Give thanks unto the Lord, call upon His name, make known His deeds among the people." I Chron. xv. xvi.

As the ark was the only dwelling-place of the Lord in the land of Israel, where His presence was consciously known, all this seems to me to be a type of that restoration to the soul of the believer, of the conscious presence of the abiding Comforter, which will always be one of the first results of the establishment of Christ's rule in the heart. And the joy which accompanied this in Israel's case, as also the feeding of the people with bread and meat, and wine, are surely symbolical of the joy of restored communion, and the feeding upon Christ which it always brings. Henceforth, as we have seen, throughout the whole of David's reign they " continually inquired of the Lord " about everything. And I believe that only those souls where Christ consciously dwells can literally in *everything* " make their requests known unto God."

Having established the ark in its proper place, as it

1 7*

were, in the heart of the nation, David next turned his
attention to the nation's enemies. "Now *after this* it
came to pass that David smote the Philistines and subdued them, and took Gath and her towns out of the
hands of the Philistines," 1 Chron. xviii. 1. Also "he
smote Moab, and Hadazezer, and the Syrians, and the
Edomites, and the children of Ammon, and the giants,
and the Lord preserved David whithersoever he went,"
see 2 Sam. v., viii., x., xviii., and xxi.; also 1 Chron.
xviii., xix., xx., for the account of his battles and victories.

David was in fact made king for this very purpose; for the Lord had spoken concerning him saying,
"By the hand of my servant David I will save my
people Israel out of the hand of the Philistines, and out
of the hand of all their enemies," 2 Sam. iii. 18. And
of our Lord also it is said that He was sent in order "that
we being delivered out of the hands of our enemies,
might serve Him without fear in holiness and righteousness before Him, all the days of our life," Luke i. 74, 75.
As far as appears, David was always victorious, and at
last he could say in that wonderful song which he
"spake unto the Lord" "in the day that the Lord had
delivered him out of the hand of all his enemies," "I
have pursued mine enemies and destroyed them; and
turned not again until I had consumed them." "For
thou hast girded me with strength to battle; them that
rose up against me hast thou subdued under me. Thou
hast also given me the necks of mine enemies, that I

might destroy them that hate me," 2 Sam. xxii. 38, 40,
41. And in all this he was, as I have said, a type of
Christ as our conquering King and Captain, leading us
on to continual victory.

But although thus victorious, David's whole reign
seems to have been a time of conflict. So much so was
this the case, that when he wanted to build a House for
the Lord to dwell in, the word of the Lord came to him
saying, "Thou hast shed blood abundantly, and hast
made great wars: thou shalt not build a house unto my
name, because thou hast shed much blood upon the
earth," 1 Chron. xxii. 8, xxviii. 3. Only in the reign of
peace, could this temple be built, and therefore David,
the man of war, was compelled to leave this work to
Solomon, the prince of peace. And it was not until the
end of his reign, as he handed over his kingdom to Solomon, that he could say, "The land is subdued before the
Lord and before His people," 1 Chron. xxii. 18. Experimentally, therefore, the kingdom of David was a type of
that stage in the soul's history, when only conflict is
known, and when Christ is apprehended only in His character as our conquering Captain, leading us on to battle.
Many souls know no other Christian life but this, and live
therefore in perpetual conflict. But David's battles were
for the purpose of conquering Israel's enemies, and
when he had accomplished this purpose, he handed
over into Solomon's control a kingdom which had "rest
from its enemies all round about" And Christ as our
Captain also meets and conquers our enemies for us, in

order that He may hand over the inward kingdom, thus
made peaceful and at rest, into the hands of Christ as
our Solomon, the Prince of Peace, who giveth "peace
always by all means." Conflict precedes peace, but conflict, if victorious, will always bring peace. And never
to pass beyond the experience of conflict into the experience of peace, would seem to prove that the soul had
not apprehended Christ as a victorious Captain, before
whom the land should be in very truth subdued, and
into whose hand all its enemies should be delivered.
Many Christians stumble here, and never pass beyond
the reign of David. They cannot believe in the accomplished victories of our Lord Jesus Christ, but think
they must fight and conquer the foe for themselves.
They lift up, not the shield of *faith* against their
enemies, but the shield of *doubt*, and are, as a consequence, sorely smitten by his fiery darts. But one
lesson taught us by this history of the kingdom under
David, seems to me to be simply this, that we must apprehend the Lord Jesus Christ as our conquering King
and Captain, in such a way as to cause us to put all our
battles into His hand to fight, and to leave all our enemies to Him to vanquish. He has overcome the world
by actual conflict. We overcome by faith, 1 John v. 4.
The fiery darts of the enemy spent their strength on
Him. He has furnished us with a shield of faith wherewith we can quench them all, Eph. vi. 16. By faith we
can say in very truth, " The land is subdued before the
Lord and before His people," and can enter into the

kingdom of rest and peace, which He has obtained for us.

The story of this peaceful kingdom will be found in our next chapter. And I would urge every one, who is travelling with me throughout the length and breadth of this land of ours, to pause here, and, before turning the page that will introduce them to the reign of Solomon, to ask themselves definitely and personally whether the kingdom of peace is their kingdom, or whether they are ready at once to enter upon it. If not, the way is plain. Crown the Lord Jesus as thy conquering David, Lord of all in thy heart and life, from this moment onward, and enter by faith into His accomplished victories. "Come unto Me," he says, "and I will give you rest." I *can* give it, for I have won it for you in a sore conflict with the enemy. Believe me that he is an already conquered foe. Let me deliver you out of his hands. Let my peace reign in your hearts, and claim a continual triumph. I have labored, enter ye into my labors. For "this is the victory that overcometh the world, even your faith;" and "who is he that overcometh the world but he that believeth that Jesus is the Son of God."

Canst thou not hear His voice saying something like this to thee, dear soul, and wilt thou not believe Him? If thou wilt, then we may together turn our page into the kingdom of peace, and may by faith enter therein and dwell there.

Texts concerning the kingdom of God :—Ez. xxxiv.
23. Luke i. 31–33. Is. ix. 6, 7. 1 Cor. xv. 25. Dan.
vii. 13, 14. Matt. xxviii. 18. Ps. ii. 6-8. Eph. i. 20, 21.
John iii. 35. Is. xxxii. 1. Jer. xxiii. 5. Hosea iii. 4, 5.
Jer. xxxiii. 14–17. Jer. xxx. 9. Zech. vi. 13. Ps. cxlv.
13. Zech. ix. 9 with John xii. 14–16. Zech. xiv. 9.
Luke xxiii. 2. Acts xvii. 7. 1 Tim. vi. 15 with Rev.
xix. 11–16 John xviii. 36. Luke viii. 1. Matt. iii. 2.
Matt. xii. 28. Mark i. 14, 15. Matt. xiii. 11. Mark x.
15. Acts i. 3. Acts viii. 12. Acts xxviii. 28–31. Luke
xvii. 20, 21. John iii. 3. Col. i. 13. 1 Cor. xv. 50.
Rom. xiv. 17. Col. iv. 11. 2 Thess. i 5. Luke xii. 32.
Luke xxii. 29. Matt. v. 3, 20. Matt. vii. 21. Matt. vi.
10, 13. Rev. i. 5, 6. Rev. iii. 21. Rev. xi. 15. Rev.
xx. 4. Matt. xix. 28.

CHAPTER XIII.

I AND II KINGS AND II CHRONICLES.

THE KINGDOM OF PEACE.

Keynote: Col. iii. 15.

THE reign of Solomon was a reign of peace. The Lord had said to David, "Behold a son shall be born to thee who shall be a man of rest; and I will give him rest from all his enemies round about: for his name shall be Peaceable, and I will give peace and quietness to Israel in his days." The result of having by faith apprehended Christ as our King and Captain, who has fought and conquered our enemies for us, will be rest and peace. " For we which have believed do enter into rest." Solomon's peaceable kingdom was the result of the victories which David had obtained. And our peace is the fruit of Christ's victories. "The chastisement of our peace was upon Him." His legacy to us is peace, " Peace I leave with you, my peace I give unto you." And the declaration of the Holy Ghost throughout the whole New

Testament Scriptures is always this, that the kingdom of God is "righteousness, peace and joy in the Holy Ghost."

In Psalm lxxii., called "A Psalm for Solomon," we have a blessed picture of this kingdom of peace, which so plainly reaches beyond Solomon to the "Greater than Solomon," and His final universal kingdom, that it is headed also in our English Bibles with the words, "Messiah's reign;" and it gives us a sufficient warrant for taking this story of the kingdom under Solomon, as a type of that glorious millennial kingdom, when in very truth there shall be a King who shall have "dominion from sea to sea, and from the river unto the ends of the earth."

At the close of this lxxii. Psalm we are told that "the prayers of David the son of Jesse are ended." All that he had hoped for and battled for, was fulfilled in the peaceable reign of his son, and in the spirit of prophecy he saw also, in the far future, the glorious kingdom, when Christ Himself would see of the travail of His soul and be satisfied, and when the need for His intercessions would be ended also.

This millennial kingdom is antedated and begun now, in the hearts of all those, who by faith enter into the "rest that remaineth for the people of God;" and such may therefore take the lessons of this glorious reign, as being lessons and promises to themselves, of practical and personal importance now and here.

One of Solomon's first announcements was a declaration of the peace and rest of his kingdom. He said to

Hiram, king of Tyre, "The Lord my God hath given me rest on every side, so that there is neither adversary nor evil occurrent," 1 Kings v. 4. And upon the dedication of the temple, he again declared it, "Blessed be the Lord, that hath given rest unto His people Israel, according to all that He promised; there hath not failed one word of all His good promise, which He promised by the hand of Moses His servant," 1 Kings viii. 56.

As a consequence of this rest, his kingdom was one of unexampled greatness. Power, wisdom, luxury and magnificence were its characteristics. 1 Kings iv. 21–34 describes it. "And Solomon reigned over all kingdoms from the river unto the land of the Philistines, and unto the border of Egypt: they brought presents, and served Solomon all the days of his life. And Solomon's provision for one day was thirty measures of fine flour, and three-score measures of meal, ten fat oxen, and twenty oxen out of the pastures, and an hundred sheep, besides harts, and roe-bucks, and fallow-deer, and fatted fowl. For he had dominion over all the region on this side of the river, from Tiphsah even to Azzah, over all the kings on this side the river: and he had peace on all sides round about him. And Judah and Israel dwelt safely, every man under his vine and under his fig-tree, from Dan even to Beer-sheba, all the days of Solomon. And Solomon had forty thousand stalls of horses for his chariots, and twelve thousand horsemen. And those officers provided victual for king Solomon, and for all that came unto king Solomon's table, every man in his

18

month . they lacked nothing.   Barley also and straw for
the horses and dromedaries brought they unto the places
where the officers were, every man according to his
charge.   And God gave Solomon wisdom and understanding exceeding much, and largeness of heart, even
as the sand that is on the sea-shore.   And Solomon's
wisdom excelled the wisdom of all the children of the
east country, and all the wisdom of Egypt.   For he was
wiser than all men ; than Ethan the Ezrahite, and Heman, and Chalcol, and Darda, the sons of Mahol: and
his fame was in all nations round about.   And he spake
three thousand proverbs: and his songs were a thousand and five.   And he spoke of trees, from the cedar-
tree that is in Lebanon, even unto the hyssop that
springeth out of the wall : he spake also of beasts, and
of fowl, and of creeping things, and of fishes.   And
there came of all people to hear the wisdom of Solomon, from all kings of the earth, which had heard of his
wisdom."

Even the Gentiles, chapter v., emblematic of the
world and its desirable things, placed themselves and
their wealth at the disposal of Solomon and helped him,
instead of hindering, in all that he undertook.   And
similarly we read concerning Christians, " All things are
yours ; whether Paul, or Apollos, or Cephas, or the
world, or life, or death, or things present, or things to
come; all are yours, and ye are Christ's, and Christ is
God's," 1 Cor. iii. 21–23.

The world was attracted by the report of the riches

and glory of this kingdom, and the Queen of Sheba came from her far country to Jerusalem to see if all that had been told her could indeed be true. And we read in I Kings x. 4-9, that when she had seen "all Solomon's wisdom, and the house that he had built, and the meat of his table, and the sitting of his servants, and the attendance of his ministers, and their apparel, and his cup-bearers, and his ascent by which he went up into the house of the Lord, there was no more spirit in her." And she said to the king, " It was a true report that I heard in mine own land of thy acts and of thy wisdom. Howbeit I believed not the words until I came, and mine eyes had seen it; and behold, the half was not told me ; thy wisdom and prosperity exceeded the fame which I heard."

And in the same way, we may be sure the world will be attracted by the report of Christian lives that are filled with spiritual riches, and power, and wisdom, and will gather from far and near to see if the story they have heard can indeed be a true one; and when they have seen it, and have witnessed the peace in the midst of trial, and the inward joy overpowering the outward sorrow, and the victory over temptation, and the overflowing wealth of grace, they will be forced to acknowledge that it is indeed true, that "eye hath not seen, nor ear heard, neither have entered into the heart of man the things which God hath prepared for them that love Him." And thus the saying of our Lord in the sermon on the mount will be fulfilled, that our light shall so "shine before men," that they, seeing our good works, may " glorify," not us, but " Our Father which is in Heaven."

Dear reader, are these things the characteristics of the kingdom in which thou art dwelling now? And is the outside world so attracted by the report of thy riches and thy spiritual power, as to come to thee to learn if what they have heard be indeed true, and to discover if possible the secret of it? Do thy children see in thee such sweetness under provocation, and such patience under trial, as to be won, by the power of these, to love and to serve thy God, who does so much for thee? Do thy servants, or thy work-people, or thy friends, have cause to know from the outward peace of thy daily life, that the God of peace reigns within, and are their hearts attracted to His service?

Alas! I am afraid that the reverse is too often the case, and that one great cause of the small number of conversions in a church or a community is to be found in the poor and meagre sort of religion that exists there; and that far oftener than we think, husbands, or wives, or children, are kept outside the fold, by what they see in those nearest them, who profess to belong to this fold. I feel sure that if we who are Christians, all lived in this kingdom of spiritual peace and of abounding spiritual plenty, we should find hundreds flocking to the church, where now there is one. How can a husband think it is a desirable thing to be a Christian, when he sees his wife with a sort of Christianity that seems only to make her uncomfortable and gloomy; or how can children be attracted to a religion, which is professed by a cross or unreasonable father? A gentleman of learning who was an unbeliever, said something to me once, which I have never forgotten. We were talking together on the subject of Christianity, and I was urging its claims upon him, when he said, with marked emphasis and yet sadness, "If you Christians want the outside world to believe in your religion, you must have a better kind. Most of you seem to carry your religion as a man carries a headache. He does not want to get rid of his head, but he is forced to confess that it causes him a great deal of discomfort and suffering. You would not I suppose want to give up your religion, but you must acknowledge it often makes you mightily uncomfortable." It was, alas, too true a criticism to be treated lightly, and I inwardly prayed then and there that the Lord would enable Christians everywhere, and myself among them, to have a better sort of religion than this. A dear old preacher used to say that when buyers went to a shop, they wanted a good article, and that sinners equally wanted a good religion, if they undertook to get any at all. And I believe this is far truer than we know. Let us then seek to realize in our own individual experience, each one of us, all the fulness of our glorious salvation, that we may attract the world around us, by the beauty and blessedness of our lives, to come, taste and see that the Lord *is* good, and that He does indeed fulfill His promises.

18*

But it is not for this reason only that we need to have the reign of peace established in our hearts. Solomon's greatest work was the building of the temple. In fact he seems to have been raised up especially for this purpose. David says concerning him in 1 Chron. xxviii. 5, 6 "And of all my sons (for the Lord hath given me many sons), He hath chosen Solomon my son to sit upon the throne of the kingdom of the Lord over Israel. And He said unto me, Solomon thy son, he shall build my house and my courts; for I have chosen him to be my son, and I will be his Father. . . . Take heed now; for the Lord hath chosen thee to build an house for the sanctuary : be strong and do it."

This temple was to be to Israel what the tabernacle had been up to this time, the dwelling-place of the Lord in their midst. While they travelled, dwelling only in tents, it was necessary that their God should travel with them, and dwell also in a "tent and a tabernacle." "For," He said, "I have not dwelt in an house since the day that I brought up Israel unto this day; but have gone from tent to tent, and from one tabernacle to another. Wheresoever I have walked with all Israel, spake I a word to any of the judges of Israel, whom I commanded to feed my people, saying, Why have ye not built me an house of cedars?" 1 Chron. xvii. 1-6, and 2 Sam. vii. 1-13.

But now that their journeyings were over, and the Israelites were settled in their own land, and dwelling in their own houses, we cannot be surprised that "as

David sat in his house," the thought should arise with
wonder, " Lo ! I dwell in a house of cedars, but the ark
of the covenant of the Lord remaineth under curtains !"
Nor that he should "set his affections " to a house for
his God, and should desire greatly to build it.

The Lord Himself also, through the mouth of David,
had recorded His own desire for a House to be built for
Him to dwell in, " For the Lord hath chosen Zion ; He
hath desired it for His habitation.   This is my rest forever ; here will I dwell; for I have desired it." "This is
the hill which God desireth to dwell in ; yea, the Lord
will dwell in it forever," Ps. cxxxii. 13, 14 ; lxviii. 16.
And in Deut. xii. 9 11, He said to His people through
the mouth of Moses, " Ye are not as yet come to the
rest and to the inheritance, which the Lord your God
giveth you.   But when ye go over Jordan, and dwell in
the land which the Lord your God giveth you to inherit,
and when He giveth you rest from all your enemies
round about, so that ye dwell in safety ; then there shall
be a place which the Lord your God shall choose, to
cause His name to dwell there ; thither shall ye bring all
that I command you; your burnt-offerings and your
sacrifices, and your tithes, and the peace-offerings of your
hand, and your choice vows which ye vow unto the
Lord.   .   .   .   Take heed to thyself, that thou offer not
thy burnt-offerings in every place that thou seest; but
in the place which the Lord shall choose in one of thy
tribes, there thou shalt offer thy burnt-offerings, and
there thou shalt do all that I command thee."

From all these passages we see, that only when Israel were at rest in their land, could this temple be built. The Lord could accompany His people in a tent throughout all their wanderings, and in all their wars, but He could not take up His *rest* among them, until they had first found rest themselves. This is in the very nature of things. The mother cannot go to rest at night, until all her little ones are securely tucked in their cribs. The shepherd cannot lie down to repose, until his flock is safely folded. A king cannot rest from war, until his people do. A captain must not secure his own safety, until the last of his crew are saved. Here as everywhere, ownership and control have their responsibilities. And the Lord Himself says, " For Zion's sake will I not hold my peace, and for Jerusalem's sake I will not rest, until the righteousness thereof go forth as brightness, and the salvation thereof as a lamp that burneth," Is. lxii. 1.

The temple, therefore, could not be built in David's reign, because it was a reign of conflict, and the Lord can dwell only in a "peaceable habitation and a quiet resting place." David must hand the conquered kingdom over to Solomon, whose name is Peaceable, before the Lord's house could be built, as we read in 1 Chron. xxviii. 7–9. " And David said to Solomon, My son, as for me, it was in my mind to build an house unto the name of the Lord my God: but the word of the Lord came to me saying, Thou hast shed blood abundantly, and hast made great wars: thou shalt not build an house unto my name, because thou hast shed much blood upon the earth in my sight. Behold, a son shall be born to thee, who shall be a man of rest; and I will give him rest from all his enemies round about; for his name shall be Solomon, and I will give peace and quietness to Israel in his days. He shall build an house to my name." And after David's death, Solomon sent to Hiram and said, " Thou knowest how that David my father could not build an house unto the name of the Lord his God, for the wars which were about him on every side, until the Lord put them under the soles of his feet. But now the Lord my God hath given me rest on every side, so that there is neither adversary nor evil occurrent. And behold, I purpose to build an house unto the name of the Lord my God," 1 Kings v. 3, 4.

The building of the Temple is described to us in 1 Kings vi., vii., viii. ; and 2 Chron. ii., iii., iv., v., vi., vii. It was indeed, as David had declared it must be, " exceeding magnifical, of fame and of glory throughout all countries," and was made after the pattern that had been given to David "by the Spirit," 1 Chron. xxii. 5, 12. When it was finished, Solomon " assembled the elders of Israel, and all the heads of the tribes and the chief of the fathers of the children of Israel unto Jerusalem, to bring up the ark of the covenant of the Lord out of the city of David." . . . "And the priests brought in the ark of the covenant of the Lord unto His place, to the oracle of the house, into the most holy place, even under the wings of the cherubims," 2 Chron. v. 1-7. The staves, by which the ark had been carried through all

the wanderings of the Israelites, were "drawn out," as a
symbol that now at last the Lord had entered into His
resting-place; and the Priests and Levites were appointed
to their rightful positions; and then we read, that "it
came to pass, as the trumpeters and singers were as one,
to make one sound to be heard in praising and thanking
the Lord; and when they lifted up their voice with the
trumpets and cymbals and instruments of music, and
praised the Lord, saying, For He is good; for His mercy
endureth forever: that then the house was filled with a
cloud, even the house of the Lord; so that the priests
could not stand to minister by reason of the cloud: for
the glory of the Lord had filled the house of God. Then
said Solomon, The Lord hath said that He would dwell
in the thick darkness. But I have built an house of
habitation for Thee, and a place for Thy dwelling forever. . . . . Now, my God, let I beseech Thee,
Thine eyes be open, and let Thine ears be attent unto
the prayer that is made in this place. Now therefore
arise, O Lord God, into thy resting-place, Thou, and the
ark of thy strength; let Thy priests, O Lord God, be
clothed with salvation, and let Thy saints rejoice in
goodness. . . . Now when Solomon had made an
end of praying, the fire came down from heaven and
consumed the burnt-offering and the sacrifices; and the
glory of the Lord filled the house. And the priests
could not enter into the house of the Lord, because the
glory of the Lord had filled the Lord's house." 2 Chron.
v. 13, 14; vi. 1, 2, 40, 41; vii. 1, 2.

All this is, I believe, typical of that which took place on the day of Pentecost, when the disciples were "all filled with the Holy Ghost." And of that, also, which takes place in every believing heart now, when it is emptied of self, and the door is opened, and Christ comes in to take up His abode there, and fills it with His manifested presence. It is a picture, in short, of the baptism of the Holy Ghost. "What, know ye not that your body is the temple of the Holy Ghost, which dwelleth in you?" "For ye are the temple of the living God, as God hath said, I will dwell in them and walk in them." "Know ye not that ye are the temple of God, and that the Spirit of God dwelleth in you?" I Cor. vi. 19; iii. 16, and 2 Cor. vi. 16.

This is in a sense true of all Christians, for on the day of Pentecost the Holy Ghost came to the Church, "which is the house of God," to abide in her midst forever. But in individual experience, the power of it is not always known, and each soul needs to come to its own Pentecost. The conscious presence of the abiding Comforter is not realized by every Christian. All of course must have the Spirit, because the new birth is impossible without His presence and power. But to some souls, there comes at a certain stage in their progress, a wonderful experience, which they seem instinctively to call the baptism of the Holy Spirit, and which lifts them up into a region of spiritual life that is as far above their former level, as the mountain top is above the valley, and from which but few ever descend. This baptism

does for souls now, just what it did for the disciples on
the day of Pentecost. It purifies; it transforms; it en-
dues with power from on high; it satisfies; it comforts;
it inspires; it controls. It bestows upon those who receive it, that "well of water springing up into everlasting
life," for the soul's own comfort, and those " rivers of living water" flowing out for the blessing of others, which
our Lord promised to all who should believe on Him.

To some this "promise of the Father" comes as a
mighty and overwhelming power, so that their very bodies
are prostrated under it; to others He comes as the tender
and gentle presence of love. But whether in one way
or the other, He always makes His presence *manifest;*
and "at that day," whenever it comes, the words of our
Lord which He spoke to His disciples concerning this
wondrous gift, are invariably fulfilled, " At that day ye
shall *know* that I am in my Father, and ye in me, and I
in you." We may have *believed* it before, because God
says it is so in the Scriptures, but then and from thence-
forth we *know* it, by the testimony of an inward consciousness, that is unassailable by any form of question-
ing or doubt. The Israelites had believed the Lord was
in their midst all along in their wanderings, and in their
years of bondage, even when no sign of His presence
was to be seen among them; but now that the temple
was built, when they all " *saw* how the fire came down,
and the glory of the Lord upon the house," they KNEW
it; and we cannot wonder that at once, without the need
of any command from Solomon, "they bowed them-

selves with their faces to the ground upon the pavement, and worshipped, and praised the Lord, saying, For He is good; for His mercy endureth forever."

But as the temple could not be built, until the land had rest from its enemies all around about, and the reign of peace had begun; so neither can the heart know this conscious indwelling of Christ, and this being "filled with the Spirit," until it has "entered into rest," and has been made more than conqueror through Him. As long as our Christian life is only one of conflict, without settled peace of soul, we cannot know this experience of being "filled with all the fulness of God." The interior life of conscious communion can only exist where peace reigns. The Comforter manifests His abiding presence only to those who have overcome the world by faith, and whose hearts are at rest. The Lord goes with us in all our wanderings, and is beside us in every battle, to fight and conquer our enemies for us; but He does not take up His abode in our hearts in conscious presence, until the kingdom of peace is established there. He cannot. He is the Prince of Peace, and His kingdom is and must be always a peaceable kingdom. If therefore we would know that experience, which answers to the building of the temple, and the Lord coming in to fill it with His glory, we must advance beyond the reign of conflict into the reign of peace, and must know what it is to have the peace of God which passeth all understanding, keep our hearts and minds through Christ Jesus continually,

19

And this can be only by faith. The Israelites entered into the enjoyment of their peaceable kingdom only by faith. David had conquered their enemies, and at the close of his reign he announced this to all the princes of Israel, saying, "Is not the Lord your God with you? and hath He not given you rest on every side? For He hath given the inhabitants of the land into mine hand: and the land is subdued before the Lord, and before His people." The princes believed the word of David, that it was indeed as he had said, and they at once crowned Solomon, whose name means peaceable, to be their king, and began to rejoice in the peace of his kingdom. "And they did eat and drink before the Lord on that day with great gladness, and they made Solomon the son of David, king the second time, and anointed him unto the Lord to be the chief governor, and Zadok to be priest. And Solomon sat on the throne of the Lord as king instead of David his father, and all Israel obeyed him. And the princes, and the mighty men, and all the sons likewise of king David submitted themselves unto Solomon the king. And the Lord magnified Solomon exceedingly in the sight of all Israel, and bestowed upon him such royal majesty as had not been on any king before him in Israel," 1 Chron. xxix. 22–25.

Had any of these princes or mighty men doubted the word of David, and refused to believe that their enemies were conquered, they might, I question not, have continued a skirmishing warfare, and would doubtless have hesitated to submit themselves to the reign of the peaceable king. But they believed, and consequently they "entered into rest."

To Christians also is the announcement made by their David, that He has met and conquered their enemies for them, and that the land is all subdued before Him. "Be of good cheer," He says, "I have overcome the world." Not I *will* overcome it, but I *have.* " I have finished the work which thou gavest me to do." " My peace I leave with you, my peace I give unto you." But unless they believe this, and by faith enter into the rest which He has conquered for them, they will fail to submit themselves to the reign of the Prince of Peace, and will miss of the gladness and the royal majesty of His kingdom of peace. Their hearts, which were meant to be His temple, and in which He desires to dwell, will be closed against His glorious fulness, and the sweetness of His conscious and abiding presence will be unknown.

But, dear friends, this need not be. The promise is sure that He will keep that man in *perfect peace* whose mind is stayed on Him, because he trusteth in Him. And if we will but trust unceasingly and without any reserves, we shall find ourselves dwelling "in a peaceable habitation, and in sure dwellings, and in quiet resting-places." Let us crown Him then, as our Prince of peace, and let us so utterly submit ourselves unto His peaceable control, as that the peace of God shall reign unrivalled throughout all our inward kingdom. And then we also, like Solomon, can build a house for the

Lord, even the temple of our surrendered hearts, at the doors of which He is knocking, knocking ever, for admittance. " Behold I stand at the door and knock ; if any man hear my voice, and open the door, I will come in to him, and sup with him, and he with me," Rev. iii. 20.

The Lord has always sought for a dwelling-place in His people's midst. He loves them with such a yearning love, that He cannot keep away from them ; and at almost the very first moment of Israel's deliverance out of Egypt, His word came to Moses, saying, " Let them make me a sanctuary, that I may dwell among them." They had not asked Him to come, but He asked them to let Him. He wanted a home amongst them. He might have made this home for Himself, by coming in power, and taking forcible possession of one of their tents. But this would not have satisfied the love that wanted to be a welcomed guest. " Of every man that giveth it *willingly* with his heart, ye shall take my offering " for the building of the sanctuary, He had said. And similarly, He will not take forcible possession of any heart now, but knocks for admittance. " Open to me," He says to each one of us; " Open to me, my sister, my love, my dove, my undefiled : for my head is filled with dew, my locks with the drops of the night," Cant. v. 2.

> " The wild-fox has his hole,
>   The sea-bird has her nest ;
>   But save in thy surrendered soul
>   I have not where to rest."

Words fail in seeking to tell out the blessedness of
this interior life of divine union, and the spirit stands
amazed before such glorious possibilities of experience!
With Solomon we exclaim, " But will God in very deed
dwell with men on the earth ?   Behold, heaven and the
heaven of heavens cannot contain thee ; how much less
this house which I have built !" 2 Chron. vi. 18.   And
the Lord answers, as He did to Solomon " in the night,"
after his prayer of dedication had been made, " I have
heard thy prayer, and have chosen this place to myself
for a house of sacrifice . . .   Now mine eyes shall be
open, and mine ears attent unto the prayer that is made
in this place.   For now have I chosen and sanctified
this house, that my name may be there for ever; and mine
eyes and mine heart shall be there perpetually," 1
Chron. vii. 12–16.   " If ye abide in me and my words
abide in you, ye shall ask what ye will and it shall be
done unto you."   " Hereby know we that we dwell in
Him and He in us, because He hath given us of His
Spirit."   " God is love; and he that dwelleth in love
dwelleth in God and God in him."   " At that day ye
shall know that I am in my Father, and ye in me, and
I in you."   These are a few of the New Testament expressions of this glorious hidden life of conscious union
and communion with God.

My dear reader, is this life thine ?   It is surely intended for thee, for it is declared in Acts ii. 39 that the
promise of this wondrous baptism is "unto you and to
your children, and to all that are afar off, even as many

19*

as the Lord our God shall call." And it is surely needed
by thee, for the Christian life without it is but poor and
dwarfed, as thy soul knoweth right well. Do not be
satisfied without it then for even so much as another day.
The steps to reach it are very simple. First, convince
thyself from the Scriptures that the baptism of the Spirit
is a gift intended for thee. Then come to the Lord in
simple faith to ask for it. Then, having put thy case into
His hands, leave it there in childlike trust, knowing that
He will attend to thy request, and that He is more willing to give thee the Holy Spirit than parents are to give
good gifts to their children. Take 1 John v. 14, 15, and
act on it. "And this is the confidence we have in Him,
that, if we ask anything according to His will He
heareth us: and if we know that He hear us whatsoever we ask, we know that we have the petitions that we
desired of Him." Thou art asking for that which is
according to His will, therefore, thou knowest that He
hears thee, and, knowing this, thou must know still
more, and must believe that thou *hast* the petitions
thou desired of Him. By faith claim it as thy present
possession. Begin to praise Him for His wondrous gift.
And it shall come to pass to thee, as it did to Israel,
that when every power of thy being is as one "to make
one sound to be heard in praising and thanking the
Lord," that *then* "the glory of the Lord will fill the house
of the Lord," and thy hungry soul will be filled and
satisfied with His presence.

Texts on the kingdom of peace:—John xiv. 27; xvi. 33; Rom. xiv. 17. Col. iii. 15. 2 Thess. iii. 16. Rom. xv. 13. Is. xxxii. 18; xlviii. 18; liv. 13; lxvi. 12. Jer. xxxiii. 6. Ez. xxxiv. 25. Haggai ii. 9. Mal. ii 5. Luke i. 79. Phil. iv. 6, 7. Eph. ii. 17. Gal. v. 22. Eph. iv. 3. Is. xxvi. 3. 2 Peter iii. 14. Matt. v. 9.

— ———

Texts on the baptism of the Spirit. Promised:—Luke xxiv. 49. John iv. 10, 14; vii. 38, 39; xiv. 16, 17; xvi. 7. Acts i. 4, 5, 8; ii. 38, 39. Eph. v. 14. Joel ii. 28–32 with Acts ii. 16–18. Bestowed -Acts ii. 1–4; v. 32; viii. 14–17; x. 44–47; xi. 15–17; xv. 8, 9; xix. 1–6. 2 Cor. i. 22; v. 5; iii. 16; vi. 19. Eph. i. 13, 14; iv. 30; v. 18, 19. Rom. viii. 9; v. 5. Gal. iv. 6. 1 John ii. 20, 27; iii. 24; iv. 13. 1 Cor. xii. 13. Titus iii. 4-6. 2 Tim. i. 14. 1 Thess. iv. 8. How to be obtained—Luke xi. 1-13.

CHAPTER XIV.

THE DIVIDED KINGDOM.

Keynote : Matt. vi. 24.

THE latter part of Solomon's reign, and the divided rule which followed, seem to me to be typical of the especial dangers that are likely to beset the experience to which we have in that reign advanced, and the temptations peculiar to it. No height of spiritual blessing or spiritual power, can for a moment absolve us from the need of obedience and watchfulness. The temptation to Antinomianism has often overwhelmed the Church or the individual, after seasons of peculiar blessing, and it needs to be especially guarded against. We can never forsake the written law of the Lord with impunity, let our advancement in spiritual life be what it may. And we need to watch, lest, when seated in heavenly places in Christ, we should feel so far lifted above the usual temptations of life, as to be tempted to be less careful of taking heed to our steps, that we walk continually in the law of our God. Some have grievously failed here.

224

And, foreseeing this danger, it was especially commanded concerning the king in Deut. xvii. 18–20:
" And it shall be, when he sitteth upon the throne of his
kingdom, that he shall write him a copy of this law in a
book out of that which is before the priests the Levites :
and it shall be with him, and he shall read therein all
the days of his life ; that he may learn to fear the Lord
his God, to keep all the words of this law and these
statutes, to do them : that his heart be not lifted up
above his brethren, and that he turn not aside from the
commandment, to the right hand, or to the left : to the
end that he may prolong his days in his kingdom, he,
and his children, in the midst of Israel." Had Solomon
kept this law before his eyes, he would not have failed
as he did. And did Christians now faithfully read and
obey the teachings of the Scriptures, they too would
escape similar failures.

Three especial things had been commanded the king
in Deut. xvii. 16, 17, " But he shall not multiply horses to
himself, nor cause the people to return to Egypt, to the
end that he should multiply horses ; forasmuch as the
Lord hath said unto you, Ye shall not henceforth return
no more that way. Neither shall he multiply wives to
himself, that his heart turn not away : neither shall he
greatly multiply to himself silver and gold." Every one
of these commands Solomon disobeyed. In 1 Kings x.
26–28 we read that he " gathered together chariots and
horsemen," and " had horses brought out of Egypt,"
and that he " made silver to be in Jerusalem as stones.'

And in 1 Kings xi. 1–8, we are further told, that he "loved
many strange women " and had "seven hundred wives;"
and that "it came to pass when Solomon was old that
his wives turned away his heart after other gods ; . . .
for he went after Ashtoreth the goddess of the Zidonians,
and after Milcom, the abomination of the Ammonites."
The result of all this was that the "Lord was angry
with Solomon, because his heart was turned from the
Lord God of Israel which had appeared to him twice,
and had commanded him concerning this thing, that he
should not go after other gods, but he kept not that
which the Lord commanded.   Wherefore the Lord said
unto Solomon, Forasmuch as this is done of thee, and
thou hast not kept my covenant and my statutes, which
I have commanded thee, I will surely rend the kingdom
from thee and give it to thy servant," 1 Kings xi. 10, 11.

The three especial dangers, that seem to me to be typi-
cally warned against in this history are, lest the heart begin to lean on earthly resources rather than on the Lord,
as symbolized by the horses from Egypt; lest it suffer its
affections to go out after things the Lord has forbidden,
as symbolized by the strange wives ; and lest it begin to
store up for its own use and enjoyment the spiritual riches
and gifts, which have been given for purposes of service
to the Lord, as symbolized in the multiplying of silver.

Solomon seemed at first to obtain by these unlawful
means, the fulfillment of the promises of prosperity made
to him ; but the fatal consequences followed none the
less surely.   He would have received the promises just

as certainly, as direct gifts from the hands of the Lord, without using these means, and no curse would have followed. But his disobedience to the commandments of the Lord, though it at first enriched him, soon led to more serious departures, and ended in a flagrant turning from the only true God to serve idols. And in our case, none the less surely will these consequences follow, if we, like Solomon, neglect the Scriptures which are able, we are told, to make the man of God perfect, "thoroughly furnished unto all good works;" and if we fail to obey the voice of the Lord by His Spirit.

The result of all this failure was a divided rule. Two kings claimed the throne, and ten tribes revolted from the house of David and set up Jeroboam, Solomon's servant, as their king, leaving only the tribe of Judah to yield allegiance to Rehoboam, Solomon's son. In these two kingdoms of Judah and Israel we have presented to us, I think, that which always results when the inward kingdom of peace has been lost through disobedience, and the heart seeks to serve two masters, alternately yielding to the one and then to the other. Our Lord says concerning this, "No man can serve two masters; for either he will hate the one, and love the other ; or else he will hold to the one and despise the other. Ye cannot serve God and mammon." Ye *cannot*. It does not say, ye must not, or ye ought not, declaring the penalties that will follow if we disobey, but simply, " ye *cannot*." Joseph Cook says that the " cans " and " cannots" of the Bible are not the arbitrary expressions of

God's will, but are simply divine announcements of the eternal nature of things. And we, all of us, know experimentally, that any effort to reverse this inexorable "cannot," always results in grievous backsliding.

The kings of Judah, for the most part, seemed to want to serve the true God, but they were weakened by the departure of the other tribes, and were continually ensnared by Israel's influence or opposition. Of most of their kings the divine sentence was of this sort: "He did that which was right in the sight of the Lord; but not with a perfect heart." But Israel was openly reprobate, and of their kings it was continually said, "He did that which was evil in the sight of the Lord." Its very first king, Jeroboam, fearing the influence of Judah and of the worship at Jerusalem, deliberately established idolatry as the legal and national worship, and has been from that time known throughout all ages as "Jeroboam, the son of Nebat, who made Israel to sin." "And Jeroboam said in his heart, Now shall the kingdom return to the house of David. If this people go up to do sacrifice in the house of the Lord at Jerusalem, then shall the heart of this people turn again unto their lord, even unto Rehoboam, king of Judah. Whereupon the king took counsel, and made two calves of gold, and said unto them, It is too much for you to go up to Jerusalem : behold thy gods, O Israel, which brought thee out of the land of Egypt. And he set the one in Bethel, and the other put he in Dan. And this thing became a sin ; for the people went ρ worship before the one, even unto Dan," 1 Kings, xii. 26-30. All this, we are told in verse 33, Jeroboam "had devised of his own heart." And it seems to me another striking illustration of what idolatry really means : that it is that sort of worship which is "after the commandments of men," and not of God, and is devised out of our own hearts, or out of the hearts of our fathers. In a divided Christian soul, such a worship is always set up sooner or later. The heart must worship, but it cannot endure the worship of the only true God; "it is too much for it," and some substitute is necessary, of the heart's own devising.

I cannot here go into the remaining details of the books we are considering. From the twelfth chapter of 1 Kings, through 2 Kings, and from 2 Chron. x. to the end, it is one long and sad story of sin and failure. There was constant war between the two kingdoms, alternated with occasional alliances. But in these alliances it was not Israel that came up to Judah, but Judah who went down to Israel, see 2 Chron. xviii. 1, 2. And the consequences of these alliances were such as always result from the effort to unite together the service of two masters; the idolatrous nation were in the ascendancy, and those who were seeking to serve the true God were deceived and betrayed. Great disasters fell upon Judah in consequence of this "joining affinity" with Israel, and the way was paved for the final fall.

The lives of the kings of Judah and Israel, and their battles, with their alternating victories and defeats, are

20

full of many practical lessons for us; but I cannot consider these at present. Neither have I space to go into
the history of the prophets raised up to preserve a faithful testimony to the Lord during this time of grievous
failure. The books written by many of these prophets,
and embodied in our Bible, should be studied carefully
in connection with this history.

The evil in the two kingdoms waxed worse and worse,
until no effort or pretence even, was made to serve the
Lord, but of both Judah's kings and Israel's we read,
each one "did that which was evil in the sight of the
Lord;" and the doom pronounced against them in
Deut. xxviii. 36, 37, 63–68, was finally fulfilled, and they
were "plucked from off" their own land, and "brought
unto a nation which neither they nor their fathers had
known." Israel's doom came first. In 2 Kings xvii.
their wickedness seemed to culminate, and we read that
"they rejected His statutes, and His covenant," and
"left all the commandments of the Lord their God."
"Therefore the Lord was very angry with Israel and
removed them out of His sight: there was none left but
the tribe of Judah only. . . . . So was Israel carried
away out of their own land to Assyria unto this day."

The doom of Judah, though somewhat later, came
none the less surely. In 2 Chron. xxxvi. we have the
account of this. They "transgressed very much," we
read, "until there was no remedy." And God brought
upon them the "King of the Chaldees, who slew their
young men in the house of their sanctuary, and had no

compassion upon young man or maiden, old man or
him that stooped for age : He gave them all into
his hand." And all the vessels and treasures of the
house of the Lord were carried away to Babylon, and
the house of the Lord was burned up, and the walls of
Jerusalem broken down, and all her palaces burned with
fire. And those who had escaped from the sword were
carried away to Babylon, where they were " servants to
the king and his sons."

Babylon was not Egypt. Egypt, I believe, is a type of
the state of nature out of which the Church is brought,
while Babylon is the state of worldliness and corruption
into which unfaithfulness brings her. Babylon seems
to be always used in Scripture to set forth Satan's counterfeit of that which the Lord has made. If the Lord
provides any good thing for His children, Satan provides
a counterfeit of it, transforming himself even into an
angel of light, if only thereby he may perchance deceive
the elect. We do not hear of Babylon while Israel were
in Egypt, nor during the early freshnesss of their joy in
escaping from Egypt. It was an enemy who came to
light only in the advanced period of their history. The
Church knew nothing of the danger which Babylon
typifies, during the early years of its existence, nor are
Christians at once upon their conversion assailed by it.
It is only when Churches or individual believers have
been drawn away from their faithful allegiance to the law
of the Lord, when they have substituted the commandments and traditions of men for the commandments of

God, and have begun to " mock the true messengers of the Lord, and despise His words and misuse His prophets," that the danger, typified by Babylon and its kings, comes in. A false and corrupt rule takes possession of the heart, and carries it captive. The precious truths, which were part of the worship of the true God, typified by the " vessels of the house of God, great and small, and the treasures of the house of the Lord," are taken for the service of the false religion; and the strength and wisdom, typified by the young men and the old men, are made to be servants to the king who has taken them captive. I am sure that our knowledge of the sad lapses into corruption of portions of the Church of all ages, and of individual Christian experiences now, can confirm all this.

A watchful walk with the Lord would have saved Judah from it all. They had had warnings without number, throughout the whole course of their declension, for we read that the " Lord God of their fathers sent to them by His messengers, rising up betimes, and sending ; because He had compassion on his people, and on His dwelling-place." 2 Chron. xxxvi. 15. And I feel sure that no soul now falls into backsliding or captivity, without continued and oft repeated warning, both from within and without. The Lord sends messengers to such now, as really as He did to Judah then, because He has compassion on them; messengers of outward sorrow, and suffering, and loss, or messengers of inward condemnation and heaviness of heart. The blessed Holy Spirit " rises up betimes" and speaks to them in a voice they cannot mistake, giving them a sight of their condition and its dangers, and drawing them back to obedience tenderly and lovingly, or seeking to drive them with stern rebuke. And the danger for such, lies just where it did for Judah's last king, of whom we read that he "humbled not him-self before Jeremiah the prophet, speaking from the mouth of the Lord."

I feel therefore that the lesson of this story calls loudly upon each one of us, and especially upon those who may have advanced in their experience as far as the reign of peace, to take heed to every warning sent in love and compassion to save us from similar backsliding, even though that warning may be but the slight inward check or call of the indwelling Spirit.

The six books of Kings, and the history of the king dom close with this captivity.   But there is, notwith-standing all, a most blessed question asked in the very last sentence of 2 Chronicles, which opens up before us a possibility of return from backsliding, and of individual faithfulness, even in the time of the nation's captivity.   It appears that 'the Lord stirred up the spirit of Cyrus, king of Persia," and charged him "to build Him an House in Jerusalem," and Cyrus made a proclamation throughout all his kingdom, and put it in writing, saying, "Who is there among you of all His people?   The Lord his God be with him and let him go up!"

In the books of Ezra and Nehemiah we have this question answered, and the remnant, whose hearts stirred

them up to individual faithfulness, are there brought before us, with the work that they did, and its blessed results.

Texts on a divided heart:—Matt. vi. 24. Luke xvi.
13. Amos iii. 2. Luke xiv. 33. John xv. 4. Luke xi.
34. Matt. vii. 18–21. James i. 22–26; ii. 10; iv. 4. 1
John ii. 15–17. Gal. i. 10. 1 Thess. ii. 4–6. John v. 44.
Eph. vi. 6. Col. iii. 22.

CHAPTER XV.

RESTORATION FROM BACKSLIDING, OR INDIVIDUAL FAITHFUL-
NESS IN A TIME OF GENERAL UNFAITHFULNESS.

Keynote : 2 Cor. vi. 16–18.

THE books of Ezra and Nehemiah contain the story of the faithful remnant, who went up out of Babylon, during the time of the captivity, to rebuild the temple and the walls of the city. They present us with a picture of restoration from backsliding, and of individual faithfulness in a time of general unfaithfulness ; and seem to me to be a type of every true effort made now, by any Christian heart, after a closer walk with God.

We live in a dispensation that seems to have failed almost as grievously as did that of the Israelites. The Church of Christ is full of worldliness, formality, and even idolatry. Many of the Lord's own people are carried away captive into the spiritual Babylon ; and there is needed now, as much as there was then, a faithful remnant, "whose spirit God has raised" to go up to build the house of the Lord, and to rebuild the walls of the spiritual Jerusalem.

These two books of Ezra and Nehemiah set before us in type, the blessed truth, that the general unfaithfulness or corruption of all around us, need be no hindrance to a faithful walk on our part, and that there is a path opened, by which we may individually separate from all that is opposed to the Lord, and may return to Him with a renewed consecration of ourselves, body, soul, and spirit, to be His temple, and to bear witness to His indwelling presence.

No especial tokens of God's power attended this work of the remnant. It was a humble, and, as it were, a hidden work; and yet the promise concerning it was, Haggai ii. 9: "The glory of this latter house shall be greater than of the former, saith the Lord of hosts: and in this place will I give peace, saith the Lord of hosts." When all Israel was faithful, it was an easy thing for each individual Israelite to be so. But in the time of Israel's captivity, it required peculiar devotedness of heart to "go up out of captivity," and was therefore peculiarly pleasing to the Lord. And just so, I believe, there is for us now, an especial sweetness and joy in a path which is one of hidden faithfulness, with but little of outward glory or honor connected with it. As our Lord says, "Blessed are ye when men shall hate you, and when they shall separate you from their company and shall reproach you, and shall cast out your name as evil,

for the Son of man's sake. Rejoice ye in that day
and leap for joy: for behold, your reward is great in
heaven: for in like manner did their fathers unto the
prophets."

In Ezra we have the rebuilding of the temple, and in
Nehemiah the walls of the city are rebuilt. The inward
restoration must come first. As the building of the
temple in the first place, seems to me to have been a
type of the soul consciously surrendering itself to be the
temple of the Holy Ghost; so now the rebuilding of this
temple, typifies, I think, the restoration of the soul from
backsliding or wandering, and a fresh surrender of the
heart to the Lord, to be possessed and indwelt by Him.
It is what is happening, I believe, in very many instances
in the present day. Believers are, as we know, being
brought to a sense of their distance from the Lord, and
are groaning under their captivity to their enemies. The
song has gone out of their hearts, and the language
used by the exiled Israelites to describe their own sad
condition, is the language found to be most appropriate
to theirs: " By the rivers of Babylon, there we sat down:
yea, we wept, when we remembered Zion. We hanged
our harps upon the willows in the midst thereof. For
there, they that carried us away captive required of us a
song: and they that wasted us required of us mirth, saying, Sing us one of the songs of Zion. How shall we sing
the Lord's songs in a strange land?" Ps. cxxxvii. 1-4.
And these have heard, as plainly as Israel of old, the
call to go up to Jerusalem to build the house of the Lord

and many have obeyed this call. To such, this book
of Ezra will be full of wonderful teaching.

A few points deserve especial notice. First of all, it was
a voluntary thing on the part of those who went. It was
only such as went willingly, who could go at all. But of
all these a loving record was kept in God's own Book;
see chap. ii. "Now these are the children of the pro-
vince that went up out of the captivity, of those which
had been carried away, whom Nebuchadnezzar the king
of Babylon had carried away unto Babylon, and came
again unto Jerusalem and Judah, every one unto his city;
which came with Zerubbabel." The whole number
being 42,360. ii. 24.

And to all the ages of believers since, has this sample-
page out of the Lord's book of record come, to teach us
that not even a cup of cold water, given in the name of
a disciple, shall lose its reward. Sometimes we have
been inclined to wonder why there should occur, now and
then, in the Bible, these long lists of names. But if we
think of them thus, as sample pages out of the Divine
book of records, they assume a deep and precious interest. Just so, doubtless, is our Father keeping the
record of those now, who, in these days of half-hearted-
ness and degeneracy, are offering themselves to Him in
a glad surrender, to be His temple, and to be filled
with His abiding presence!

None were allowed to serve who were strangers to Israel, Ezra iv. 1-3, nor even those among the Israelites
themselves, who " could not show their Father's house,

and their seed, whether they were of Israel," see
ii. 59-62. So only the true children of God, and those
moreover also, who know of a certainty that they *are* His
children, can ever enter upon this glorious work of consecration and restoration. It is essential to notice this.
It is not conversion we are speaking of here, but restoration. The children of Israel were not now being brought
out of Egypt, but restored from Babylon. And the first
point to be settled always, in every such restoration, is that of assurance, the knowledge that our sins
are forgiven, and that we *are* in very truth the children
of God. We must be able to " shew our Father's house,"
and to " declare our genealogy," or we, too, shall be
" put from the priesthood."

In chapter iii. the children of Israel, who were thus a
numbered and recognized people, " gathered themselves
together as one man to Jerusalem ; " and under the direction of Joshua and Zerubbabel, they " builded the
altar of the God of Israel to offer burnt offerings thereon."
This must always be the first step in the restoration of
any backslidden heart. The burnt offering altar represented Christ as the atoning sacrifice, making us at one
with the Lord. The whole thought of this offering was
at-one-ment. It was " an offering by fire of a sweet sa-
vour unto the Lord," Lev. i. 9; and proved to the offerer,
in a way he could not mistake, his acceptance with
God. To set up the burnt offering altar, for us, therefore, signifies a realization of our perfect acceptance,
or at-one-ment with the Lord. And the returning

heart needs this assurance, before any other step can be taken.

They next laid the foundations of the Lord's house, iii. 10–13 ; and so great was the joy of Israel at this, that we read " all the people shouted with a great shout, when they praised the Lord, because the foundation of the house of the Lord was laid." But they were not allowed to proceed with their work unmolested. In chapter iv. we read, that when their "adversaries" heard that "the children of the captivity builded the temple unto the Lord God of Israel," they came to them and said, " ' Let us build with you. ' " And when this was re- fused, they sought to " weaken their hands," and trouble them, and to " frustrate their purpose." Satan, who is our adversary, cannot endure to see any soul surrender- ing itself to the Lord to be His temple, and he always puts forth his utmost efforts to hinder all such. At first he seeks to mar the work by his co-operation, trying to bring wrong motives and unlawful means into play ; and when this fails through the believer's faithfulness to his Lord, he then rouses opposition and persecution ; see iv. 1–16. The result of this was that the " work ceased," and for many years, until the " second year of the reign of Darius," the burnt offering altar, and the foundations of the temple, were all that existed among the Israelites as a witness for the Lord their God. It is true, a pro- hibition came finally from the king ; but many years had passed before this, and it is evident that it was want of faith in the Israelites, that was the real hindrance. Their enemies "weakened their hands," and " frustrated their purposes," and they were discouraged from their work.

I think this is a true picture of that which often happens in the history of a returning soul. The believer restored from backsliding, realizes his acceptance with the Lord, and the foundations of the inward temple are afresh laid with joy. But discouragements arise; the hands are weakened by fear, and the adversary stirs up opposition on every side. Friends grow anxious lest there should be danger of fanaticism; the Church turns a cold shoulder; older Christians remonstrate; until finally the believer "ceases his work," and the temple remains unfinished: the soul stops short of the fulness of the blessing.

The Lord, however, was not content with this state of things. He longed still, as always, to *dwell* among His people; and in the "second year of the reign of Darius," He sent Haggai to stir them up. "Then came the word of the Lord by Haggai the prophet saying, Is it time for you, O ye, to dwell in your ceiled houses, and this house to lie waste?" Hag. i. 3, 4. Moreover he showed them what were the sad results of this neglect. " Now therefore thus saith the Lord of hosts; Consider your ways. Ye have sown much, and bring in little; ye eat, but ye have not enough; ye drink, but ye are not filled with drink; ye clothe you, but there is none warm; and he that earneth wages, earneth wages, to put it into a bag with holes. Thus saith the Lord of hosts; Consider your ways. Go up to the mountain, and bring wood, and build the house ; and I will take pleasure in it, and I will be glorified, saith the Lord. Ye looked for much, and lo, it came to little ; and when ye brought it home, I did blow upon it. Why? saith the Lord of hosts. Because of mine house that is waste, and ye run every man to his own house. Therefore the heaven over you is stayed from dew, and the earth is stayed from her fruit. And I called for a drought upon the land, and upon the mountains, and upon the corn, and upon the new wine, and upon the oil, and upon that which the ground bringeth forth, and upon men, and upon cattle, and upon all the labor of the hands." Hag. i. 7–11.

I believe these words will find an echo in many disappointed hearts, whose restoration from backsliding has not brought the spiritual prosperity they had hoped for, and who yet have failed to suspect the cause. Spiritual drought and poverty must always be more or less the portion of every believer, who does not know fully the inward building of the temple of the heart, for the Lord to dwell in.

We read, however, concerning Israel, that, at the prophesying of Haggai, "they obeyed the voice of the Lord their God," and "that the Lord stirred up the spirit of all the remnant of the people; and they came and did work in the house of the Lord of hosts," Haggai i. 12–14. Their fear and discouragement had ended many years before in a decree being issued against them ; but now their faith was so strong, that, without waiting for the reversal of this decree, they began to build at once.

And the effect of this faith was such, that even their "adversaries," who had stopped them before, were the means of a decree in their favor now, and were even compelled to help them. See chaps. v. and vi., especially vi. 6-9. "And the elders of the Jews builded, and they prospered through the prophesying of Haggai the prophet, and Zechariah the son of Iddo : and they builded and finished it." vi. 14.

They then "kept the dedication of this house of the Lord with joy;" and offered abundance of sacrifices, vi. 17, and set the priests and Levites in their rightful places "for the service of God," "as it is written in the book of Moses," vi. 18. When the heart is fully surrendered to the Lord to be His temple, there will always come abundance of sacrifice, and priestly service, according to His own commandments.

Moreover they kept the Passover, the memorial of their redemption out of Egypt, of which all might par take who were purified, and who had " separated themselves from the filthiness of the heathen of the land," vi. 19, 20, 21. And finally, they kept the "feast of unleavened bread with joy ; for the Lord had made them joyful," vi. 22. The feast of unleavened bread was a type of holiness, and the joy of being made a partaker of Christ's holiness, will always come to the believer, who has reached this stage in his experience, and who knows that his heart is indeed the " temple of the Holy Ghost."

In chapters vii. and viii. we have the account of Ezra's

return to Jerusalem with a further remnant, who were " minded of their own free-will to go up to Jerusalem ;" and of this remnant also a faithful record is kept, all of them we read, being "expressed by name," viii. 20. This return of Ezra was for the purpose of instructing the people in the law; for Ezra " was a ready scribe in the law," and we are told that he " had prepared his heart to seek the law of the Lord, and to do it, and to teach in Israel statutes and judgments," vii. 6–10. A heart-whole dedication will open the inward ear to listen to the law of the Lord, and He will always send teaching therein. Even as we read in John xiv. 26: " But the Comforter, which is the Holy Ghost, whom the Father will send in my name, he shall teach you all things, and bring all things to your remembrance, whatsoever I have said unto you."

The coming of Ezra to teach the law of the Lord, at once made manifest the sins into which the remnant had fallen, ix. 1, for " the word of God is quick and powerful, and sharper than any two-edged sword, piercing even to the dividing asunder of soul and spirit, and of the joints and marrow, and is a discerner of the thoughts and intents of the heart," Heb. iv. 12. The necessity for a practical outward separation, to correspond to the inward separation, forced itself upon the consciences of the people; and the princes came to Ezra and said, " The people of Israel and the priests, and the Levites, have not separated themselves from the people of the land, doing according to their abominations; . . . yea, the hand of the princes and rulers hath been chief in this trespass." Ezra was confounded at this discovery, and "sat down astonished until the evening sacrifice," ix. 3, 4. At the time of the evening sacrifice he fell upon his knees and poured out his heart in confession and prayer, ix. 5–15. The hearts of the people also were touched, and they "wept very sore." And they said, " We have trespassed against our God, and have taken strange wives of the people of the land ; yet now there is hope in Israel concerning this thing. Now therefore let us make a covenant with our God to put away all the wives, and such as are born of them." And at once they set themselves to the work of separation and obedience. All Israel was summoned to gather themselves "together unto Jerusalem" within three days, and " all the people," we read, "sat in the street of the house of God trembling, because of this matter, and for the great rain," x. 9. "Then Ezra arose and made a proclamation :" Now therefore make confession unto the Lord God of your fathers, and do His pleasure ; and separate yourselves from the people of the land, and from the strange wives. And all the congregation answered and said with a loud voice, As thou hast said, so must we do." Under the direction of Ezra this work of separation from their "strange wives" was at last accomplished ; and here the book of Ezra leaves them.

It remains true throughout all generations that " holiness becometh thine house, O Lord, forever." And invariably, from the place where the Lord dwelleth, all

21*

evil must be put away. When the soul, therefore, has afresh surrendered itself to the Lord to be His dwelling-place, the searching power of His Holy Spirit begins to reveal the evil, and calls for an entire separation from it.

This matter of the "strange wives" seems to me to be a type of that wandering of the heart from the Lord, which is called "setting our affections on earthly things." The New Testament speaks of it as the "friendship of the world," and in Jas. iv. 4, we are told that this friendship is "enmity with God;" for whosover will be a "friend of the world, is the enemy of God." Also, in 1 John ii. 15, we read, "Love not the world, neither the things that are in the world. If any man love the world, the love of the Father is not in him." The life of sepa ration to the Lord must be real. All that answers to this union with strange wives, must be put away, and also all that which is the fruit of it. The Lord must have our whole hearts, for our love is precious to Him, and any-thing which entices our hearts from our allegiance to Him must be given up. "He that loveth father or mother more than me is not worthy of me; and he that loveth son or daughter more than me is not worthy of me." "So likewise whosoever he be of you that forsaketh not *all* that he hath, he cannot be my disciple."

A poor woman, living alone in a country neighbor-hood, who supported herself by keeping a little country shop, was greatly stirred on the subject of her soul's sal-vation, but was continually hindered in all her prayers and efforts, by an indulged sin. She sold ale without a license, and it was by far the most profitable part of her business; but her conscience was uneasy with it, and whenever she prayed or thought of being a Christian, this illicit trade would start up between her soul and the Lord. The struggle went on for many months, and over and over she resolved to give up the ale, but could never quite bring herself to the actual point. Finally, she attended a meeting one night, where the subject of the preacher was the blessedness and the joy of Christ's indwelling presence in the heart and in the life. She listened with delight. Nothing was said about giving up anything; and she said to herself, "Ah, that is just what will suit me, to have Christ always with me in my lonely cottage!" And in the utmost simplicity of faith she began at once to ask Him to come, and believed that He did. The preacher had spoken about His knocking at our hearts for admittance, and about our opening to let Him in, and this poor woman caught the idea at once, and began to say over and over, "I open to Thee, Lord Jesus, and now I believe Thou dost come in, and I am going to take Thee home with me to-night, and keep Thee there. Mind Thee, Lord Jesus, I have let Thee in;" and all the way home, in her lonely walk across the fields, she kept repeating, "Now I am taking Thee home with me, Thou knowest. Remember, Lord Jesus, I am taking Thee home." Gradually, as she thus by faith claimed His presence, she began to feel a sweet consciousness of it; and by the time she had reached her own door, He had become so precious to her, that all else seemed worthless in comparison. All this time she had not once thought of the ale. But as she opened her cottage door, the first thing she set her eyes upon was a large pot of ale standing on the table. At once the thought came, "Oh, the Lord Jesus won't stay if I keep that ale!" And so sweet had His presence become to her by this time, that the ale was as nothing. She kneeled right down beside the table and said, "Now, Lord Jesus, I have brought Thee home with me, and here is this ale, and I know Thou won't stay if the ale does. So please give me strength to heave that ale right out into the road." She rose and lifted the heavy pot, and it was soon emptied of all its contents. Then she returned into her cottage and kneeled down again and said, "Thank Thee, Lord Jesus, for giving me strength to get rid of that ale. And now, if there is anything else in this house, that Thou cannot stay here with, please show me, and that shall go too."

It remains to be true throughout all ages, that as the presence of light must inevitably drive out darkness, so the realized presence of Christ in any heart or any life must inevitably drive out sin. "Whosoever abideth in Him sinneth not."

This entire separation from all evil, with a list of those who "gave their hands that they would put away their wives," closes the book of Ezra; leaving Israel thus prepared for the work, which Nehemiah chronicles in the next book.

Does it leave us also prepared for a similar work, dear readers? Has the presence of Christ in our hearts, driven

out the sin there, and have we "given our hands" to
put away all that is contrary to His will?

————

Texts on restoration from backsliding, and separation
from all evil:—Jer. iii. 12, 14, 22. Hosea xiv. 4. Ps. li.
12. Is. lvii, 18. Jer. xxx. 17. Joel ii. 25. Gal. vi. 1.
Is. x. 21 ; xxv. 10. Jer. xxiv. 7 ; xxx. 10; xxxv. 3, 7.
Hosea iii 5; vi. 1; xiv. 1, 2. 1 Pet. ii. 25. 2 Tim. ii.
21. 2 Cor. vi. 17, 18. John xvii. 6, 14–18. Rom. xii. 2.
2 Cor. vii. 1. Matt. x. 37–39. 1 John ii. 15–17. Jas. iv.
4. Is. lii, 11, 12. Eph. v. 1–11.

CHAPTER XVI.

NEHEMIAH.

RESTORATION FROM BACKSLIDING, OR FAITHFUL SERVICE IN
A TIME OF GENERAL UNFAITHFULNESS.

Keynote: 1 Cor. iii. 8–15.

THE book of Nehemiah gives us the rebuilding of the walls of Jerusalem. Like Ezra, it shows us in type, a picture of restoration from backsliding, and of individual faithfulness in a time of general unfaithfulness. The city of Jerusalem had been ravaged and destroyed by the King of the Chaldees, and, as we read Neh. i. 3, "the wall of Jerusalem was broken down, and the gates thereof were burned with fire."

While dwelling in the palace of King Artaxerxes, the heart of Nehemiah was stirred up by the account he received of the desolate condition of his beloved city, and he cried to the Lord to grant him His favor, and to incline the heart of the king to permit him to return unto

Judah, and unto the city of his fathers' sepulchres, that he might rebuild its walls, i. 1-11. The king granted the request, and Nehemiah returned to Jerusalem, and went out by night to view the wall. He found it was indeed as it had been reported to him, and he went to the elders of the city and said unto them, " Ye see the distress that we are in, how Jerusalem lieth waste, and the gates thereof are burned with fire ; come, and let us build up the wall of Jerusalem, that we be no more a reproach." Then he told them how the hand of the Lord was on him for this work ; and, stirred by his words, they said, " Let us rise up and build. So they strengthened their hands for this good work," ii. 12-18.

The temple having been built, in Ezra, and God's dwelling-place having been thus provided for, the people now can turn their thoughts to their city. Inward restoration always paves the way and prepares the heart for outward restoration ; and this rebuilding of the walls of Jerusalem seems to me to typify the outward work and service of the Christian, in whose heart the Lord dwells. Jerusalem may be taken as a figure of the Church, and the building of her walls and gates, as symbolizing that building up of the Church now, of which the Apostle speaks when he says, " Even so ye, forasmuch as ye are zealous of spiritual gifts, seek that ye may excel to the edifying (building up) of the Church," 1 Cor. xiv. 12. "And He gave some apostles; and some prophets; and some evangelists; and some pastors and teachers; for the perfecting of the saints, for the work of the ministry ; for

the edifying (building up) of the body of Christ," Eph.
iv. 11, 12.

In chapter iii. we have a detailed account of the work
that was done, and the names of the men who did it.
This is another sample page out of the Lord's book of
records, similar to the one we noticed in Ezra. How
precious to see Him thus taking note of each man, and
of all the details of each man's work. Men may pass
over lightly the work which their brethren do for the Lord,
and may even think their own work not worth remember-
ing; but the Lord never forgets the smallest thing. How
little did Jehoiada the son of Paseah, and Meshullam the
son of Besodeiah, as they "laid the beams of the old
gate, and set up the doors thereof, and the locks thereof,
and the bars thereof," amid the sneers and assaults of
their enemies, think that the record of their work was to
go down to untold millions; and that, wherever the Bible
should go, there would it be told as a memorial of them,
iii. 6. But "God is not unrighteous to forget your work
and labor of love which ye have showed to His name,"
and the weakest laborer may be sure that he is honora-
bly mentioned in that blessed book of records, which is
kept in the Lord's own house on high.

It is very striking also to notice how often it is said
that they built "every one over against his own house,"
and even "over against his chamber. See iii. 10 23, 28,
29, 30. This teaches us the comforting truth, that we
never need seek far for an acceptable service, or for one
that will be valuable to our Lord; for if each one of us

will but build over against our own house, or, if we
possess but a chamber, over against that, the work of
one will join on to the work of another, and the result
will be a completed wall around the whole city. As
we read in vi. 15, "So the wall was finished in the
twenty and fifth day of the month Elul, in fifty and two
days."

But although thus successfully finished, the work had
been carried on through great difficulties, for a disappointed enemy beset them on every side. At first they
came with sneers, saying, "What do these feeble Jews?
will they fortify themselves? will they sacrifice? will they
make an end in a day? will they revive the stones out
of the heaps of the rubbish which are burned? . . . .
Even that which they build, if a fox go up, he shall even
break down their stone wall," iv. 2, 3. And so likewise
will our enemy seek to discourage us, when he sees us
entering into the Lord's service with earnest hearts. He
will come whispering in our hearts his sneers, and
doubts, and mocking questions, "What do these feeble
Christians? will such as they be able to accomplish
anything? Even that which they build, shall it not after
all come to naught?" But we must meet all such taunts
as Nehemiah did, not with angry replies, nor even with
arguments to prove our own strength and capability,
but by simply committing our cause to the Lord, and
leaving it with Him to deal with our enemy; "Hear, oh
our God, for we are despised, and turn their reproach
upon their own head," iv. 3-5. And we must only build

22

on all the more resolutely, having as they had a "mind to the work."

Sneers and taunts having failed, their enemies assailed the faithful builders in another way. For it came to pass that when they "heard that the walls of Jerusalem were made up, and that the breaches began to be stopped, then they were very wroth, and conspired, all of them together, to come and fight against Jerusalem, and to hinder it." If the enemy of our souls fails to discourage us by his sneers, then he assaults us with outward difficulties and oppositions, and with his fiery darts of temptation. But, as it was with Israel, the only effect must be to cause us to "make our prayer unto our God," and to set a watch against him day and night, iv. 7-9. Their adversaries thought to surprise them, saying, "They shall not know, neither see, till we come in the midst among them and slay them, and cause the work to cease," iv. 11. But Nehemiah set a watch, and armed his people with armor, so that "every one with one of his hands wrought in the work, and with the other hand held the weapon," iv. 16-18, and he said, "Be ye not afraid of them; remember the Lord which is great and terrible; and fight." "In what place therefore ye hear the sound of the trumpet, resort ye thither unto us: our God shall fight for us."

Surely the New Testament counterpart of all this is to be found in such words as "Watch and pray lest ye enter into temptation;" "Fight the good fight of faith:" "Resist the devil and he will flee from you." "Finally, my brethren, be strong in the Lord, and in the power of his might. Put on the whole armor of God, that ye may be able to stand against the wiles of the devil. For we wrestle not against flesh and blood, but against principalities, against powers, against the rulers of the darkness of this world, against spiritual wickedness in high places. Wherefore take unto you the whole armor of God, that ye may be able to withstand in the evil day, and having done all, to stand. Stand therefore, having your loins girt about with truth, and having on the breastplate of righteousness; and your feet shod with the preparation of the gospel of peace; above all, taking the shield of faith, wherewith ye shall be able to quench all the fiery darts of the wicked. And take the helmet of salvation, and the sword of the Spirit, which is the word of God: praying always with all prayer and supplication in the Spirit, and watching thereunto with all perseverance and supplication for all saints."

I am aware that those who teach a life of perfect rest and peace, are sometimes supposed to mean that there are no more assaults from our enemy in such a life. But this is so manifestly a misunderstanding, that it hardly seems necessary to say anything about it. And yet it is so difficult to explain just what we do mean, that I do not wonder we are misunderstood. For it is one of those marvellous paradoxes, in which two apparently irreconcilable things exist at the same moment, and perfectly harmonize. Peace and war, rest and labor, are one here. We fight, but it is the fight of faith, not of effort, for

"our God fights for us," and therefore we are at perfect
peace. We work, but it is not we who work, but God
who worketh in us and through us, and therefore we
rest. But to understand this, it must be experienced.
We work as the instrument works in the hand of the
skilful workman. We fight as the baby fights, who hides
its head in its mother's bosom.

> " The dove hath neither claw nor sting,
> 　Nor weapon for the fight;
> She owes her safety to the wing,
> 　Her victory to flight;
> The Bridegroom opes His arms of love,
> And in them folds the panting dove."

As the result of these faithful labors on the part of
Nehemiah and the people, the wall was at last finished,
and the Lord according to His promise that He "will
bring forth our righteousness as the light, and our judgment as the noonday," if we but commit our way unto
Him, and trust Him fully, made even the very enemies
who had begun by mocking them, confess that the work
they had so much despised, was after all of God. "And it
came to pass that when all our enemies heard thereof,
and all the heathen that were round about us saw these
things, they were much cast down in their own eyes;
for they perceived that this work was wrought of God,"
vi. 16.

In chapter viii. we find that the immediate and blessed
result of the work of restoration, which had been ac-

complished, was to bring the people to a renewed
acquaintance with the law of the Lord. It had been
many years since Ezra had come up to Jerusalem, for the
express purpose of instructing Israel in His statutes and
judgments. But the condition of things in which he
found them, had unfitted them for hearing or understanding it. They were such as Paul describes in Heb.
v. 12. " For when for the time ye ought to be teachers,
ye have need that one teach you again, which be the
first principles of the oracles of God: and are become
such as have need of milk and not of strong meat."
During times of captivity and of unfaithfulness, the law
of the Lord is lost sight of, and indeed, cannot even be
understood. But when the soul is again restored to
communion, and the presence of the Lord is afresh
realized in our midst, then the Divine law becomes most
precious. In truth, I think its preciousness is felt then as
never before. And to my mind this chapter in Nehemiah gives us in picture a truer apprehension of the
sweetness of the will of God, and of what it means to
have that will perfectly done in our lives, than almost
any other chapter in the Bible.

The eagerness with which " all the people gathered
themselves together as one man into the street that was
before the water-gate," to hear the reading of the book
of the law, is a picture of that " hungering and thirsting
after righteousness," which comes to every soul that has
been drawn near to the Lord. Since we have found
Him so precious Himself, we begin to realize that His

22*

will must be precious also, and we begin to long to
know it.

From morning until midday they stood and listened
to the reading, "both men and women, and all that
could hear with understanding," while Ezra " read the
law distinctly, and gave the sense, and caused them to
understand the reading." And we are told that "the
ears of all the people were attentive unto the book of
the law." During the years of their captivity, this law
had been but a vaguely remembered tradition among
them, and it is no wonder that it should come to them
now like a fresh and wondrous revelation.

Their first impulse as they listened was to grieve.
"For all the people wept when they heard the words of
the law." Doubtless their grief had two causes, regret
at their neglect of so wonderful a law, and fright at the
discovery of their own great distance from its perfect
righteousness. And so also, to souls in the present day,
the fresh discovery of the will of God may perhaps at first
cause tears and fright, as they see how great is their want
of conformity to its blessed requirements. But in our
case, as in theirs, if we only saw it aright, this very Will
is our cause of deepest rejoicing. For Nehemiah said
to the people, " This day is holy unto the Lord your
God; mourn not nor weep. . . . Go your way, eat
the fat and drink the sweet, and send portions unto
them for whom nothing is prepared; for this day is
holy unto our Lord; neither be ye sorry, for the joy of
the Lord is your strength. So the Levites stilled all the

people, saying, Hold your peace for the day is holy; neither be ye grieved. And all the people went their way, to eat, and to drink, and to send portions, and to make great mirth, because they had understood the words that were declared unto them," viii. 1–11.

A strange cause for mirth, some would say; even among those who profess to know and love the Lord, whose will they so dread. But to my mind the greatest cause of rejoicing that our poor world can have, lies just in this, that God has chosen to give to us His holy, and blessed, and lovely law, and has taught us to say, "Thy will be done." Without the will of God, this world would indeed be a place of concentrated misery. But the presence and accomplishment of His will, transforms it into an outer court of heaven.

And did we but know our God and His love, I am sure we, too, as they did, "would make great mirth," as soon as we understood the words that are declared unto us.

I confess I feel more deeply than I can express, the grievous wrong that is done to our Heavenly Father, by the evident dread His own children have of His blessed will. If they, who profess to know Him and trust Him, feel so about it, we cannot wonder that the world looks upon the will of God as something to be feared and resisted more than anything else, and we need not question why they are driven away from Him. If His own children regard Him as a tyrant, what can His enemies be expected to think? It is indeed most grievous, that Satan should have so veiled the loveliness of the will of God from the eyes of many Christians, that, instead of clinging to it as their chiefest good, they should so often shrink from it in fear and sorrow. Yet it is a fact which cannot be ignored, and which I would gladly meet and overcome, were it possible.

For the will of God is always and under all circumstances good and best. He is love, and His will can be nothing but love. He is full of wisdom, and His will must always be wise. He is omnipotent, and His will is baffled by nothing that can oppose. He is just, and His will must be truly and perfectly just. The truth is, when I think of who and what our God is, I am amazed that it ever entered into the head of any one of us to fear or combat His will. We do not know what we are doing, when we indulge in such feelings. The idea that our Father, who loves us, *can* want anything but our best and truest happiness is inconceivable. His will for us *must* be all that is best, and sweetest, and most satisfying, and surely we can trust ourselves to it without a single shrinking or fearing thought.

And when once we have opened our ears to listen to this will, we shall find, as the children of Israel did, that "His commands are not grievous," as perhaps we may have feared they would be; but that peace, and rest, and even "very great gladness" follow quickly in the keeping of His law. For the very second day of their reading, "they found written in the law which the Lord had commanded Moses, that the children of Israel

should dwell in booths in the feast of the seventh month,"
viii. 14. This feast of tabernacles was a feast of joy. It
was the celebration of their rest and possession of the
land, after their journey through the wilderness. And
thus they, who had expected perhaps commands which
might cause them sorrow, found instead that their first
duty was to joy and gladness. Not since the days of
Joshua, had they known such joy!

It is indeed true, as some one says, that "God's will
on earth is always joy, always tranquility;" and so
every soul finds it, whose surrender is absolute and unconditional. "Great peace have they that love Thy
law, and nothing shall offend them."

The result of this reading of the law, was great searching of heart among the Israelites, and in chapter ix.
they tell their experience, and make their confession
unto the Lord, and agree together solemnly to dedicate
themselves unto Him, ix. 38. Chap. x. 1–27 gives us a
roll of the names of "those that sealed" themselves
unto this covenant, another blessed list, in which it is
an everlasting glory to have been enrolled. And this list
is, I believe, only a sample of the long and ever-increas-
ing one, where are written the names of all who since
then, have "sealed themselves" to be wholly the Lord's.

The terms of their consecration are given us in x.
28–39, ending with the significant words, " and we will
not forsake the house of our God." All depends upon
this. As long as the dwelling-place of the Lord is in the
midst of any people, or in any heart, holiness of life will

necessarily follow. And sin, if it comes, will nearly always result from the heart having first forsaken the Lord's dwelling-place.

In chaps. xi. and xii. there is given us another list of those who "willingly offered themselves to dwell at Jerusalem;" and also of those who "praised and gave thanks" at the "dedication of the wall of Jerusalem." See xii. 27–42. They could not sing while in captivity in Babylon, as we read in Ps. cxxxvii. 1–4. "By the rivers of Babylon, there we sat down, yea, there we wept when we remembered Zion. We hanged our harps upon the willows in the midst thereof. For there they that carried us away captive required of us a song: and they that wasted us required of us mirth, saying, Sing us one of the songs of Zion. How shall we sing the Lord's song in a strange land?" But now that their captivity had been turned, their mouths were filled with singing, as it had not been since the days of David and Asaph of old. We even read that they "sang loud," and that they "rejoiced with great joy; so that the joy of Jerusalem was heard even afar off." The soul in captivity cannot sing, but when the "Lord turns again the captivity of Zion," then are our "mouths filled with laughter, and our tongue with singing." The praises of His people are acceptable to the Lord, and this record of those who here praised and gave thanks is therefore very significant.

The result of this joy, was a renewed and still deeper consecration. Again the book of the law was brought out, and read in the audience of the people, and it was

found written therein, "that the Ammonite and the Mo-
abite should not come into the congregation of God forever," xiii. 1. At once Israel set themselves to obey this
command, and separated from themselves "all the mixed
multitude," 1–3. And it was discovered that this evil
had crept even into the very inner courts of God's house ;
for the "stuff of Tobiah," the Ammonite, had filled the
chambers of the temple, where aforetime they had kept
the meat offerings and the frankincense. But this was
now cast forth, and the chambers cleansed, and restored
to their proper use, xiii. 4–9. So deep-seated was this
evil of fellowship with those from whom the Lord had
commanded entire separation, that even the priest, who
had the oversight of the chamber in the house of the
Lord, was " allied with Tobiah," and had been left un-
disturbed in his alliance, vs. 4, 7. But all hidden and
even unsuspected sins are brought to light, when the
law of the Lord is yielded to in simple obedience; and
the soul is then enabled to cleanse its innermost chambers of all the "stuff" belonging to the enemy, and to
present the heart to the Lord, for His use only.

Besides all this, it was found that the rest of the
Sabbath was being habitually broken, by tradesmen of
different kinds, who "brought all manner of burdens
into Jerusalem on the Sabbath day." This, Nehemiah
remedied, commanding the gates to be kept shut, and,
setting some of his servants at the gates to watch "that
there should no burden be brought in on the Sabbath
day," xiii. 15–22. The Sabbath is a type of the rest of

soul, Christ promises to all the wearied and heavy laden who come unto Him ; and to break the Sabbath, there-fore, symbolizes the breaking of this spiritual rest, by bearing burdens, which we are commanded to lay on the Lord. This is a very important point; for of all the declarations of God's will given us in the Gospel, none is more distinct and positive than this, that His people are to bear no burdens and carry no cares. " Be careful for nothing;" "Take no thought for your life, what ye shall eat, or what ye shall drink ; nor yet for your body, what ye shall put on." " Let not your heart be troubled, neither let it be afraid." " Cast all your care upon Him, for He careth for you." And I doubt whether we even *begin* to know the grief that we give to our Lord, by our disobedience to these commands. When we, who are strong, tenderly love any one who is weak and helpless, how it delights our hearts to bear their burdens and do their work for them, and how it grieves us, if they will not permit us the privilege. And this should make us understand the longing of our Lord's heart towards us, His poor weak and helpless little ones, whom He knows to be so unable to care for anything aright for themselves.

A weary missionary lady in Persia went into a church there one Sabbath afternoon, and was obliged to sit down on a mat near the middle of the floor, as there were no other seats. She was very tired with her previous labors that day, and longed for rest; but with no support to her back, it seemed impossible to obtain it.

In a moment a broad-backed native woman, noticing her look of extreme weariness, moved quietly up, and, planting her strong shoulders squarely behind her, whispered, "Lean on me." The lady leaned, but not with her whole weight. The fear of oppressing her kind friend, made her feel delicate about abandoning herself to the luxury of the support. But the native woman, with a look of longing love, leaned around and whispered to her in intensest tenderness, "Do you *love* me? If you love me, you will lean hard!" And then to that poor, weary body came rest, and to the weary spirit also came the sweet words from the Master, saying, "If you love *Me*, you will lean hard on Me also." Soul and body were rested, and from that time the dear missionary lady kept unbroken the blessed "Sabbath of rest," upon which she then entered.

> Child of my love, "lean hard,"
> And let *Me* feel the pressure of thy care;
> I know thy burden, child; I shaped it,
> Poised it in Mine own hand, made no proportion
> In its weight to thine unaided strength:
> For even as I laid it on, I said,
> "I shall be near, and, while she leans on *Me*,
> This burden shall be mine, not hers.
> So shall I keep my child within the circling arms
> Of Mine own love." Here lay it down, nor fear
> To impose it on a shoulder which upholds
> The government of worlds. Yet closer come—
> Thou art not near enough, I would embrace thy care
> So I might feel My child reposing on My heart.
> Thou lovest Me? I know it. Doubt not then,
> But, loving Me—*lean hard.*

23

Finally, the Lord's rest having been restored, a com·plete separation was made from all the "strange wives," who had either been left when Ezra made the former separation, or who had been married since; and Nehemiah closes his book with the words: "Thus cleansed I them from all strangers, and appointed the wards of the priests, and the Levites, every one in his business; and for the wood offering at times appointed, and for the first-fruits. Remember me, O my God, for good."

And as Nehemiah dealt with the Israelites, so, I believe, will the blessed Holy Spirit deal now in faithful and loving rebuke with every soul that returns afresh to the law of the Lord, teaching us and enabling us to "cleanse ourselves from all filthiness of the flesh and spirit, perfecting holiness in the fear of God."

What comfort there is for thee · here, beloved Christian. Thou mayest have wandered far from thy Lord, and have been taken captive by cruel enemies. His law may have been lost to thee, and thy heart may have formed many close alliances with strangers. But a path is here opened before thee, by which thou mayest return, and which will lead thee out of all that is contrary to His will. Do not therefore be afraid to face the truth as to thy present spiritual condition; and do not admit the thought that thou hast been carried captive too far and too long for restoration to be possible to thee. For in the swift transitions of our spiritual life, the very time that reveals a failure, may reveal the remedy also, and at once that remedy may be applied, and the soul delivered. And that which took years for the children of Israel, may be accomplished for thee in a Divine moment.

" Who is there therefore among you of all his people? His God be with him and let him go up."

Texts illustrating faithful service in times of unfaithfulness :—Matt. x. 16. Luke x. 3. Heb. xiii. 14. 2 Cor. vi. 14–18. Acts xx. 28–31. Matt. vi. 24. Luke i. 74, 75. John xii. 26'; xv. 19–21. Dan. iii. 12–18, 28, 29. Eph. vi 5, 6. Rom. vi. 16. Luke v. 11; xix. 12–26; xiv. 33. Matt. xix. 27–29; x. 37–39. Mark i. 18. Ps. xlv. 10, 11.

CHAPTER XVII.

ESTHER.

GOD'S HIDDEN PROVIDENTIAL CARE OVER HIS PEOPLE IN THEIR CAPTIVITY.

Keynote: Heb. xiii. 5, 6.

THE book of Esther closes the series of the historical books of the Old Testament. It takes up the condition of the Jews, who "had been carried away from Jerusalem with the captivity," ii. 5, 6, and who had remained behind in the land of their enemy, when the faithful remnant under Ezra and Nehemiah had returned to Jerusalem to rebuild the temple and the walls of the city. These captives are shown here, to be still the objects of God's care, although they would seem to have forfeited all right to it, by their failure to return to their own land when an opportunity was afforded them.

The details of this story are very simple. The Gentile wife of Ahasuerus, having been set aside because of her disobedience, the king chose for her successor a lowly

Jewish maiden, belonging to the captive race; and her
uncle and protector Mordecai "sat in the king's gate,"
ii. 19. One of the king's servants, Haman the Agagite,
was advanced to a place of great honor, and all the
king's servants bowed and reverenced him, but we read
that "Mordecai bowed not nor did him reverence." In
this no doubt Mordecai as a Jew, was governed by a
command of the Lord, which was more binding to him
than even the command of Ahasuerus. For Haman
was an Agagite, and the family of Agag were of the nation of Amalek, whom Israel as far back as Exodus had
been commanded utterly to destroy. See Ex. xvii. 14–16;
Deut. xxv. 17-19. The wrath of Haman at this disre-
spect, led him to desire the destruction of the whole
nation to which Mordecai belonged. For Haman
"thought scorn to lay hands on Mordecai alone;"
wherefore he "thought to destroy all the Jews that were
throughout the whole kingdom of Ahasuerus, even the
people of Mordecai." "And Haman said unto King
Ahasuerus, There is a certain people scattered abroad
and dispersed among the people in all the provinces of
thy kingdom : and their laws are diverse from all people.: neither keep they the king's laws : therefore it is
not for the king's profit to suffer them. If it please the
king, let it be written that they may be destroyed."
King Ahasuerus consented, and posts were immediately
sent out into all his provinces with commandment to destroy "all Jews, both young and old, little children and
women, in one day." iii. 11-15.

Mordecai at once made application to Esther to inter-
cede with the king on behalf of her nation; and Esther
braved the king's displeasure, by going into his presence
unsummoned, and requesting him to come that day
with Haman to a banquet she would prepare for them.
At this banquet she invited them to a second one on the
following day, where she promised to tell out her petition. Meanwhile, on that very night, the king could not
sleep, and he commanded them to bring the book of records to be read to him, vi. 1, 2. There "it was found
written " that Mordecai had saved the king's life from a
conspiracy, and his gratitude was so stirred at the remembrance of it, that he bestowed upon Mordecai great
honor, unconsciously making use of his worst enemy,
Haman the Agagite, to carry out the plans. And at the
second banquet the whole story of Haman's cruelty was
brought out, and Haman was hanged, and the king issued
a decree giving the Jews permission to "gather themselves
together, and to stand for their life, to destroy, to slay, and
to cause to perish all the power of the people and provinces that would assault them, both little ones and women, and to take the spoil of them for a prey," vii. 10, 11.
The result of this was a general deliverance to the Jews
throughout all the provinces which were from India unto
Ethiopia; and the "Jews had light, and gladness, and joy,
and honor," viii 16, 17. And "Mordecai the Jew was next
to King Ahasuerus, and great among the Jews, and accepted of the multitude of his brethren, seeking the wealth
of his people, and speaking peace to all his seed," x. 3.

Such is the story of the book of Esther. Some seem to have seen in it a typical picture of the Kingdom of God upon earth ; taking Ahasuerus as a type of the Most High Jehovah, Vashti as a type of rejected Israel, Esther as a type of the chosen Church, Mordecai as a type of the Lord Jesus, and Haman as a type of Satan. But this seems rather fanciful to me ; and I confess that I have no clear apprehension of any especial typical teaching as intended here. The story of Esther, like that of Ruth, is the story of a bride. In both a lowly maiden is exalted to a place of honor and wealth. And it seems probable, although one was a Gentile and the other a Jew, that they were both meant to typify in some way the future story of the Church of Christ, chosen from her low estate, and called to the glorious destiny of sharing the throne with her heavenly Bridegroom

But I incline to think that the lesson to be drawn from this little book, is rather moral than typical. We have given to us here, the secret and providential care of the Lord over His people, even when they were in captivity in an enemy's country, and at a time when they seemed to be utterly unmindful of Him. God's people may forget Him, but He cannot forget them, and wherever they may be, He watches over and cares for them.

The book of Esther, therefore, seems to me to teach the much-needed lesson that even at times, when, on account of their unfaithfulness, the Lord may seem to have hidden Himself, or to have forsaken His people, His care over them is as real as ever, although it may be

a secret care, which is altogether hidden from their eyes.
The name of the Lord is not once mentioned in this book,
because His agency in their deliverance could not be
made manifest to a people so far off from Him, and yet
to the anointed eye there can be traced plainly throughout the whole of it, His providential care. Behind all
their neglect of Him, and His seeming forgetfulness of
them, He held the reins of His providence, and by a
series of apparently natural events, and by most un-
likely means, using the king's sleeplessness even as one
link in this chain, He brought to pass His will concerning them, and saved them in the time of their need,
see vi. 1-3.

I have said that the name of the Lord was not once
mentioned in this book, yet that the thought of Him was
there, and that His hand was recognized in the events
that took place, is very evident from the fact of a fast
being proclaimed by Esther and Mordecai, iv. 16, which
could have no other meaning than that of prayer to the
Being whose Name is left unspoken; and also from
the establishment of the "feast of Purim" which has
been celebrated by the Jews for all the centuries since,
as the memorial of a great national deliverance, ix.
17, 26. Even as I write, the daily papers are calling attention to the fact that at this very time the feast of Purim is being kept. One paper says, "By the unanimous
consent of the entire body of the Jewish people, the festival of Purim has been observed for a period of about
2500 years. Devoted to rejoicing and hilarity, without

sinking into Bacchanalian orgies, it has taken deep hold on the affections of the Jews, and its annual return is hailed with such marked demonstrations of pleasure, as to show that it occupies no inferior position in their estimation. In pious gratitude for the joyful termination of Haman's plot, Esther and Mordecai enjoined all Israelites and their descendants to celebrate the 14th and 15th day of Adar as " days of feasting and joy, of sending presents one to another, and gifts to the poor." In the spirit in which the festival was instituted, it is observed at the present day. On the eve of Purim, and again on the following morning, the Jews assemble in their synagogues to offer prayers and hymns of thanksgiving to God, and to listen to the reading of *Megillah*, or Book of Esther. The rich distribute alms bountifully to their poorer brethren, presents are interchanged, social reunions take place, and no Jew permits the day to pass without devoting some portion of it to domestic comfort and happiness."

The teaching of this book is therefore, that the Lord, though hidden, still cares for His people. And it is a teaching of great practical importance for every one of us.

The natural heart finds it hard to trust in an unseen Care-taker ; and when Christians wander away from the Lord and forget Him, they can hardly believe that He does not forget them. They talk about being forsaken ; and, because their own love has grown cold, they imagine that His has also. They judge Him to be altogether such as themselves in their unfaithfulness, and

measure His truth by their own falseness. But the
Scriptures reveal a far other God than this. They reveal One who "having loved His own, that were in the
world, loved them to the end," even though they forsook
Him and fled. They show forth a Shepherd who does
not leave His sheep on the cloudy and dark day, nor
when the wolf cometh ; but who draws nearer than ever
in such times of need, and who always goes after the
ones that wander. They tell us of a Saviour who saves
the lost, not the found, and of a Physician who heals
the sick, not the well. They declare to us the glorious
fact that He never leaves nor forsakes us, and that
always and everywhere He is watching over us and
caring for us in tenderest love, and with infinite wisdom. Our sins separate us from Him, but they do not
separate Him from us ; and we never get from under
His providential care. This care may be hidden, but it
is none the less real, and all things in the daily events of
our lives are made to work subservient to the Lord's
gracious purposes towards us. "Can a woman forget
her sucking child that she should not have compassion
on the son of her womb? Yea, they may forget, yet
will I not forget thee. Behold, I have graven thee on
the palms of my hands : thy walls are continually before
me," Is. xlix. 15, 16.

This thought would have wonderful power to restore
the soul of the backslider, were it but fully realized continually. Coldness, and neglect, and indifference we can
resist and resent, and be only driven away the further ;

but who can turn always from the persistent love and
care that will not be rebuffed, and that never forgets
our need? And even backsliding Israel will at last be
won by this love that has so followed them throughout
all their rebellions and backsliding, and will, when
the final and crowning proof of undying love has come
in their restoration and establishment in their own land,
be brought to "remember their own evil ways, and
their doings that were not good, and shall loathe themselves in their own sight for their iniquities and for their
abominations," Ez. xxxvi. 31. "And they shall look
upon Me whom they have pierced, and they shall mourn
for Him as one mourneth for his only son, and shall be
in bitterness for Him as one that is in bitterness for
his first-born," Zech. xii. 10.

No doubt, in Esther we have an insight into the
Lord's providential care of His people from that time
onward. The day of their "scattering" still continues,
but the Lord still watches over them as faithfully as He
did then, though as secretly. And in every country or
nation where a single one of His chosen nation are to-
day abiding, His providential care is, I doubt not, order-
ing all outward events to work together for their preservation and their final deliverance. Only in this way
can we account for their marvellous history down to the
present time. They are still His people, beloved and
blessed, in spite of their long-continued unfaithfulness;
and His sovereign unfailing care, come what will, is
unceasingly exercised in their behalf.

But if all this is true of the Lord's people, when living afar off from Him in the land of their captivity, how much more true must it be of those who are seeking to follow Him closely, and to abide continually in the land of promise which He has given them!   Surely to all such, no single doubt of His constant watchfulness and care ought ever to be permitted to come, even though no manifest token of His presence is discernible!   And the lesson of Esther to each one of us must be, to teach us to rest in a serene and unwavering trust, even in the midst of the most mysterious dispensations, sure that He overrules and controls it all, and that nothing that affects us, whether seen or unseen, whether in the minds of others or in our own, escapes His care.

————————

Texts on the Lord's over-ruling and providential government:—Dan. iv. 35. Ps. cxv. 3; cxxxvi. 6; ciii. 19. Prov. xxi. 1. Is. xl. 15, 17; xliii. 13; xliv. 24–28: xlv. 5–9. Jer. xviii. 6; xxiii. 24. Job xii. 9, 10, 16; xxxiv. 29; xxxvii. 5–19. Ps. xxii. 28; xxxiii. 10–15; lxxxix. 6–14; xciv. 7–10. 2 Chron. xx. 6. Rom. ix. 14–23. Heb. xiii. 5, 6.

CHAPTER XVIII.

JOB.

THE DEATH OF SELF.

Keynote: Heb. xii. 5-11.

THE book of Esther, as we have seen, closed the historical series of books in the Old Testament. In Job we now enter upon another series, containing, I think, the inward exercises of the hearts of God's people, as to sanctification. This series consists of Job, Psalms, Proverbs, Ecclesiastes and the Song of Songs; and seems to give us a progressive development of heart experience, beginning with the death of self in Job, and culminating in a realized union with the Lord in the Song of Songs.

In Job we have the death of self. Man is taught to see himself as he really is in the Lord's presence. His utter weakness and need are here revealed to him, and he is brought to an end of the self-life. In Psalms we

24

have the resurrection life, the "life hid with Christ in God." Man is there taught to know the Lord, and is shown how to draw from Him the supplies for his weakness and need. In Proverbs we have this dead and risen man surrendering himself to the teachings of Divine wisdom, by which he is shown the path to walk in. In Ecclesiastes the world is sought in vain for an object to satisfy this deeply-taught soul. And in the Song of Songs this Object is found, and the heart rests eternally in a realized union with its Beloved. Job is the first step in the soul's experience, and Canticles is the last; and Canticles can never be reached, until Job has been first passed through. These steps are more or less marked in the experience of every sanctified soul, I think, and come mostly in the same order. We must first be brought to an end of self, as in Job, before we can learn what it is to live the life hid with Christ in God, as in Psalms. But in this resurrection life, we realize the need of guidance in order to walk safely through the crooked paths of the world, and must therefore yield ourselves up to the teachings of Divine wisdom, as in Proverbs. The world will then drop from our hands as an utterly unsatisfying thing, as in Ecclesiastes. And finally the soul will find itself prepared to be united to its Lord in a blessed oneness, which forever satisfies its needs and its longings, as in Canticles.

The first step in this developing series of heart exercises is, as I have said, that man should be brought to an end of self; and the Lord's first dealings with him, therefore, will be directed to this. In the book of Job we seem to have these dealings plainly set before us, and are there shown, as it were, the Lord's *processes* with His saints. We get behind the scenes here, into His secret counsels, and are made to understand the hidden mystery of trial, and see how it all has its spring in God, let the instrumentalities be what they may ; and is all meant to make us " partakers of His holiness." It is the work of the Refiner that is here revealed to us. And I feel that it is unspeakably blessed for us, thus as it were, to get a glimpse into His work-shop, and see His processes of refining the gold committed to His care. The mystery of suffering is so unfathomable to most of us, and the questions it asks are so unanswerable, and often so agonizing, that we cannot be thankful enough for the glorious and satisfying answer given us in this book of Job ; nor can we rest our hearts too utterly upon the revelation here made. " No chastening for the present seemeth to be joyous, but grievous. Nevertheless afterward it worketh the peaceable fruits of righteousness to them that are exercised thereby." This is the lesson of Job.

Job was a righteous man, coming under the refining and purifying hand of the Lord, in order that he might be brought to an end of self, and might have a revelation of God to his soul. And in this he was a sample and a foretelling of the thousands of saints since, who have had to go through similar processes, for the same glorious and blessed end. " There was a certain

man in the land of Uz whose name was Job; and that
man was perfect and upright, and one that feared God,
and eschewed evil," i. 1.

It was necessary that a righteous man should have
been chosen for that which was to follow, since it is the
training of God's saints that is here set forth ; and none
but a good man could have understood the lessons or
profited by them.   Moreover it is plain to the simplest
comprehension, that a wicked man needs to be brought
to the end of himself.   But that an upright man, who
" fears God and eschews evil," should also need this, is
not so clear.   And some who can look, with a com-
placent comprehension of the divine purposes, on the
trials that fall to the lot of the sinners around them, are
yet unable to discover any reason for the mysterious dispensation of suffering to themselves.   They are conscious,
it may be, of the integrity of their hearts, and cannot see
the justice or the need of their trials.   " I was doing
what I believed to be right," such a one will say, and
" why should these things come upon me?"   But the subtle forms of self-life that would ruin us, if left undiscovered
and unchecked, are often most vigorous in those whose
outward walk is all that could be desired ; and it needs
sometimes a very sharp discipline to uproot them.   And
in this fact lies hidden, doubtless, the secret of much that
is mysterious in the dealings of the Lord with the souls
of His servants.   He loves us too much to permit any
evil to linger undiscovered and uncured in our natures,
and He will probe us to the very bottom by His dispensa-

tions, before He will suffer the hurt of His people to be slightly healed. This is not severity, but mercy. For the great object of all the discipline of life here, is character-building. We are to be the "friends of God" throughout all eternity, and to be His *friends* means something far grander than merely being saved by Him, and requires a far deeper harmony with His will. Therefore it is an unspeakable boon for us, that He loves us enough to take the necessary pains to make us meet for companionship with Himself. How well we know the strength of love it requires for us to discipline our children, in order to make them what they ought to be, and how often we fail just through a selfish weakness. Let us be thankful, then, that we have to do with a God who is of purer eyes than to behold iniquity with any toleration, and whose love is so strong that He will not withhold the hand of His discipline, until He has purely purged away all our dross, and taken away all our tin, and has presented us to Himself a "glorious Church, not having spot, or wrinkle, or any such thing."

Job, as I have said, shows us the divine process by which all this is accomplished. It is "baptism unto death." By all that happened to Job, he was brought to a knowledge of his own heart, and was made to abhor himself in dust and ashes. The instrument used was Satan, but the Hand that used this instrument was the Lord's. In both cases, when Job's possessions were taken, and also when his own body was smitten with sores, Satan's power extended only so far as the Lord permitted, and not

24*

one hair's breadth further. At first the Lord said, " Be·
hold, all that he hath is in thy power, only upon himself
put not forth thy hand," i. 12. And afterward he said, ' Behold he is in thine hand ; but save his life," ii. 6. Therefore, while Satan seemed to do it all, there was One behind
Satan, who overruled everything, and made it all work
together to accomplish His purposes of grace toward Job.

First, the Sabeans fell upon Job's oxen and asses, and
the servants who were ploughing with them, and destroyed them all. Then; ' the fire of God " fell from
Heaven and consumed his sheep and their shepherds.
Next, the Chaldeans made out three bands, and fell
upon his camels, and carried them away. Then, there
came a great wind from the wilderness and caused the
house to fall upon his children and kill them, i. 13–19.
And finally Satan smote Job himself " with sore boils
from the sole of his foot unto his crown," ii. 7. To all
these trials were added the reproaches and misunderstanding of his friends; until Job's life seemed to be
utterly ruined, and as though it must end in nothing but
humiliation and defeat on every hand. But it was only
the " seen thing " which was thus ruined. The " unseen
thing " in the mind of the Lord, was the "exceeding and
eternal weight of glory " which was to be the outcome
of this ruin. The outward man, it is true, seemed to
perish, but the inward man was renewed day by day.
And by all that Satan was thus permitted to do, Job was
brought at last to the place of emptying, where the
Lord could reveal Himself in glorious fulness.

The Sabeans, and the Chaldeans, the fire, the wind, and the sore sickness, were the agencies employed to accomplish this blessed result. And man, judging by "feeble sense," would have seen only these. But the curtain has been lifted for us, and we see behind these fires of trial, One who sits as a Refiner and Purifier of silver, and who controls and guides it all. He knew the heart of His servant Job, and that his successful and prosperous career, and even his very righteousness, were in danger of building up a subtle form of self-life, that would in the end, if unchecked, drag him down into the miry clay. Therefore He used Satan to spoil i·, that in the spoiling, Job himself might be saved.

This story of Job is, I believe, enacted over and over in our midst now. The righteous suffer, and we cannot tell why. "Mysterious providences," as we call them, darken and apparently ruin the lives of those who have seemed too good to need such discipline. Even to ourselves come afflictions that we cannot understand. And Satan seems so busy in the matter, that it is hard to trace the hand of the Lord in it at all. But His hand *is* in it nevertheless, and He overrules everything. Not a trial comes except by His permission, and for some wise and loving purpose, which, however perhaps, only eternity will disclose.

The Sabeans and the Chaldeans may carry away our property. Fires and storms may deprive us of all that we love and value. Sore sickness may lay its hand upon us. Friends may misjudge and reproach us. But behind them all, our Father sits, measuring out each bitter drop with His own unerring wisdom and unspeakable love.

Earthly parents deal thus continually with their children. Their watchful eyes discover incipient diseases, long before the children perhaps feel any uncomfortable symptoms themselves, and they administer the needed medicines, often when it seems very mysterious and unreasonable to the child. And yet the parent's closet may be full of medicines, and all remain untouched for months, if no need is discovered. A parent's love is too tender to inflict unnecessary doses, and too strong to spare the dose that is needed.

We may be sure, therefore, that here lies the secret of all that seems so mysterious in the discipline of our lives, whether it is outward or inward trial. Our loving and wise Physician has discovered in us some incipient disease, that He knows will ruin us, if it remains unchecked, and He is applying the remedy. Would we stay His hand, even if we could? Surely not. For more than anything else we, too, want for ourselves soul health; and any remedy that will bring it to us, is more than welcome. Above all do we want to have that done for us which was done for Job, and to be brought to the end of self as he was, and have, as he had, a revelation of God to our souls. We sing, and we mean it,

> "Oh! to be nothing, nothing,
> Only to lie at His feet,
> A broken and emptied vessel,
> For the Master's use made meet.

Emptied, that He might fill me,
As forth to His service I go;
Broken, that so unhindered,
His life through me might flow."

But when the Lord takes us at our word, and begins to empty us, and to break us, the means He is obliged to use, puzzle us, and seem unreasonable, and even often unkind and unjust. No chastening for the present *can* seem joyous to us; but must necessarily be grievous, and we ought not to think it "mysterious" that it should be so. We must not question, therefore, nor admit the slightest inward rebellion against it, but thankfully submit to that which our Lord permits to come, let the instrumentality be what it may, whether Satan directly, or the wickedness and treachery of men. For not a sparrow falls without our Father's notice, and all that He permits to come upon us is meant to make us "partakers of His holiness," if only we are rightly exercised thereby. For it is the cross, and the cross alone, that brings us out of self. And lives that we are apt to call wasted, which have ended in sorrow and humiliation, are not really wasted, but are simply being stripped of that which separated them from the Lord, and from a perfect conformity to His likeness. And that man is happy who goes into the next world emptied of self, no matter how painful the humbling may have been.

But Job's friends, as so many now, saw nothing of all this. They thought they entirely understood the Lord's dealings, and that what He did must simply be a just reward for Job's sins. Eliphaz said, "Remember, I pray thee, who ever perished being innocent? Or where were the righteous cut off?" iv. 7. Bildad also said, "If thou wert pure and upright, surely now He would awake for thee, and make the habitation of thy righteousness prosperous," viii. 6. And finally Zophar said, "Know therefore that God exacteth of thee less than thine iniquity deserveth," xi. 6. See also xxii. 3-11. These three friends coldly reasoned concerning the Lord, that His outward dealings towards men are an adequate representation of His relationship with them, and that an eye for an eye and a tooth for a tooth is always His way; therefore, because Job was in trouble, it manifested the Lord's disapproval and anger. We, who see behind the scenes, know how mistaken was this view, for it was really the Lord's love and approval of Job, that was at the secret source of all that had happened. For the Lord said to Satan, "Hast thou considered my servant Job that there is none like him in the earth, a perfect and an upright man, one that feareth God and escheweth evil?" i. 8. As the potter will cast aside the poorest vases, as not worth any further trouble, but will expend all his energies on perfecting and beautifying one that is already beautiful, so the Lord chose Job out of all the men living on the earth at that time, as being the one most worthy of His utmost skill to fashion and mould to His will. It is the old rule, "For whosoever hath, to him shall be given, and he shall have more abundance." Because Job had so much righteousness already, the Lord desired to make him altogether right down to the very bottom ; and his trials, therefore, if they had been rightly understood, were but a proof of that blessed sort of approval, that cannot be satisfied with anything but complete perfection in the object of its love. But Job's friends had not such a knowledge of God as would have enabled them to dream of this. Their view of Him was the shallow outward view of hearts, who have not yet gone into the depths, either for themselves or others. They looked upon Him as a hard and exacting Master, instead of a loving and tender Father, and construed the blessed justice of One who knows the weakness and the infirmities of those He judges, into the stern and revengeful injustice of a tyrant, who makes no allowance for human need. They lost sight of the Saviour in the Judge. "Behold God will not cast away a perfect man, neither will He help the evil-doers," was the whole of their creed. It was all works, works, works: "this do, and thou shalt live." And in this they were a fitting type of every legalist since, who will not believe in any justification but the justification of works.

Job, conscious of the integrity of his heart, and roused by the unjust reproaches of his friends, appealed from them to the Lord. His friends, he felt, did not understand him, but he knew the Lord did, and he was not afraid to pour out all his heart before Him. The very freedom of his complaints and reproaches revealed the depth of his childlike confidence in Him. "Oh that I

might know where I might find Him! that I might
come even to His seat! I would order my cause before
Him and fill my mouth with arguments. I would know
the words which He would answer me, and understand
what He would say unto me. Will He plead against me
with His great power? No; but He would put His
strength in me," xxiii. 3-6. Job was sure that if he could
only see the Lord, and get at His reasons, all would be
made plain. "Surely I would speak to the Almighty,
and I desire to reason with God. . . . Then call
thou, and I will answer: or let me speak and answer
thou me. How many are my iniquities and sins?
Make me to know my transgressions. Wherefore hidest
thou thy face, and holdest me for thine enemy? Wilt
thou break a leaf driven to and fro? and wilt thou
pursue the dry stubble?" xiii. 3, 22-24. And through it
all he trusted. His mouth was full of complaints and of
anguish, and even of reproaches; but they were, after
all, the complaints and the reproaches of a soul who knew
that his Redeemer lived, and who at the bottom trusted all
the time. "Though He slay me, yet will I trust in Him,"
xiii. 15. "For I know that my Redeemer liveth, and
that He shall stand at the latter day upon the earth;
and though after my skin, worms destroy this body, yet
in my flesh shall I see God: whom I shall see for myself
and not another; though my reins consume within me."
xix. 25-27.

Job proved moreover, that outward prosperity was no
test of righteousness, by pointing out the prosperous cir-

cumstances of the wicked. "The tabernacles of robbers prosper, and they that provoke God are secure ; into whose hand God bringeth abundantly," xiii. 6. "Their seed is established in their sight with them, and their offspring before their eyes. Their houses are safe from fear, neither is the rod of God upon them," xxi. 7-14. And he showed that if righteousness were indeed the test of prosperity, none could be prosperous, because none in the sight of the Lord are really righteous. "If I wash myself with snow water, and make my hands never so clean, yet shalt thou plunge me in the ditch, and mine own clothes shall abhor me," ix. 30, 31.

Notwithstanding all his rebellious complaints, Job knew the Lord so much better than his three friends, and set forth His character and His ways so much more truly, that the Lord's own verdict, given to Eliphaz the Temanite was, "My wrath is kindled against thee, and against thy two friends ; for ye have not spoken of me the thing that is right as my servant Job has," xlii. 7. The resignation of these three friends to Job's sorrows, and their exalting of the Lord's rigid justice in His dealings with men, sound to a surface reader far more pious than poor Job's rebellious complaints ; but the fact remains that the Lord Himself was angry with them for not speaking the thing that was right, as He declared His servant Job did. And when we look below the surface, we get at the secret. Job believed in a Saviour, they believed in a Judge. And all the rest was included in this. Job knew something of God's love ; they were ignorant of it.

25

To Job He was a Father, to them He was only a Law-
giver.   Job trusted Him, although he did not understand Him ; they thought they understood Him, but were
afraid of Him.   Theirs was a salvation of works ; Job's
was a salvation of faith.   They misjudged the Lord, and
ascribed to Him a character that He could not but hate.
Therefore Job, with all his complaints and his questionings, was far more acceptable, because through it all,
and in spite of it all, he trusted.   And doubtless this is
so still, and the man who trusts, even in the midst of
utter darkness, and while acknowledging that he cannot
understand, pleases the Lord far better than the cold
reasonings of hearts who know Him not, and who attri-
bute to Him therefore characteristics that grieve. Him.
More than anything else, I feel sure, He wants our utter
confidence, and would far rather we would trust that
His ways are right, than try to explain them.   It is not
comprehension we desire from our children, but *confidence*.   And we can love even the very complaints that
come from this confidence, far better than the con-
strained and stiff backwardness that is our homage from
those who know us not.   Love, love, love ! is the one
universal cry of every heart, whether Divine or human,
and no homage but love can satisfy.

But although Job had thus spoken of the Lord that
which was right, in comparison with his three friends, yet
the deep-seated evil of his heart came out at last in his
self-justifications.   Sinful self had been conquered in
him, but righteous self was mighty.   Chapters xxix.

xxx., xxxi. bring this to light: " When the ear heard
me, then it blessed *me;* when the eye saw *me*, it gave
witness to *me;* because *I* delivered the poor that cried,
and the fatherless, and him that had none to help him.
The blessing of him that was ready to perish came upon
me : and *I* caused the widow's heart to sing for joy. *I*
put on righteousness, and it clothed *me: my* judgment
was as a robe and a diadem." Job was satisfied with
himself. He was good, and he knew it, and his heart
was lifted up within him. This was a very subtle, but a
very fatal form of self-life, and nothing would have
reached it and destroyed it but those very "mysterious"
dealings, against which poor Job so rebelled. " He was
righteous in his own eyes," we are told," and " justified
himself rather than God," xxxii. 2. And this was more
disastrous than any other form of evil; therefore it
must be rooted out at whatever cost. I believe that just
here many fail, and need sore discipline. Their very
righteousness and religious success builds up self in
them, and nothing but a complete overthrow of all will
root it out. Sometimes the contrast between chapters
xxix. and xxx. is experienced now, and Christians who
once could say with Job, " Unto me men gave ear, and
waited, and kept silence at my counsel ;" afterwards
are driven to say as he did, "But now am I their song:
yea I am their byword. They abhor me, they flee from
me, and spare not to spit in my face." Such know not
why this is, and their friends know not, and perhaps reproach them. But the Lord knows, and, behind all the

wrath of the enemy, He is at work, sitting " as a refiner and purifier of silver," watching for the moment when the perfect reflection of His own image in the molten metal, shall assure Him that the work is accomplished, and the dross is all purged away.

That moment came when Job could say from the depth of a convicted heart, " I have heard of thee by the hearing of the ear, but now mine eye seeth thee. Wherefore I abhor myself, and repent in dust and ashes," xlii. 5, 6. But it did not come, until the Lord had revealed Himself. That which all the re-proaches and accusations of his friends had failed to do, one sight of God accomplished in a moment. Job had prayed that he might but see Him and hear Him speak, and the answer had come, bringing with it a revelation of self, which Job could hardly have expected, and yet which he found to be the beginning of richest blessings. He saw the Lord, but he also saw himself, as he was in the Lord's presence, and all his self-righteousness turned into filthy rags in an instant.

Chapters xxxii. to xli. give us this revelation, first through the lips of Elihu, and then directly from the mouth of the Lord Himself. These chapters are un-speakably grand revelations of the Almighty. They show us His infinite greatness and His infinite goodness in such a glorious union, as to give to every heart that receives their teaching, an eternal rest. His ways are here declared to be ALWAYS RIGHT, let them look as they may to the eyes of men. And we are shown, therefore, that there is nothing left for us to do but to trust Him : " Although thou sayest I shall not see Him, yet judgment is before Him, therefore trust thou in Him," xxxv. 14. Yes, trust Him always, everywhere, and through everything. We must not question His dealing, for He is too great for us to comprehend, and yet too wise to make a mistake. " Behold God is great and we know Him not; neither can the number of His years be searched out," xxxvi. 26. " God thundereth marvellously with His voice ; great things doeth He which we cannot comprehend," xxxvii. 5. " Touching the Almighty, we cannot find Him out : He is excellent in power, and in judgment, and in plenty of justice : He will not afflict." xxxvii. 23. " Yea, surely God will not do wickedly, neither will the Almighty pervert judgment." xxxiv. 12. Such was the testimony of Elihu who spoke to Job " in God's stead " and on His behalf. And the Lord Himself also spoke. " Then the Lord answered Job out of the whirlwind and said, . . " Gird up now thy loins like a man : for I will demand of thee and answer thou Me. Where wast thou when I laid the foundations of the earth ? Declare, if thou hast understanding. . . . Wilt thou also disannul my judgment ? Wilt thou condemn Me that thou mayst be righteous ? Hast thou an arm like God ? Or canst thou thunder with a voice like Him ? Deck thyself now with majesty and excellency ; and array thyself with glory and beauty. . . . Then will I also confess unto thee that thine own right hand can save thee." Who can wonder that his rebellious reasonings silenced forever

25*

by such a revelation of God's greatness and his own unspeakable nothingness, Job should exclaim, "Behold I am vile : what shall I answer thee ? I will lay my hand upon my mouth." xl. 4. In such a Presence we may well be dumb. But not with fear, only with adoring love. "For this God is our God even for ever and ever ; He will be our guide even unto death."

Job did, however, at last "answer the Lord," but it was simply by a confession of the Divine omnipotence, and his own nothingness. All his self-justifications were over forever, and from henceforth he would have eyes and ears for none but the Lord and His glory. "Then Job answered the Lord and said, I know that Thou canst do everything, and that no thought can be with-holden from Thee. Who is he that hideth counsel without knowledge ? Therefore have I uttered that I under-stood not, things too wonderful for me which I knew not. Hear I beseech Thee and I will speak : I will de-mand of Thee, and declare Thou unto me. I have heard of Thee by the hearing of the ear : but now mine eye seeth Thee. Wherefore I abhor myself, and repent in dust and ashes." xlii. 1–6.

Upon the lap of God's greatness Job could now lie down in perfect content, satisfied to be nothing in him-self, since he belonged to the omnipotent One.

> "For greatness which is *infinite*, makes room
>   For all things in its lap to lie ;
>   We should be crushed by a magnificence
>   Short of eternity.

*   *   *   *   *   *

" But what is infinite must be a home,
    A shelter for the meanest life,
  Where it is free to reach its greatest growth,
    Far from the touch of strife.

*   *   *   *   *   *

" Thus doth Thy hospitable greatness lie
    Outside us like a boundless sea;
  We cannot lose ourselves where all is home,
    Nor drift away from Thee.

*   *   *   *   *   *

" Great God ! our lowliness takes heart to play
    Beneath the shadow of Thy state;
  The only comfort of our littleness
    Is that Thou art so great.
  Then on Thy grandeur I will lay me down:
    Already life is heaven for me;
  No cradled child more softly lies than I,—
    Come soon Eternity ! "

One deeply important lesson to be drawn from this experience of Job's is this, that all true knowledge of self and abhorrence of self must come, not from self-examination, but from beholding the Lord. Until Job had his eyes opened to see the Lord, he was very well satisfied with himself, and all his self-examination seemed to lead only to self-justification. But the moment the Lord was revealed, all was changed, and the man, who, while looking at self had seen nothing but good, now abhors himself in dust and ashes.

Self-examination is sometimes extolled among Christians as a most commendable and necessary duty; but in my view it is often a very great evil. It leads either to self-justification and self-commiseration, or else to discouragement and despair. It fills our lives with chapters full of the personal pronoun "I" and "my," as Job's was. While the soul that looks away from self, and examines the Lord instead, finds its mouth filled with His name, and His praises, and His glorious power. Compare Job xxix. with Psalm lxxi. In the one it is all, I, my, me. In the other it is all, Thou, Thy, Thee. If you will take a pencil and mark these respective words underneath, you will see how striking is the contrast.

I feel very sure that the commands to look unto Jesus, to behold His glory, to have our eyes ever toward the Lord, mean something exceedingly literal. And it is very certain that when we are looking unto Jesus, we cannot see ourselves, for if our face is to the One, our back will necessarily be to the other. It is by "beholding as in a glass the glory of the Lord," that we are to be "changed into His image." It is by keeping our eyes "ever toward the Lord," that our feet are to be plucked out of the net. It is by looking unto Him, that all the ends of the earth are to be saved.

And practically we know that nothing hinders us more in our christian life, than to keep our eyes fixed on ourselves, trying to search out evidences of our own goodness and fitness for the mercy of the Lord, or tokens of our growth in grace. If we think we find any, then at once we are frightened at the danger of pride; and if we do not find any, then we are plunged into the depths of discouragement. The true way is to give up self at first, as Job did at last, as hopelessly bad, and to have no eyes nor thoughts for anything but the Lord and His salvation. This, I think, is what the Scriptures mean by self-denial and self-crucifixion. It is to say to this "I," "I am a stranger to you," and to refuse to listen for a moment to its pretensions or its claims.

I am afraid but few will understand this, and fewer still will act upon it. Self is so enticing to us, and self-examination such an interesting and absorbing occupation, that it is very difficult for us really to take in the thought that we are to have no more of it. But experimentally I can say, that I never have any peace nor find any victory, except when I utterly ignore even the existence of self, and turn my eyes and thoughts only on the Lord.

Job's end was a glorious triumph. The discipline had accomplished its work of purification, and the Lord could now bestow upon him double of all his blessings. "And the Lord turned the captivity of Job, when he prayed for his friends; also the Lord gave Job twice as much as he had before," xlii. 10. The turning point was "when he prayed for his friends;" and it seems to me that it is because this fact was the sign of the inward death to self that had taken place. They had utterly misunderstood and misjudged him, and had heaped undeserved reproaches upon him. But now that he abhorred himself, he felt no resentment towards them, and so partook of the mind of the Lord as to pray for those who had thus "despitefully used him and persecuted him." In the New Testament, our Lord speaks of this as one of the marks of being "perfect even as our Father which is in Heaven is perfect." And I doubt not, it is one of the last surrenders of self and self-love made by any soul.

Thus was Job's discipline completed, and he was brought out of self and into God. The process had been painful and mysterious, but the end that the Lord had in view, could have been reached by no other means; and could Job have seen into the secret counsels of the Lord from the beginning, he would doubtless have rejoiced at every blow. The "exceeding and eternal weight of glory" worked out for him by what he had passed through, a thousand times more than com pensated for it all.

Let us learn the lesson, dear friends; and without a question let us accept the sorrows, and trials, and crosses of our lives, directly from the hands of our loving Father, as being His own choice for us, in order for our being made "partakers of His holiness," no matter what instrumentality may be used to bring them upon us. What if they are mysterious? The ways of the infinite God *must* be mysterious to the finite creature. Even the ways of earthly parents are often mysterious to the minds of their children, and cannot be explained in any terms that the children could comprehend, even if the parent should be willing to make the explanation. But the day comes, when the children have been trained

into such maturity of character, as to be able to understand the needs-be for the process of their training,
and to understand it by an intuitive perception without
any explanation. And the day will come to us, I am
sure, if we yield ourselves unresistingly to our Lord's
training, when His ways with us will all be vindicated
and made glorious, and when we will praise Him for
every dispensation of His providence, and for 'every
stroke of His rod.

> "God moves in a mysterious way,
>   His wonders to perform;
> He plants His footsteps in the sea,
>   And rides upon the storm.
> Deep in unfathomable mines
>   Of never failing skill,
> He treasures up His bright designs,
>   And works His sovereign will.
>
> "Ye fearful saints, fresh courage take i
>   The clouds ye so much dread
> Are-big with mercy, and shall break
>   In blessings on your head.
> Judge not the Lord by feeble sense,
>   But trust Him for His grace:
> Behind a frowning providence
>   He hides a smiling face.
>
> " His purposes will ripen fast,
>   Unfolding every hour;
> The bud may have a bitter taste,
>   But sweet will be the flower.

> Blind unbelief is sure to err,
>   And scan His works in vain;
> God is His own Interpreter,
>   And He will make it plain."

———

Texts illustrating the Lord's refining processes with his children, and their blessed fruits:—Jas. v. 10, 11. Heb. xii. 5–11. Rev. iii. 19. Prov. xiii. 24. Luke vi. 21–26. Matt. v. 10–12. Ps. xciv. 12, 13. 1 Pet. iv. 12, 13. James i. 2, 3, 12. John xv. 19–21. Matt. x. 22–25. Phil. i. 29. 1 Peter ii. 19–23. 1 Cor. xi. 31, 32. Job v. 17. Deut. viii. 2–5. Prov. iii. 11, 12. Jer. xxxi. 18, 19. Ps. xxxviii. Rom. v. 3. John xvi. 33. Acts xiv. 22. Rev. vii. 14. **Matt. xviii. 8.**

CHAPTER XIX.

PSALMS.

THE LIFE HID WITH CHRIST IN GOD.

Keynote: Col. iii. 1-3.

THE Book of Psalms gives us the resurrection-life of the believer. It is the illustration of the latter part of Rom. vi. 4. "Therefore we are buried with Him by baptism into death; that like as Christ was raised up from the dead by the glory of the Father, even so we also should walk in newness of life." In Job we have seen the christian "buried into death," and here we see him "raised up from the dead," to walk, as Christ walked, in "newness of life." This book is therefore the natural sequence of the book of Job, or the next step in the soul's progress. In Job man had been taught to know himself, here he is taught to know the Lord. This book shows us human nature in all its weakness, as it is seen in God's presence, but reveals at the same moment the all-sufficient

supply there is in the Lord for its every need. It is the
necessary and immediate outcome of Job's death to self.
It is life in God. Its language throughout is, " I am
nothing ; Christ is all."

And my feeling is that no heart is fitted to enter fully
into an understanding of this wonderful book, until it
has passed through the discipline, and reached the
result which the book of Job reveals. None but a soul
that has come to the end of self and of all self-depend-
ence, *can* enter into the blessed sweetness of the twenty-
third Psalm, or dwell in the fortress of the ninety-first ;
for the grace which these Psalms reveal, and the blessings they set forth, are all grace and blessings for the
weak and the helpless, and none but these can possibly
receive or enjoy them. The man who speaks here, is
the man of faith, and the life revealed, is the life of
trust. " Many there be which say of my soul, There is
no help for him in God. But Thou, Lord, art a shield
for me ; my glory and the lifter up of my head." ii. 2, 3.
" But mine eyes are unto Thee, O God the Lord ; in
Thee is my trust ; leave not my soul destitute." cxli 8.
" It is better to trust in the Lord than to put confidence
in man: it is better to trust in the Lord than to put confidence in princes." cxviii. 8, 9. " O taste and see that
the Lord is good: blessed is the man that trusteth in
Him." xxxiv. Such are a few out of the numberless
declarations of helplessness and of trust that are found in
this book.

The Psalms are the expression of the inward feelings produced in the heart of each writer by the varied circumstances and events of his life. They were written mostly by David, though some of them are ascribed to other writers, and the prayer of Moses is included among them. But whoever may have been the authors, of each one it is true that he was evidently prepared by the Lord, through personal or public events, for expressing the mind of the Spirit of God, who "wrote by him, and whose words were upon his tongue." And moreover, whoever speaks, it is true, as Augustine says in his exposition of this book, that "the voice of Christ and His Church are well nigh the only voices to be heard." In some instances Christ Himself is the sole speaker, in others His people only speak; but generally it is the Head and the members together, who "use the harp and utter the song."

Many of the Psalms refer so manifestly to Christ that they are sometimes called Messianic Psalms. And these may be looked upon as a sort of diary, as it were, kept by our Lord for the purpose of letting His people know a little of the deep, inward emotions He experienced as a Man, bearing the awful burden of humanity, partaking of our nature, and tempted with our temptations. In other parts of the Bible we have the details of His outward life while on earth, and learn what He did, and what was done to Him. But here we have the record of what He thought and felt, while going through all these.

The writer of a little book called "Short Meditations

on the Psalms " says concerning this, " The cries, and
tears, and praises of Jesus, His solitary hours, His
troubles from man, and His consolations in God, all
these are felt here in their depth and power. What was
passing in His soul when He was silent as to man, led
as a lamb to the slaughter: what they who surrounded
Him did not hear, we listen to in this wondrous Book.
His thoughts of men, His worship of God, with all the
incense of His various and perfect affections, are understood here. The New Testament tells us that He prayed
and sung, but this Book gives us His prayers and songs
themselves."

If this then be indeed true, what blessed intimacy
does it declare, that our Lord should thus permit us to
enter into the wonderful secrets of His deepest emotions
while living on this earth, for us, and in our nature.
And I think nothing so makes us realize His actual
humanity, as to listen to these cries of human suffering
and anguish, and to feel our hearts thrill over His
yearning for human sympathy and appreciation.

One example will illustrate what I mean. In Psalm
xxii. we have the emotions of our Lord's heart as He
hung on the cross, bearing the sins of the whole world.
The opening verse proves this, " My God, my God,
why hast Thou forsaken me? why art Thou so far from
helping me, and from the words of my roaring?" The
first sentence of this cry is all that we hear in the New
Testament, Matt. xxvii. 46; but the Speaker who utters
that, must also utter all the rest likewise. Some compa-

rison of other verses in the Psalm will confirm this. Compare verse 6 with Is. liii. 3 ; verses 7, 8, with Matt. xxvii. 39–44; verse 16 with John xx. 25–27; verse 17 with Is. lii. 14; verse 18 with Luke xxiii. 34; verse 22 with Heb. ii. 11, 12. See also,

Ps. ii. 7, compared with Matt. iii. 17 ; xvii. 5 ; Acts xiii. 33.

Ps. ii. 2, and xxxi. 13, compared with Matt. xxvii. 1.

Ps. xvi. 8–11, compared with Acts ii. 25 ; iii. 15 ; Matt. vii. 14 ; xxv. 33.

Ps. xxxviii. 11, 12, compared with Matt. xxvi. 56 and verse 13 with Is. liii. 7.

Ps. xxxix. 9, compared with Matt. xxvi. 62, 63 ; Acts viii. 32–35.

Ps. xl. 6–8 ; li. 16, compared with Heb. x. 5–9 ; Luke xxiv. 44 ; John v. 39.

Ps. lxix. 5–9, compared with John ii. 17 ; xv. 25 ; vii. 5 ; Rom. xv. 3.

Ps. cx. 1, compared with Matt. xxii. 44 ; Acts ii. 34 ; 1 Cor. xv. 25 ; Heb. i. 13.

Ps. xli. 9, compared with John xiii. 18, 25, 26, 27.

Ps. xlv. 1–17, compared with Luke iv. 22 ; Heb. 1. 8 ; Is. lxi. 1.

But besides those Psalms which thus expressly refer to the Lord Jesus, there are many others whose praises, desires, hopes and deliverances could have in Him alone their truest realization. Only by seeing this, I think, can we understand much here written. And only by understanding that the desires for vengeance upon

26*

His enemies and for the destruction of all His foes, is to be interpreted as referring to Christ's great enemy, Satan, and all his host of evil spirits, and to the dreadful effects of sin in the hearts and lives of men, can we be relieved from the painful sense of vindictive cruelty that otherwise would oppress many tender hearts in their perusal. The Lord, who has told *us* to love our enemies, and to do good to them that hate us, could surely not do otherwise Himself; and I cannot but feel that we must read of His wrath as being directed against the sin, and not against the sinner, and His vengeance as being poured out upon the cruel Enemy, who carries captive His helpless flock, and not upon the poor flock, thus attacked and enslaved.

And, taken in this sense, we, His people and the flock of His pasture, can unite with our whole hearts in His cries for vengeance, and can rejoice with Him in the promised downfall of every foe. I do not of course state this view of mine as an infallibly correct one; but simply as the best explanation I can find of all that is so difficult to understand in the Psalms, and as containing experimentally much blessed help to my own soul. If it is Christ and His Church who speak here, it must be that the expressions are such as the Church can unite in, without disobeying the commands of her Lord as to her treatment of her enemies; and only by taking the view I present can this be done. But I feel that the Holy Spirit alone can teach us concerning this.

The Psalms might be called the *heart* of the Bible.

They lie in the midst of it, and express its secret and hidden life. The central verse of the whole divine volume is found here, the keystone of the arch, as it were; and this verse reveals the point upon which all else turns. It is the eighth verse of Ps. cxviii., and reads as follows: "It is better to trust in the Lord, than to put confidence in man." And throughout the whole book the universal teaching consists only of different changes rung upon this same theme. For it contains, as I have said, the heart exercises of the dead and risen man. "Not I, but Christ" is its constant language. It is the second stage in the series, beginning with Job and ending with the Song of Songs, and is the second stage in the experience of every soul, which has been brought by the cross and the revelation of God, to the end of self.

No other dependence but the Lord God of Israel is thought of or permitted here. "Some trust in chariots, and some in horses; but we will remember the name of the Lord our God. *They* are brought down and fallen, but *we* are risen and stand upright," Ps. xx. 7. "Except the Lord build the house they labor in vain that build it, except the Lord keep the city, the watchman waketh but in vain," Ps. cxxvii. 1. And no possibility of disappointment to those who do thus trust, is for a moment admitted. "They that trust in the Lord shall be as mount Zion, which cannot be removed, but abideth forever," cxxv. 1. "The Lord redeemeth the soul of His servants; and none of them that trust in Him shall be desolate," xxxiv. 22. "In God have I put my trust : I will not be afraid what man can do unto me," lvi. 11. From beginning to end, the voice that speaks here tells of only one Refuge and one Defence. All dependence upon self seems to have been taken from him, and, with Paul, his realization is throughout, " My grace is sufficient for thee : for my strength is made perfect in weakness. Most gladly therefore will I rather glory in my infirmities, that the power of Christ may rest upon me. Therefore I take pleasure in infirmities, in reproaches, in necessities, in persecutions, in distresses for Christ's sake : for when I am weak then am I strong." This experience is not generally the first, nor the second, nor even the third step in the christian life. Much has to be passed through before this is reached. The deliverance out of Egypt, the wilderness journey, the going into the land, the failures there, the bondages and the restorations, need often all to be experienced according to our measure, before we are ready to come to the death of self, as in Job, and to know this life of utter dependence upon the Lord. I do not say that all these experiences need to be gone through, but that which they teach must, and ft seems as though souls but seldom have simplicity enough, and faith enough, to learn these lessons directly from the Lord, without this outward discipline of failure and trial. But whether by the inward crucifixion only, or by that also which is outward, in one way or the other, all must come here, before the Lord can work in them perfectly the good pleasure of His will ; and happy shall we be if we can submit ourselves so unresistingly and so thoroughly to the forming hand of our Lord upon us, as to pass rapidly, and with the ease of a passive and yielding soul, through the necessary stages that precede this.

A poor woman was once scoffed at by an infidel for supposing that she, in her weakness and ignorance, could ever travel over the long and weary road from earth to heaven. "Ah, master," she replied, "it is a very short road, and easily travelled. There are only three steps in it." "Three steps," he repeated scornfully, "and what are they?" The answer was a memorable one,—"Out of self, into Christ, and into glory." If then to some of my readers the road to present peace and victory may look long and hard, let me assure you that after all it needs but two of these steps to take you there. Out of self, and into Christ! That is all! And that is enough for the deepest experiences and the richest blessings. The process that brings this about may be hard to flesh and blood, as Job's experience surely was, but the end is worth it all. And, although hard, it need not be long, for entire consecration and perfect faith will hasten every stage. Job's lesson was learned in one year, but he suffered truly the loss of all things to reach it. *We* often are many years learning our lesson, because we are not able to bear such rapid and severe strokes of the Divine chastising Hand. "Out of self" is a step to be taken by faith, but it is also a step to be taken actually and experimentally as well, and the Lord's part is to turn our faith into a reality, by His dealings with us, both inward and outward. The life of trust looks beautiful to us, and we long to live it, but we forget that something must be done first. No soul can trust utterly in the Lord, it is manifest, who has anything of self left in which to trust, and we must therefore come out of the self-life entirely, before we can fully enter into this life hid with Christ in God. For it is utter weakness alone that can bring any soul to the point of utter trust. And many a "messenger of Satan" may have to be sent "to buffet" some of us, before we come here. But if our faith will but grasp it now, and if we will but let the Lord work as He pleases, without any shrinking or hindrance on our part, who can say by what rapid steps He may bring us out into this place of perfect peace, nor how soon He may make the language of absolute trust our language also.

In the Hebrew Bible this Book is divided into five books, the first ending with Ps. xli. ; the second, with Ps. lxxii.; the third, with Ps. lxxxix.; the fourth, with Ps. cvi. and the fifth with Ps. cl. Probably each of these books would be found to contain some especial line of teaching, if our eyes were spiritually enlightened enough to see it. But I do not feel prepared to go into this.

The book of Psalms opens with blessing and ends with praise. The very first Psalm introduces us to the man who is the speaker throughout. It is the godly man; that is, the man who is like God, "conformed to the image of Christ." He not merely obeys the law of the Lord, but his *delight* is in it; it is "written on his heart." Therefore he has found the river of living water, and is planted beside it, and whatsoever he doeth cannot but prosper.

The introduction to the Psalms in the Commentary by Canon Cook of Exeter, England, says concerning the ideal man of the Book of Psalms that "he has these characteristics: unshaken trust in God; entire devotion to His service; submission to His will; reliance on His love, met by a corresponding affection, a more than filial tenderness; a longing for His presence in the sanctuary, and for fruition of that presence in Heaven; a thorough appreciation of the righteousness of all His dispensations; a confident, nay certain anticipation of a full manifestation of His righteousness. Faith, hope. and love assume thus their true relative position in the development of the spiritual man."

And to this godlike man are revealed secrets concerning the Lord and His ways, that have not heretofore in the progressive teaching of the Bible found any fitting hearer. "The secret of the Lord is with them that fear Him; and He will show them His covenant." Only the man who is like God, can understand God. And therefore in this book of Psalms, for the first time in the progress of the Bible development, does the sanctified soul find an adequate expression of its worship and its praise. All the previous revelations of the Lord had been but one-sided and limited, for there were no hearts prepared to understand any other. "As it is written, Eye hath not seen, nor ear heard, neither have entered into the heart of man, the things which God hath prepared for them that love Him. But God hath revealed them unto us by His Spirit: for the Spirit searcheth all things, yea, the deep things of God. For what man knoweth the things of a man, save the spirit of man which is in him? even so the things of God knoweth no man but the Spirit of God. Now we have received not the spirit of the world, but the Spirit which is of God; that we might know the things that are freely given to us of God. Which things also we speak, not in the words which man's wisdom teacheth, but which the Holy Ghost teacheth; comparing spiritual things with spiritual. But the natural man receiveth not the things of the Spirit of God; for they are foolishness unto him: neither can he know them, because they are spiritually discerned. But he that is spiritual judgeth all things, yet He himself is judged of no man. For who hath known the mind of the Lord, that He may instruct him? But we have the mind of Christ." To none but the spiritual man therefore do the secrets of this book lie open.

One of the most blessed of these secrets thus revealed to this "godly man," is that concerning the claim of the weak upon the strong. The language of his heart is always, "Have mercy upon me, O Lord, for I am weak." "Turn Thee unto me, and have mercy upon me; for I am desolate and afflicted." "Have mercy upon me, O Lord, for I am in trouble." "Attend unto my cry; for

I am very low ; deliver me from my persecutors, for they
are stronger than I." This speaker recognizes that the
plea of weakness and of need is the most effectual plea
that the soul can make. And do not our hearts also recognize it at once, as the one irresistible plea all the world
over, as far as the knowledge of the true God has gone.
Wherever there is weakness, there strength hastes to the
rescue. In times of danger the weakest are the first
cared for. If suffering must come, the strong endure it,
that the weak may be spared. " *Noblesse oblige*" is the
universal Christian law. And the Strong and Mighty
One who inhabiteth eternity, who is at once the Fountain
and the Power of this noble necessity, must therefore
charge Himself with the care of all who are weak and
needy. But none can know this, save those who have
been made " partakers of His divine nature," for none
else know God. Therefore it is, that, in the book of
Psalms for the first time, He has fully revealed it ; for
until this stage is reached, there are no eyes that can see
it, nor ears that can hear it. But the man who speaks
here has learned it all. " For the oppression of the
poor, for the sighing of the needy, now will I arise, saith
the Lord," xii. 5. " The Lord also will be a refuge for
the oppressed, a refuge in times of trouble," ix. 9. " He
will regard the prayer of the destitute; He will not despise their prayer," cii. 17. " The Lord executeth righteousness and judgment for all that are oppressed." ciii.
6. " He raiseth up the poor out of the dust, and lifteth
the needy out of the dung-hill ; that He may set him

27

with princes." cxiii. 7. "The Lord preserveth the simple; I was brought low, and He helped me." cxvi. 6.
"The Lord upholdeth all that fall, and raiseth up all
those that be bowed down." cxlv. 14. "The Lord
executeth judgment for the oppressed; He giveth food
to the hungry. The Lord looseth the prisoners; the
Lord openeth the eyes of the blind; the Lord raiseth
them that are bowed down; the Lord loveth the righteous; the Lord preserveth the strangers; He relieveth
the fatherless and the widow." cxlvi. 7-9. "He gathereth
together the outcasts of Israel. He healeth the broken
in heart, and bindeth up their wounds." cxlvii. 2.

Throughout all the varied experiences of this book, it
is still always this man who knows the Lord, that speaks
to us, whether in the voice of Messiah, or of His people.
And through it all he is led, doubtless by a series of
deepening and widening revelations, to the pæan of victorious praise that closes the Book. For only he who
knows the Lord, and has seen the King in His beauty,
could thus extol Him and praise His holy name.

The last six Psalms are a series of continually
rising songs of thanksgiving, beginning with, "I will
extol Thee, my God, O King; and I will bless Thy
name for ever and ever;" and closing with that wonderful, and to me most precious and comforting command,
"Let everything that hath breath praise the Lord."
As Bonar has written concerning this, "Praise is now
gathered in from every creature; every instrument of
joy, and gladness, and triumph, and jubilee are sum-

moned to sound loud praise ; and every voice and heart
are engaged to help the choir." And another also says
concerning it, " Every voice now teems with praise;
every thought is about praise; every object awakens it;
every power uses itself to produce it. And no wonder,
when we remember that we have been ushered into the
Kingdom at last. . . . These are the days of heaven
upon the earth! The kingdom has come ; and the will
of the Blessed One is done here as there. The mystic
ladder connects the upper and the lower sanctuaries.
Praise crowns the scene. The vision passes from before
us with the chanting of all kinds of music. Man has
taken the instrument of joy into his hand; but it is only
to God's glory he strikes it. The creature is happy ; God
is glorified. Yes, praise, all praise ! Untiring, satisfying fruit of the lips, uttering the joy of creation, and
owning the glory of the Blessed One."

All sorts of instruments are needed in this universal
chorus, the trumpet, the psaltery, the harp, the stringed
instrument, the organ, the loud cymbal, and the high-
sounding cymbal; the cymbal which can give but one
note only, being as necessary as the stringed instrument
which can give many. And all voices are needed here
also, the voices of young men and maidens, of old men
and children; the voices of those who are able only to
sound one note of praise, as well as of those who can
sound many. The heart-felt, " Praise the Lord," of the
humble washer-woman, is as necessary to the grand harmony, as the reverberating eloquence of the great

preacher, or the melody of the gifted singer. For the word is, " Let *everything* that hath breath praise the Lord." Yes, everything,—" Ye dragons and all deeps ; fire and hail; snow and vapors; stormy wind fulfilling His word; mountains and all hills; fruitful trees and all cedars; beasts and all cattle; creeping things and flying fowl; kings of the earth, and all people ; princes and all judges of the earth ; both young men and maidens ; old men and children ;" all must praise Him, for He is good to all.

And the day will come when this blessed command shall be literally obeyed. John saw it, and thus described it in Rev. v. 13, " And every creature which is in heaven, and on the earth, and under the earth, and such as are in the sea, and all that are in them, heard I saying, Blessing, and honor, and glory, and power, be unto Him that sitteth upon the throne, and unto the Lamb for ever and ever."

Let us join in this anthem, beloved friends, now and here. Let us praise Him, whether we understand Him or not. Let us praise Him, even though His ways with us may seem to be too mysterious ever to be understood. Let us praise Him out of our weakness, and out of our ignorance, and out of our very vileness itself. Let us praise Him that we *are* weak, and ignorant, and covered with infirmity, because this is our most irresistible claim upon Him, and because so, and so only, can His power rest upon us. Let us praise Him that we are nothing and that He is all.

" Praise ye the Lord.

" Praise God in His sanctuary:

" Praise Him in the firmament of His power.

" Praise Him for His mighty acts:

" Praise Him according to His excellent greatness.

" Praise Him with the sound of the trumpet:

" Praise Him with the psaltery and harp.

" Praise Him with the timbrel and dance:

" Praise Him with stringed instruments and organs.

" Praise Him upon the loud cymbals;

" Praise Him upon the high-sounding cymbals.

" Let every thing that hath breath praise the Lord.

" Praise ye the Lord."

Texts concerning the resurrection life of the believer:
—Col. iii. 1–4; ii. 12, 20. Gal. ii. 20; iv. 19; v. 16, 25.
2 Cor. iv. 10, 11; vi. 16. 1 John iv. 12–16; v. 11, 12:
iii. 24. Rom. vi. 11; viii. 2, 10. 1 Cor. vi. 17. John
vi. 53–57; xi. 25, 26; iii. 15, 16; iv. 14; v. 24; xiv. 20–23;
xv. 4–7; xvii. 21–23. Eph. ii. 5, 6, iii. 16–19. Phil. iii.
8–10. Col. iii. 9. 10. Eph. iv. 21–24. Rom. vi. 13. Ez.
xxxvi. 26, 27,

CHAPTER XX.

PROVERBS.

THE REDEEMED AND SANCTIFIED SOUL GUIDED BY DIVINE WISDOM IN THE DAILY WALKS OF LIFE

Keynote: James i. 5, 6.

THE book of Proverbs gives us the application of Divine wisdom to the practical details of our walk through the labyrinth of this evil world. It is the third step in the developing series concerning sanctification, which we are considering. The soul having experienced a measure of the death of self, and having begun to live the "life hid with Christ in God," needs now, according to the prayer of the Apostle in Col. i. 9, 10, to be " filled with the knowledge of His will in all wisdom and spiritual understanding," that we may "walk worthy of the Lord unto all pleasing, being fruitful in every good work, and increasing in the knowledge of God." For this there must be Divine teaching. The life in selfhood depends upon the natural wisdom of the human heart for guidance;

but the man who is emptied of his own wisdom, needs to
have Divine wisdom to supply its place, or he will fall
into all manner of evil. This book, therefore, reveals
the Father teaching His children how to walk safely and
wisely through this world of sin and danger. "My
son, hear thou the instruction of thy father, and forsake
not the law of thy mother," i. 8. " Hear, ye children,
the instruction of a father, and attend to know understanding," iv. 1. " My son, attend unto my wisdom, and
bow thine ear to my understanding," v. 1.   " Hear
me now therefore, O ye children, and depart not from
the words of my mouth," v. 7.   It is not teaching as
to how we are to *become* children, but teaching given
to us because we *are* children, that we may know how
to live and walk as children should.   It is essential
to notice, therefore, that it is not the question of redemption that is touched upon in this book ; but
simply a walk according to the wisdom and will of
the Lord.   And I cannot but believe that Christians
would make far fewer mistakes in their daily walk, if
they were only in the habit of more frequently consult-
ing this guide-book provided for them.   It is surely a great
privilege in the labyrinth of this evil world, to have
a path set before us, marked out by divine wisdom,
walking in which, we are assured, a practical happiness
would be secured to us.   How eager we are to run for
advice to those whom we call wise in human affairs, yet
how often we neglect to consult this compendium of divine wisdom, which would teach us far more unerringly

I feel assured that the careful study of this book would enable us to understand the Psalmist's rejoicing, when he said: " Thou through thy commandments hast made me wiser than mine enemies, for they are ever with me. I have more understanding than all my teachers ; for thy testimonies are my meditation. I understand more than the ancients: because I keep thy precepts," Ps. cxix. 98–100.

This book was written by Solomon, of whom we read in 1 Kings iv. 29-34, "And God gave Solomon wisdom and understanding exceeding much, and largeness of heart even as the sand that is on the sea-shore. And Solomon's wisdom excelled the wisdom of all the children of the East country, and all the wisdom of Egypt. For he was wiser than all men: than Ethan the Ezrahite, and Heman, and Chalcol, and Darda, the sons of Mahol: and his fame was in all nations round about. And he spake three thousand proverbs ; and his songs were a thousand and five. . . . And there came of all people to hear the wisdom of Solomon, from all kings of the earth which had heard of his wisdom."

Its object is announced to us in the opening verses : " The proverbs of Solomon, the son of David, king of Israel ; to know wisdom and instruction ; to perceive the words of understanding ; to receive the instruction of wisdom, justice, judgment and equity ; to give subtilty to the simple, to the young man, knowledge and discretion," i. 1-4. And in the closing verse of this chapter we are told what will be the blessed results of hearkening to this teaching: "Whoso hearkeneth unto me shall dwell safely, and shall be quiet from fear of evil." See also iv. 20–22; iii. 21–24; vi. 20–23; xxii. 17–21.

But it is not human wisdom and prudence that are to bring about these blessed results. These continually lead astray. It is submission to the mind and will of the Lord. We are expressly told to "lean not on our own understandings," "but in all our ways to acknowledge the Lord and He will direct our paths," iii. 4, 5. "For it is written, I will destroy the wisdom of the wise, and will bring to nothing the understanding of the prudent. . . . . . . Because the foolishness of God is wiser than men; and the weakness of God is stronger than men." 1 Cor. i. 19–29. Therefore we must turn from the teachings of our own wisdom, and submit ourselves in all things to that wisdom which is from above.

And for this reason the "fear of the Lord" is put before us here as the one grand constraining motive, and power. "The fear of the Lord is the beginning of wisdom," ix. 10. "The fear of the Lord prolongeth days," x. 27. "He that walketh in his uprightness feareth the Lord: but he that is perverse in his ways despiseth Him," xiv. 2. "By the fear of the Lord men depart from evil," xvi. 6. "By humility and the fear of the Lord are riches, and honor, and life," xxii. 4. "Favor is deceitful, and beauty is vain; but a woman that feareth the Lord shall be praised," xxxi. 30. In the very first chapter the contrast is drawn between the folly of self-will and this spirit of submission to the Lord. "For that they hated knowledge, and did not choose the fear of the Lord: they would none of my counsel; they despised all my reproof; therefore shall they eat of the fruit of their own way and be filled with their own devices. . . . But whoso hearkeneth unto me shall be quiet from fear of evil," i. 29–33. The different forms of the expression " fear of the Lord " or " fear the Lord," are used over one hundred and twenty-five times in the Scriptures, and always, in connection with richest blessings. It is said of those who "fear the Lord"—that the secret of the Lord is with them; the eye of the Lord is on them; the angel of the Lord encampeth round about them; His salvation is nigh to them; His mercy is great towards them; He will fulfil all their desires; He taketh pleasure in them; and finally that there is "no want to them that fear Him." Moreover we are told that it is the beginning of wisdom, and the beginning of knowledge; that it causes us to hate evil; that it gives us strong confidence; that it is a fountain of life; that it is the instruction of wisdom; that it brings riches and honor; and that he that feareth the Lord shall come forth of every trouble.

The fear meant in all these passages is not the fear of fright, but the fear of love. It is the fear we feel lest we should in any way grieve or wound the heart of a beloved one; and is not the fear of the consequences to ourselves, but of the sorrow to them. It is a fear which can exist only in connection with the highest and tenderest forms of love, for all lower forms of affection are indifferent to it, and cannot even comprehend it. And therefore I believe that it is only the Christian who has passed through the death to self in Job, and has learned the life of trust in Psalms, who can understand this sweet and constraining "fear of the Lord," which brings forth such results of blessedness. Others may perhaps be *afraid* of Him, but these only can *fear* Him. Others may dread His anger, these alone can fear His grief. Only these in fact know that He can be grieved, for they alone know how He loves. It is because His love for us is so deep and so tender that we are able to grieve Him, for no other affection or passion of the soul can be grieved but love. None can truly fear Him therefore who do not know something of His love, and none can, I believe, truly follow Him who do not know this sweet constraining fear. For His voice is so gentle and low, and His will comes to us so much oftener in the form of suggestion rather than in that of a command, that unless our love makes us fear the slightest neglect of His sweet requirements, or the least deviation from His will, we shall often overlook them and miss them altogether. No wonder that we are told here that the " fear of the Lord is the beginning of wisdom." For he alone is wise who follows the Lord whithersoever He leadeth, and such a following is the outcome only of this lovely fear.

The soul in Proverbs is brought here, and consequently we find a great deal said about "wisdom" in this Book. The word is used thirty-six times, and it is exalted to a place of such great prominence, as to lead us to inquire, if it has not a much deeper meaning

than at first appears. In 1 Cor. i. 24 we are told that
Christ is the "wisdom of God." Then we read here
" The Lord by wisdom hath founded the earth," and in
John i. 3 we read concerning Christ, "All things were
made by Him;" and in Heb. i. 2 " By whom also God
made the worlds"; and in Heb. xi. 3 " the worlds were
framed by the word of God." All these passages seem
to me to point to the thought that Christ is hidden
here under the figure of wisdom, and that it is a fulfilling of that declaration of the apostle, that "He is made
unto us wisdom," as well as righteousness, and sanctifi·
cation, and redemption. Chapter viii. seems to make
this even more clear and unmistakable, especially if
the marginal references are carefully considered. It
begins with, "Doth not wisdom cry?" and then gives
us the words of this cry, "Unto you, O men, I call; and
my voice is to the sons of men. . . . The Lord possessed me in the beginning of His way, before His works
of old. . . . When He prepared the heavens, I was
there; . . . when He appointed the foundations of the
earth. Then I was by Him, as one brought up with
Him; and I was daily His delight, rejoicing always
before Him; rejoicing in the habitable parts of His
earth; and my delights were with the sons of men."
Surely to none but Christ can all this apply.

If by wisdom then in this book is meant Christ, and if
the indwelling of wisdom means His indwelling, what a
lesson we are here taught concerning the practical
effect of the abiding presence and teaching of the Divine

Comforter, of whom we are told in the New Testament, that He is to "lead us into all truth." "My son, if thou wilt receive my words, and hide my commandments with thee; so that thou incline thine ear unto wisdom, and apply thine heart to understanding; yea, if thou criest after knowledge, and liftest up thy voice for understanding; if thou seekest her as silver, and searchest for her as for hid treasures; then shalt thou understand the fear of the Lord, and find the knowledge of God. For the Lord giveth wisdom; out of his mouth cometh knowledge and understanding. He layeth up sound wisdom for the righteous; he is a buckler to them that walk uprightly. He keepeth the paths of judgment, and preserveth the way of his saints. Then shalt thou understand righteousness, and judgment, and equity; yea, every good path. When wisdom entereth into thine heart, and knowledge is pleasant unto thy soul; discretion shall preserve thee, understanding shall keep thee; to deliver thee from the way of the evil man, from the man that speaketh froward things; who leave the paths of uprightness, to walk in the ways of darkness; who rejoice to do evil, and delight in the frowardness of the wicked; whose ways are crooked, and they froward in their paths; to deliver thee from the strange woman, even from the stranger which flattereth with her words; which forsaketh the guide of her youth, and forgetteth the covenant of her God. For her house inclineth unto death, and her paths unto the dead. None that go unto her return again, neither take they hold of the paths of

28

life. That thou mayst walk in the way of good men and keep the paths of the righteous." ii. 1–20.

All this, and more, will most certainly be true of that life which is ordered by the Lord, and guided by His blessed Spirit; and the path of obedience to the divine requirements will always prove to be a path of richest blessing.

Our Lord has declared that His sheep shall "know His voice," but we shall need to live very near Him, and have much close communion with Him before this can be. For amid the multitude of voices abroad, it is not easy to distinguish the Shepherd's voice, unless we have become familiar with its sound. At first all voices are alike to the infant, and some time must pass before it can learn to distinguish even its mother's tones; and doubtless in the learning it makes many mistakes. But the time comes when the child knows that dear voice from every other, and cannot mistake it, and when the voice of a stranger makes it afraid. And for us also, if we but follow on to know unwaveringly, "applying our hearts" as our book says, and "inclining our ears," "seeking for it also as for silver and for hid treasure," the time will surely come when we likewise shall be able to distinguish the Shepherd's voice, and shall "flee from the voice of a stranger."

Not long ago a friend related to me the following story. A farmer, wishing to purchase some sheep, made a selection from the flocks of a neighbor, and started to drive them home. But he found it impossible to induce a single sheep of them all to leave its owner s sheep-fold by any force or persuasion. In despair he called upon the shepherd, who told him the trouble was that the sheep did not know his voice, and going outside of the fold himself, the owner of the sheep stood and called them, when immediately every one bounded eagerly and joyfully out. He walked on, the sheep following him through strange and unknown roads, calling out continually to let them know that he was their leader, until he had secured them safely in the sheep-folds of their new owner. No doubt in time these sheep would learn to know the voice of the shepherd who from this time had the care of them, but, until they had learned it, they could not follow him willingly, nor yield a ready obedience to his commands.

Subjection to a voice is one of the sweetest ways of learning to know it, and experimentally we shall find that each time we obey the voice of our Shepherd, when we do recognize it, it will become easier for us to distinguish it the next time. As our book tells us, " My son, keep thy father's commandment, and forsake not the law of thy mother : Bind them continually upon thine heart, and tie them about thy neck. When thou goest, it shall lead thee ; when thou sleepest, it shall keep thee ; and when thou awakest, it shall talk with thee. For the commandment is a lamp ; and the law is light ; and reproofs of instruction are the way of life:" vi. 20–23.

We must therefore bow our necks to the yoke of this Divine guidance, if we would learn to walk in the true

"way of life." But none can do this fully, I believe,
who have not learned the previous lessons of our series.
Self must be dead, and Christ must be known to be all
in all, before the soul can everywhere and always take
His yoke upon it, and learn of Him. Our own wisdom
must have failed utterly, before we can submit in all
things to Divine wisdom. And therefore but few comparatively reach this stage. Believers are crying out
everywhere, "Oh! that I might know the Shepherd's
voice!" But they shrink from the steps that must be
taken in order to learn it. Their bemoanings are like
the bemoanings of Ephraim, "Thou hast chastised me,
and I was chastised, as a bullock unaccustomed to the
yoke." For there is no other way. If we would walk
where Christ walks, we must have on His yoke, and if
we will not *take* it on lovingly and gladly, He will be
compelled to *put* it upon us with chastisements and severity. A farmer's wife once said to me, that it had
often been a great lesson to her, to watch the young oxen
being trained to wear the yoke, and to see how much severe discipline was needed, which might all have been
spared, had the animals but been docile enough to have
bowed their necks to the yoke willingly and without
resistance.

To take the yoke of Christ upon us, means, I think
that we give up utterly our own freedom of will to Him,
and consent to be in all things led and guided by His
voice. This voice will be made known to us, I believe,
in three ways; through the Scriptures, through providen-

tial circumstances, and through a divine conviction produced in the soul by the Holy Spirit; and we have a right to ask that we may clearly distinguish it, before being required to act. But when once we know it, nothing but obedience will do, and to the truly obedient soul the yoke proves to be indeed an easy one, and the burden light.

> " Dole not thy duties out to God,
>   But let thy hand be free;
>   Look long at Jesus, His sweet blood,
>   How was it dealt to thee?
>
> " The perfect way is hard to flesh,
>   It is not hard to love;
>   If thou wert sick for want of God,
>   How swiftly wouldst thou move!
>
> " No outward helps perfection needs;—
>   Keep thy heart calm all day,
>   And catch the words the Spirit there
>   From hour to hour may say.
>
> " Then keep thy conscience sensitive;
>   No inward token miss:
>   And go where grace entices thee;—
>   Perfection lies in this.
>
>   " Be docile to thy unseen Guide,
>   Love Him as He loves thee;
>   Time and obedience are enough,
>   And thou a saint shalt be."

The " voice of the stranger " is warned against in this book under the figure of the " strange woman," whose house we are told "inclineth unto death," and "whose guests are in the depths of hell," ii. 16–19; v. 3–5; ix. 13–18. Some have thought this "strange woman" means the Babylon of Revelation, that "great whore which did corrupt the earth with her fornication," and which is plainly a corrupt form of religion; Rev. xix. 2. See also Rev. xvii. 1–6, and xviii. But whether this be so or not, the warnings against this "strange woman" apply to any form of evil that draws away the heart from the voice of heavenly wisdom, whether this divine voice is heard inwardly in the soul, or comes to us outwardly in the written word of our Lord, or in His providential dealings.

The practical teaching of divine wisdom given us in this book, reaches into many details of private and public life, and is worthy of far more careful study than it generally receives, teaching us also that nothing is too insignificant for His notice or advice. We are shown here what things are an abomination to the Lord. "These six things doth the Lord hate; yea, seven are an abomination unto Him: a proud look, (or, as the margin has it, haughty eyes,) a lying tongue, and hands that shed innocent blood, an heart that deviseth wicked imaginations, feet that be swift in running to mischief, a false witness that speaketh lies, and he that soweth discord among brethren," vi. 16–19. Also in other verses we are told that "they of a froward heart," a "false balance," "divers weights and divers measures," the "sacrifice of the wicked," the "way of the wicked," the "thoughts

of the wicked," " every one that is proud in heart ," he
that justifieth the wicked, and he that condemneth the
just," all these are declared to be an "abomination to
the Lord."

We are also taught what are the things likely to
bring us into outward trial and difficulty, and are
warned against them; and are encouraged in paths
that will lead to outward prosperity and peace. I cannot
go into these details here. But I would repeat again,
what I said at first, that this book is a blessed gift of
wisdom to us, who feel ourselves so far from wise, and
that it is great grace in our Lord to have condescended
to apply His wisdom, thus, to the details of our lives, in
the midst of this world's confusion, because of sin.

Let us come to it, then, beloved readers, with receptive
and submissive hearts, prepared to yield a glad obedience
to what we find here ; and prepared also to listen more
attentively and obediently than ever to the inward voice
as well, relying with perfect confidence upon our Lord's
own promise, "When He, the Spirit of truth, is come,
He will guide you into all truth ; ' and " He shall teach
you all things, and bring all things to your remembrance
whatsoever I have said unto you." This blessed doctrine of the direct and personal teaching and guiding
of the Holy Spirit has been too much neglected in the
Church, and great loss has been the result. But that it
is a glorious reality, and within the reach of even the
most unlearned believer, thousands of witnesses can
testify, who have given themselves up to a " walk in the

Spirit," and who have found themselves led, perhaps by ways they knew not, into the green pastures and beside the still waters, where the little flock who follow the good Shepherd whithersoever He leadeth, always feed. "For wisdom's ways *are* ways of pleasantness, and all her paths are peace." And the heart that "wholly follows" the Lord, as Caleb did, shall, like him, enter into the possession of an inheritance, which none others can conquer. Joseph Cook says, "Whenever your conscience is made fully supreme, its yoke by irresistible natural law will transform itself into a crown. This constant experience you will have at every fork of the way; and rising through such continual steppings, we may, even in our present low estate, approach the bliss of the upper ranges of being, even of those who have never sinned, and of that Nature which was revealed on earth once as the fullness of Him that filleth all in all."

If any doubt the truth of this, let them try the experiment of an utter yielding to God at every step of their way, and I feel sure they will be amazed at the rapidity with which their souls will climb toward these wondrous heights of divine fellowship and bliss. Let our obedience but keep pace with the outmost verge of our light, and our happiness *will* reach even here and now, to the joys of the "upper ranges of being," and a blessed foretaste of Heaven will be granted us. But without this utter surrender, we cannot expect to advance in the divine path ; and the lesson of Proverbs therefore must necessarily be learned, before the soul can take the next step in its progress, and come to know the vanity of the world and all it has to give, as in Ecclesiastes.

"Happy, therefore, is the man that findeth wisdom, and the man that getteth understanding : for the merchandise of it is better than the merchandise of silver, and the gain thereof than fine gold. She is more precious than rubies, and all things thou canst desire are not to be compared unto her."

Texts illustrating Divine guidance :—John xiv. 16, 17 xv. 26 ; xvi. 13–15 ; Luke i. 79 ; John x. 3, 4 ; Ps. xxv. 9 ; Ps. xxxii. 8 ; Ps. xxxi. 3 ; Ps. xlii. 3 ; Ps. xlviii. 14 ; Ps. lxxviii. 52, 72 ; Ps. cxxxix. 10, 24 ; Isaiah xlii. 16 ; Isaiah xlviii. 17 ; Is. xlix. 10 ; Is. lvii. 18 ; Is. lviii. 11 ; 1 John ii. 20, 27 ; Matt. x 19, 20 ; Acts ii. 4 ; x. 10–16, 19, 20, with xi. 7–9, 12 ; Gal. v. 16, 18 ; Acts xiii. 2 ; xvi. 6, 7 ; viii 29 ; xxi. 4 ; 1 Cor. xii. 4–11 ; ii. 10 ; Rom. viii. 5. Gal. v. 25 ; 2 Pet. i. 21 ; 1 Cor. ii. 13 ; Type, Num. xi 15 -22.

CHAPTER XXI.

ECCLESIASTES.

THE VANITY OF ALL EARTHLY THINGS; AND THEIR POWER-
LESSNESS TO SATISFY THE REDEEMED SOUL.

Keynote : 1 John ii. 15-17.

THIS book shows us the utter vanity of the world and all it contains, apart from God. It is the illustration of those words of our Lord to the woman of Samaria, " He that drinketh of this water shall thirst again." The world is here searched for an object to satisfy the heart, but in vain. All is proved to be only vanity and vexation of spirit. It is the fourth stage of the developing series concerning sanctification, and shows us the soul completely delivered from the love of the world and the things that are in the world. It is that inward escape from the world's allurements, which comes from the discovery of its utter hollowness and vanity. It is the heart made " dead " to its power. Many give up the world outwardly, who yet long after it inwardly. But

334

this man hates it. It has no longer any charms for him. In the marvelous maturing of his inward life, he has outgrown it. Its greatest gifts are but childish toys to him, and to go back to them would be for a man to return to the rattles and rings of his babyhood. This is the only true deliverance, for it weans the heart. It is the divine way of cutting the cords and breaking the bonds that chain the soul to earth, and of setting it free to soar into infinity. When we love the world, it is hard to give it up, but when it has lost its charms, it drops from our hands unheeded. And if our affections are thus weaned from earthly things, it is easy then to set them on heavenly things. Nor can a heart that has once tasted of divine joys, be ever again satisfied with the joys of earth.

This book gives us the experience of the man who has found the wisdom spoken of in the preceding book of Proverbs, and who has tried the world by this wisdom, and has proved it all to be only vanity of vanities. "I the Preacher was king over Israel in Jerusalem: and I gave my heart to seek and search out by wisdom concerning all things that are done under heaven: this sore travail hath God given to the sons of man to be exercised therewith. I have seen all the works that are done under the sun ; and, behold, all is vanity and vexation of spirit." i. 12-14. It is the wise man trying the world by his wisdom, for others less wise, that he " might see what was that good for the sons of men, which they should do under heaven all the days of their life." The effect of this trial was to prove that all was "vanity and vexation of spirit, and there was no profit under the sun." And yet this man had tried the world at its brightest and best, under the most favorable possible circumstances for proving its worth. "I made me great works," he says; "I builded me houses; I planted me vineyards: I made me gardens and orchards, and I planted trees in them of all kinds of fruits: I made me pools of water, to water therewith the wood that bringeth forth trees: I got me servants and maidens, and had servants born in my house; also I had great possessions of great and small cattle above all that were in Jerusalem before me: I gathered me also silver and gold, and the peculiar treasure of kings and of the provinces: I gat me men singers and women singers, and the delights of the sons of men, as musical instruments, and that of all sorts. So I was great, and increased more than all that were before me in Jerusalem: also my wisdom remained with me. And whatsoever mine eyes desired I kept not from them, I withheld not my heart from any joy; for my heart rejoiced in all my labor: and this was my portion of all my labor." But at the end of it all his sentence concerning it still was : "Then I looked on all the works that my hands had wrought, and on the labor that I had labored to do: and, behold, all was vanity and vexation of spirit, and there was no profit under the sun." ii. 1–11.

This book gives us an insight into what the world is to a really sanctified heart; and it has been placed, I believe.

by our loving Father in the Bible, as a beacon-light to warn us, before we enter upon them, from the seducing temptations of the world. But for this book of experience, we might have been tempted perhaps to think that there must be some satisfying portion somewhere in earthly things, although we ourselves have never found it. But here a man speaks who had tried everything, and who is so sure he had left no earthly joy untried, that he asks confidently, "What can the man do that cometh after the king? even that which hath been already done." ii. 12. No one can ever again be in circumstances more favorable for earthly happiness than was this man, and yet he says, from the stand-point of experimental knowledge, that " all is vanity." He has tried it for everyone who was to come after him, and, if we would but believe his testimony, and would renounce the world without trying it for ourselves, we would none of us need to go through the same disappointing experiment.

It may seem to some a sad thing that the world should be so unsatisfactory. But when we understand the reason of it, and the blessed result, we will surely praise the Lord with all our hearts that He has so arranged it. For He has commanded us to hate the world and to forsake it, and how could we obey Him if it was attractive and satisfying? If there should be poison in our food, would we not be thankful if it had so bitter a taste as to make it impossible for us to eat it? And, since there is a fatal poison in the world to all who

29

love it, shall we not be thankful that the Lord has given
it such a bitter taste as to make it too nauseous to be enjoyed? If we understood this, dear friends, I think we
should not grieve so bitterly over the spoiling of our
pleasant pictures, nor think it so mysterious that disappointments should come. For it is a grand victory not
to love the world; and the soul that has gained this victory finds itself set in a large place, and cannot but be
thankful for whatever disappointment may have brought
it there.

And not only is the soul here set free from the seduc-
tions of outward earthly things, but even also from the
more subtle snares of earthly wisdom. There are many
who scorn the physical enjoyments of earth in the shape
of riches or tangible pleasures, who yet take refuge in
the exercise of wisdom and knowledge. But these also
are here shown to be vanity and vexation of spirit.
"I communed with mine own heart, saying, Lo, I am
come to great estate, and have gotten more wisdom than
all they that have been before me in Jerusalem: yea,
my heart had great experience of wisdom and knowledge. And I gave my heart to know wisdom and to
know madness and folly: I perceived that this also is
vexation of spirit. For in much wisdom is much grief:
and he that increaseth knowledge increaseth sorrow,"
i. 16–18. "Then said I in my heart, As it happeneth to
the fool, so it happeneth even to me; and why was I
then more wise? Then I said in my heart, that this also
is vanity," ii. 15.

Man is made for a divine destiny, and nowhere short of this can he be satisfied. It is not that he *ought not* to be, but he *cannot.* This is in the eternal nature of things. A learned man cannot be satisfied in the company of fools, neither can a man of culture and refinement be happy with coarse and brutal associations. They ought not, it is true, but there is something deeper than ought in the case, they *cannot.* And the soul that has tasted of divine wisdom, can never be happy with anything on a lower level.

> " God only is the creature's home;
>   Though rough and strait the road,
> Yet nothing else can satisfy
>   The soul that longs for God,
> Oh, utter but the name of God
>   Down in your heart of hearts,
> And see how from the world at once
>   All tempting light departs."

Therefore upon all that man tries of earthly things there can be but the one same universal sentence, which is here repeated over and over, " This also is vanity." See i. 2, 14; ii. 1, 11, 15, 17, 19, 21, 23, 26; iii. 19; iv. 4, 8, 16; v. 10; vi. 2, 9; vii. 6; viii. 10, 14; xi. 8; xii. 8.

But viewed from this earthly standpoint, all is not only seen to be vanity, but utter confusion as well. Apart from the thought of God, all is darkness beyond this present life, and all is mystery here. Neither wisdom nor reason can explain the sad perplexity of life. Everything seems to go wrong. Wickedness triumphs, and

righteousness suffers loss, and there is no explanation.
"When I applied mine heart to know wisdom, and to
see the business that is done upon the earth : (for also
there is that neither day nor night seeth sleep with his
eyes): Then I beheld all the work of God, that a man
cannot find out the work that is now done under the sun :
because though a man labor to seek it out, yet he shall
not find it; yea farther; though a wise man think to
know it, yet shall he not be able to find it," viii. 16, 17.
"I returned, and saw under the sun, that the race is not
to the swift, nor the battle to the strong, neither yet bread
to the wise, nor yet riches to men of understanding, nor
yet favor to men of skill; but time and chance happeneth
to them all,' ix. 11. "All things come alike to all: there
is one event to the righteous, and to the wicked; to the
good and to the clean, and to the unclean: to him that
sacrificeth, and to him that sacrificeth not: as is the good,
so is the sinner; and he that sweareth, as he that feareth
an oath," ix. 2. "So I returned, and considered all the
oppressions that are done under the sun: and behold the
tears of such as were oppressed, and they had no comforter; and on the side of their oppressors there was
power; but they had no comforter," iv. 1.

It is the lesson of Job repeated here, that the outward
works of the Lord are not an adequate expression of His
heart towards us, and that therefore nothing is left to us
but the sublime silence of faith, which can calmly await
the day of His explanations, and can meanwhile sit
down contentedly before the greatest mysteries. To

judge of things by what we see, there seems often to be
no God. But faith can always claim His presence.

>   " Thrice blest is he, to whom is given
>   The instinct that can tell,
>   That God is on the field, when He
>   Is most invisible."
>   *   *   *   *   *
>   " God's glory is a wondrous thing,
>   Most strange in all its ways,
>   And, of all things on earth, least like
>   What men agree to praise.
>
>   " As He can endless glory weave
>   From what men reckon shame,
>   In His own world He is content
>   To play a losing game.
>
>   " Muse on His justice, downcast soul;
>   Muse, and take better heart;
>   Back with thine angel to the field
>   And bravely do thy part.
>
>   " God's justice is a bed, where we
>   Our anxious hearts may lay,
>   And, weary with ourselves, may sleep
>   Our discontent away.
>
>   " For right is right, since God is God,
>   And right the day must win;
>   To doubt would be disloyalty,
>   To falter would be sin."

Our book, therefore, not only teaches us the vanity and
confusion of all things "under the sun;" but it also lets
us know that there is one way of relief, one outlet from
the oppressive sense of universal emptiness and mystery,

29*

and that this is to be found in the fear of the Lord, and in doing His will. There *are* "bags which wax not old" and treasures which do not fail, and these are bestowed upon the Lord's faithful servants. All other things are vain, but "he that feareth the Lord shall come forth of them all," vii. 18. Therefore the lesson of our book is all summed up at last in one short sentence, "Let us hear the conclusion of the whole matter: Fear God, and keep His commandments: for this is the whole duty of man," xii. 13.

All that is really necessary is declared to us in this one sentence. We cannot understand the world, we cannot find any comfort in it; it is all hopelessly empty and mysterious. But the Lord reigns, and holds the clue; and to fear Him and keep His commandments is the only thing needed to make everything straight. Obedience is the golden key to every mystery. They that do His will, shall always come, sooner or later, to know of the doctrine; and to the obedient soul, God, with His infinity, fills every void. A walk with Him is a walk through a region of grandeur, and life is transfigured before us. Let us praise Him, then, that the one only thing which is declared to be our duty, is also the one only thing which it is possible for us to do, or the doing of which can bring us any abiding peace or rest. For the "world passeth away, and the lust thereof: but he that doeth the will of God abideth forever."

A dear little girl of my acquaintance, whose life was the truest picture of childlike faith I ever saw, said one

morning, as she kneeled in prayer, " Dear Lord, I thank
Thee that I have nothing to do all day to-day, but just to
mind." Nothing to do but to mind! Ah! this is the
blessed secret ! We need not plan, we need not worry;
we need only to obey, and all will come right.

Such is the lesson of our book. It is the judgment of
heavenly wisdom on all that happens " under the sun,"
and the decision of that wisdom as to the only relief from
it all. It shows us the world as it looks to the man who
has died to self, as in Job, and who is living the resurrection life, as in Psalms, and has been taught the "wisdom
which is from above," that belongs to that life, as in
Proverbs. It is the fourth stage in the progressive steps
of sanctification given us in the series of books beginning with Job and ending with the Song of Songs:
and is the necessary prelude to the beautiful lesson of
the Canticles. Here the world is searched to find an object to satisfy the heart, but in vain. There that Object
is found. And until our hearts have learned the lesson
of Ecclesiastes, we shall not be prepared to receive the
lesson of that wondrous mystic Song.

Hast thou learned this lesson, dear reader? Is the
world "vanity of vanities " to thee, or has it yet charms
to attract thee and win thy heart? Thou hast heard the
command, "Love not the world, neither the things that
are in the world." Hast thou obeyed it? If not, I
would sound in thy ears the accompanying sentence :
" If any man love the world, the love of the Father is
not in him." The love of the Father may be believed

in and trusted by many christians, who yet have never
known it to be shed abroad *in* their hearts by the Holy
Ghost, and it is this inward experience and manifestation of it that is meant here. In the very nature of
things this way of divine love cannot be known by the
heart that loves the world ; and therefore it is that the
experience of Ecclesiastes must be realized before the
Song of Songs can be reached.

May the Lord Himself teach and lead us here!

Texts illustrating the necessity of giving up the world,
and being delivered from its bondage :—1 John ii. 15-17.
Rom. xii. 2.   Jas. iv. 4, 14.   Matt. vi. 24.   Gal. i. 10.
Ps. xxix. 6.   John xv. 18, 19.   1 John iii. 13.   Gal. vi.
14.   John xvii. 14-16.   Jas. i. 27.   1 John iii. 1 ; v. 4,
5 ; iv. 17.   Titus ii. 12.   Mark viii. 36, 37.

CHAPTER XXII.

DIVINE UNION, OR THE LOVE OF CHRIST AND THE CHURCH.

Keynote 2 Cor. xi. 2.

"Oh! bless thee, bless thee, treacherous world
That thou dost play so false a part;
And drive, like sheep into the fold,
Our loves into our Saviour's heart."

THE Song of Songs is in wonderful contrast to the book of Ecclesiastes. There the world is searched for an object to satisfy the affections of the sanctified heart, but it is not found. Here the Object is revealed, and the heart has entered into the richest enjoyment of it. This little book gives us the fifth and last stage in the developing series concerning sanctification, and is the consummation of all the soul's deepest longings. It can only be understood, I believe, by those who have passed through all the preceding stages. Self must die, as in Job, and

345

the hidden resurrection life must be known, as in Psalms
divine wisdom must be submitted to, as in Proverbs; and
the world must be tried by this wisdom, and found to be
utter vanity, as in Ecclesiastes; before the heart is prepared for the experience set forth in this mystic song.
Through emptying to fulness is always the Divine
way. And the heart must have learned for itself, the
hollowness of all earthly things, before it is able to
receive that fulness of the love of Christ, and to realize
that conscious union with Him, which are typified in
this wonderful little book. The world must go out,
before Christ can come in. And in Ecclesiastes, the
departure of the world has prepared the way for this
allegorical picture of Christ's incoming. He that
drinketh of the water the world giveth, shall thirst
again, but he that drinketh of *this* water, shall never
thirst.

This Song would seem to be the Old Testament
typical expression of the truth set forth in Eph. v. 23-
33 of the wondrous union of Christ and His Church.
"For the husband is the head of the wife, even as Christ
is the head of the church: and He is the Saviour of the
body. Therefore as the church is subject unto Christ, so
let the wives be to their own husbands in every thing.
Husbands, love your wives, even as Christ also loved the
church, and gave Himself for it: that He might sanctify
and cleanse it with the washing of water by the word.
That He might present it to Himself a glorious church,
not having spot, or wrinkle, or any such thing; but that

it should be holy and without blemish. So ought men to love their wives as their own bodies. He that loveth his wife loveth himself. For no man ever yet hated his own flesh; but nourisheth and cherisheth it, even as the Lord the church: for we are members of His body, of His flesh, and of His bones. For this cause shall a man leave his father and mother, and shall be joined unto his wife, and they two shall be one flesh. This is a great mystery: but I speak concerning Christ and the church."

The same figure is also used in many other places in Scripture to express this glorious oneness. The Church is called "the Bride, the Lamb's wife;" the Lord Jesus speaks of Himself as the "Bridegroom;" and the moment of the final union in Heaven is called the "marriage supper of the Lamb." In answer to the question as to why His disciples did not mourn or fast, Jesus said: "Can the children of the bride-chamber mourn as long as the Bridegroom is with them? But the days will come when the Bridegroom shall be taken away from them, and then shall they fast in those days." Matt. ix. 15, see also Mark ii. 19, 20, and Luke v. 34, 35. John the Baptist speaks of Christ as the Bridegroom, when asked who he himself was. "Ye yourselves bear me witness," was his answer, "that I said, I am not the Christ, but that I am sent before Him. He that hath the bride is the Bridegroom; but the friend of the Bridegroom, which standeth and heareth Him, rejoiceth greatly because of the Bridegroom's voice: this, my joy, therefore, is fulfilled." John iii. 28, 29. Our Lord Himself speaks of His own return as the return of the Bridegroom, " Then" (that is in the day of His return) "shall the kingdom of Heaven be likened to ten virgins which took their lamps and went forth to meet the Bridegroom. . . . While the Bridegroom tarried, they all slumbered and slept. And at midnight there was a cry made, Behold, the Bridegroom cometh; go ye out to meet Him. . . . And while the foolish went to buy, the Bridegroom came; and they that were ready went in with Him to the marriage: and the door was shut. . . . Watch, therefore, for ye know neither the day nor the hour when the Son of Man cometh." Matt. xxv. 1-13. And, finally, in the Revelation of John, the voice of the great multitude is heard to say: "Alleluia! for the Lord God omnipotent reigneth. Let us be glad, and rejoice, and give honor to Him: for the marriage of the Lamb is come, and His wife hath made herself ready. And to her was granted that she should be arrayed in fine linen, clean and white: for the fine linen is the righteousness of saints. And He saith unto me, Write, Blessed are they which are called unto the marriage supper of the Lamb. And he saith unto me, These are the true sayings of God." Rev. xix. 7, 8. Also John describes what he saw, "And I, John, saw the holy city, new Jerusalem, coming down from God out of heaven, prepared as a bride adorned for her husband. . . . And there came unto me one of the seven angels which had the seven vials full of the seven last plagues, and talked with me, saying, Come hither, I will shew thee the bride, the Lamb's wife:" Rev. xxi. 2, 9.

In the Old Testament, also, this figure of the Bridegroom and the Bride is prophetically used. "Thou
shalt no more be termed Forsaken; neither shall thy
land any more be termed Desolate; but thou shalt be
called Hephzi-bah, and thy Land Beulah: for the Lord
delighteth in thee, and thy land shall be married For
as a young man marrieth a virgin, so shall thy sons
marry thee: and as the bridegroom rejoiceth over the
bride, so shall thy God rejoice over thee." Is. 62: 4, 5.
And again in Hosea ii. 14–20. "And it shall be at that
day, saith the Lord, that thou shalt call me Ishi" (that is
my husband); "and shalt call me no more Baali" (that is
my Lord). "For I will take away the names of Baalim out
of her mouth, and they shall no more be remembered by
their name. . . . And I will betroth thee unto me for
ever; yea, I will betroth thee unto me in righteousness,
and in judgment, and in loving-kindness, and in mercies.
I will even betroth thee unto me in faithfulness; and
thou shalt know the Lord." And yet again in Isaiah 54:
5, is the assertion made with unmistakable clearness,
"For thy Maker is thy husband; the Lord of hosts is
His name; and thy Redeemer, the Holy One of Israel;
the God of the whole earth shall He be called."

Such, then, is the mystery of the soul's divine Bridegroom, and the Song of Songs tells us about it. Well
may it be called the Song of Songs, for never before, nor
since, has any song, containing such a wondrous story
as this, been sung by human lips. It is the revelation of
a love that does indeed "pass knowledge," the love be·

30

tween Christ and the soul of the believer. It is the fulfilling of the Lord's own marvellous words : "*As* the Father hath loved me, *so* have I loved you."

But it is not every Christian heart that can sing this song. Origen says, concerning it : "As we have been taught by Moses that there are not only holy places, but a Holy of holies, that there are not only Sabbaths, but Sabbaths of Sabbaths, so now we are taught, by the pen of Solomon, that there are not only songs, but a Song of songs. Blessed, truly, is he who enters into the holy place, but more blessed he who enters into the Holy of holies. Blessed is he who keepeth the Sabbath, but more blessed he who keepeth the Sabbath of Sabbaths. So, too, blessed is he who understands songs, and sings them, for no one does sing save on high festivals ; but much more blessed is he who sings this "Song of songs." And as he who enters into the holy place, still needs much ere he is able to proceed into the Holy of holies ; and as he who keeps the Sabbath enjoined on the peo- ple by the Lord, yet wants many things that he may keep the Sabbath of Sabbaths, so, too, he who traverses all the songs of Holy Writ, finds it no easy thing to ascend to the Song of songs. Thou must needs go out of Egypt, and issued thence, cross the Red Sea, that thou mayest sing the first song, saying : "I will sing unto the Lord, for He hath triumphed gloriously." Ex. xv. And even though thou mayest have sung this first song, thou art still far from the Song of songs. Pass spiritually through the wilderness, till thou comest to the well which the

princes dug, that thou mayest there sing the second song.
Afterwards approach the borders of the Holy Land, and,
standing on Jordan's bank, sing the song of Moses:
"Give ear, oh ye heavens, and I will speak; and hear,
O earth, the words of my mouth." Yet again, thou
needest soldiers, and the inheritance of the holy land,
and that Deborah should prophesy to thee and judge
thee, that thou mayest utter that hymn also, which is contained in the book of Judges: "Praise ye the Lord for
the avenging of Israel, when the people willingly offered
themselves." Ascending to the record of the Kings,
come to the song when David escaped from the hands
of all his enemies, and from the hand of Saul, and said:
"The Lord is my rock, and my fortress, and my deliverer." Thence thou must reach Isaiah, that thou mayest
say with him: 'I will sing to my Beloved, a song of my
Beloved touching His vineyard.' And when thou hast
traversed all these, go up yet higher, that thou mayest,
with pure soul, cry unto the Bridegroom this Song of
songs."

For in truth, this song utters holy secrets, which
only God's Spirit can teach, and which none but the
deeply spiritual can understand. And these secrets are
the secrets of an infinite and Divine love St. Bernard
says concerning it, "This song excels all other songs of
the Old Testament; they being, for the most part, songs
of deliverance from enemies, Solomon for such had no
occasion. In the height of glory, singular in wisdom,
abounding in riches, secure in peace, he here, by Divine

Inspiration, sings the praises of Christ and His Church, the grace of holy love, the mysteries of the Eternal Marriage; yet all the while, like Moses, putting a veil before his face, because at that time there were few or none that could gaze upon such glories. . . . This song is not heard without; it is not sounded forth in public concourse ; she only hears its notes who sings it, and He for whom it is sung—the Bridegroom and the Bride."

In the very latest Commentary on the Bible, edited by Canon Cook, of Exeter, Eng., we find in the Introduction to the Song of Solomon this passage, "And shall we then regard it as a mere fancy which for so many ages past has been wont to find in the pictures and melodies of the Song of Songs, types and echoes of the actings and emotions of the highest Love, of Love Divine in its relations to Humanity ; which if dimly discerned through their aid by the Synagogue, have been amply revealed in the Gospel to the Church. Shall we not still claim to trace in the noble and gentle history thus presented, foreshadowings of the infinite condescensions of Incarnate Love ?—that Love which first stooping in human form to visit us in our low estate in order to seek out and win its object, Ps. cxxxvi. 23, and then raising along with Himself a sanctified Humanity to the heavenly places, Eph. ii. 6, is finally awaiting there an invitation from the mystic Bride to return to earth once more and seal the Union for Eternity."

It is manifest from all these extracts, that the spiritual

mind of the Church in all ages has received this Song
as the expression of a mystic Divine union, and that as
such it has brought richest blessings to many childlike
souls.

There are many forms of love between heart and heart,
there is filial love, and brotherly love, and parental love,
and the love of friendship. But besides all these, and
different from them all, there is the love of espousals,
and it is of this sort of love our little book speaks. It is
true that we do love our Lord as children love a parent,
as brethren love brethren, as a friend loves a friend.
But all these do not after all completely meet our need,
nor fill our capacity. Our hearts are susceptible of a
more absorbing affection than any of them, and Christ
is the offered Object of it. He has loved us Himself
with a love passing knowledge, and He wants our utmost love in return. He wants us to be *one* with Him,
as He is one with the Father. He has bought us for
Himself at infinite cost and pains, and now He seeks to
win our whole soul's devotion. It is intended that there
should be an *interchange* of affection between our hearts
and His. We love Him, it is true, because He first
loved us, but we are commanded nevertheless to love
Him absorbingly, unutterably, supremely. "Thou shalt
love the Lord thy God with all thy heart, and with
all thy soul, and with all thy might," is the "first and
great commandment." And when we have been enabled
to obey this command, and have found our hearts
possessed by this supreme affection, we need some

30*

fitting expression of it, such as we find here. "Let
Him kiss me with the kisses of His mouth; for Thy
love is better than wine." "As the apple-tree among
the trees of the wood, so is my Beloved among
the sons. I sat down under His shadow with great delight, and His fruit was sweet to my taste. He brought
me to the banqueting house, and His banner over me
was love. Stay me with flagons, comfort me with
apples: for I am sick of love. His left hand is under
my head, and His right hand doth embrace me. I
charge you, O ye daughters of Jerusalem, by the roes,
and by the hinds of the field, that ye stir not up, nor
awake my love till He pleases." "My Beloved is white
and ruddy, the chiefest among ten thousand. . . .
His mouth is most sweet; yea, He is altogether lovely.
This is my Beloved, and this is my Friend, O, daughters
of Jerusalem." i. 3–7 and v. 10–16.

Such is the impassioned language of this mystic song.
The soul here makes her boast in the Lord's love. She
does not refuse to listen to the tenderest expressions
of it, nor to tell out her own deepest emotions. "My Beloved is mine, and I am His," is the underlying consciousness through it all, which warrants the most blessed
confidence and freedom.

An English writer, whose name I do not know, has
written a very delightful book entitled, "Introduction to
the Canticles,"* in which he says:—"The Canticles
do not give us the ways of filial affection, nor of the

* J. B. Bateman, London, Publisher.

affection due to a benefactor. But they give us, I
believe, the actings of the love of espousals, in both
Christ's heart and ours. The joy of hearing the Bridegroom's voice, I may say, is fulfilled here in the heart
of the saint, as it was in the soul of John the Baptist.
. . . . It is the love which warrants personal intimacy of the nearest and dearest kind that breathes
in this lovely little book; and if these affections be
not understood as passing between Christ and the
saint, if we do not, without reserve, allow this satisfaction in each other, our souls will not enter into
much of the communion which the Scriptures provide
for. . . . Love takes different forms in the heart
and regards its object in many different ways; but the
love of which this Song speaks has a glory peculiarly its
own. It warrants the deepest intimacies. There is no
settling of oneself for the other's presence. There is full
ease in going out and coming in. Expressions of love
are not deemed intrusive here; nay, they are sanctioned
as being due and comely. The heart knows its right to
indulge itself over its object, and that, too, without check
or shame. This is the glory of this affection. The love of
pity, of gratitude, or of complacency must act decorously,
and in proper form. But the love of kindred, the love of
those who dwell in one house, and whom nature or the
hand of God has bound together, feels its right to gratify
itself, and is not fearful of being rebuked. This is its
distinguishing boast. Nothing admits this but itself.
This is in a full and deep sense, personal affection.

. . . And it is the richest feast of the heart. . . .

"It is a love which commands the whole being of the one in whom it seats itself. As to *service*, it makes it welcome. To say that service for the object of this affection is perfect freedom, is far too cold. It makes service infinitely grateful, even though it call for self-denial and weariness. And it can render its offering without caring for any eye or heart to approve it, but that of the one whom it has made its object. It cares not that others should be able to esteem its ways. It has all the desired fruit of its service, if its object approve it, and give but His presence at the end of it. As to *society*, this affection wants none but that of its object. If there be no weariness felt in service, as we have been saying, so is there no irksomeness known in solitude. All that is cared for is the presence of that One who commands the heart. There is no sense of solitude, if that One alone be present; there is no sense of satiety, though that One be alway present. As to *authority* in the soul, it holds its place, I need not say, unrivalled. It is the man of the heart. It breaks the bands, and cuts the cords of other desires. It makes us to undervalue all things but the one. . . . Other things are esteemed only according to their connection with this. And it will control the wrong, and cultivate the right tendencies of the heart. For occasions which might wound vanity or gratify pride are not valued nor pursued, while we retain it; and yet to approve ourselves there, we will nerve the heart and hand to great and generous ways.

"What intenseness is here, and what purity also. It re-
freshes the soul to think that we have been created
susceptible of such an affection, and to know that Christ
is the offered Object of it. He proposes Himself to it.
He claims the supreme place in our hearts. 'He that
loveth father or mother more than me, is not worthy of
me.' Whatever passion of the soul be moved, it is God's
right to have the highest exercise of it towards Himself.
. . . This may sound a solemn truth, but it is a happy
one. Is it not blessed to know, that our Lord claims our
hearts and their affections? Have any of us read the
'first and great commandment' without at least sometimes rejoicing in the grace that would make such a demand upon us? Is it nothing to us that God Himself
values our love, that He says to us, 'My son, give me
thy heart'? . . . And we want these affections to
make us happy, and to set us free. It is the divine
method of delivering us from the tyranny of carnal or
worldly desires. It is the Spirit's way of spoiling other
attractions of their power to seduce and fill the heart, and
of lifting the soul above the frettings of low anxieties.
"Would that this love were more shed abroad in our
hearts, beloved! How should we learn, then, to enter-
tain Christ as this affection entertains or embalms its
object. And what a Heaven it will be, when He is ours
in this way, feeding this fire in our souls, and giving us
to know in Himself and His beauties, this seraph love,
without chill, for ever and ever!"

Such is the Song of songs. It is the soul's longing

after, and satisfaction in her Beloved. " Tell Him that
I am sick of love " is its cry. " Tell me, oh thou whom
my soul loveth, where thou feedest, where thou makest
thy flock to rest at noon."

The question of the ground of our acceptance with
God, is not touched upon in this book. The whole expression is that of a soul that *knows* its place of union,
but longs for a fuller manifestation of it; and the faults
mourned, are all only such faults as are based upon the
closest intimacy. No open transgression or conscious
disobedience are lamented, or even apparently thought
possible, only a little hesitation in responding to His call,
a momentary coldness, a temporary slothfulness of soul;
faults, the very nature of which reveal the fine spiritual
sense of the heart that can mourn them.

There is a manifest development of the " apprehending
of that for which we are apprehended of Christ Jesus "
in the experience of this bride. In the first chapter
she longs after the Beloved. In the second chapter
He is found, and her heart is made conscious of His
manifested love, and exclaims rapturously, " My beloved
is mine, and I am His." In the third chapter something,
a little slothfulness of spirit, perhaps, has caused a temporary loneliness and darkness, and the soul has again
to seek her Beloved, and again she finds Him and rests
in His love. "By night on my bed I sought Him whom
my soul loveth : I sought Him, but I found Him not. I
will rise now, and go about the city in the streets, and
in the broad ways I will seek Him whom my soul loveth:

I sought Him, but I found Him not. The watchmen that go about the city found me: to whom I said, Saw ye Him whom my soul loveth? It was but a little that I passed from them, but I found Him whom my soul loveth: I held Him, and would not let Him go, until I had brought Him into my mother's house, and into the chamber of her that conceived me. I charge you, O ye daughters of Jerusalem, by the roes and by the hinds of the field, that ye stir not up, nor awake my love, till He please."

In chapter iv. He declares what she is to Him, that her heart may be reassured, after its temporary slothfulness. "Thou art all fair, my love, there is no spot in thee." "Thou hast ravished my heart, my sister, my spouse; thou hast ravished my heart with one of thine eyes, with one chain of thy neck. How fair is thy love, my sister, my spouse! how much better is thy love than wine! and the smell of thine ointments than all spices!" It is hard for the natural man to accept such love as this, as really existing in the heart of the Lord towards His people. We can comprehend how it is that we should love Him, but that He should love us, literally and actually *love* us, with the intensity and delight here expressed, seems an impossibility. And yet it is all, and far more, contained in our Lord's own words, "*As* the Father hath loved me, *so* have I loved you." Thou, O Father, hast loved them *as* Thou hast loved me." What an " as " and " so " are here! And how little of this road have our souls as yet travelled, beloved, that we find it so hard to comprehend this lovely mystic song!

Chap. v. gives us another experience. Again a little
hesitation to respond to the call of the Beloved for communion, deprives the bride of His presence, and in the
desolation of her heart she goes out a second time to seek
Him. " I sleep, but my heart waketh : it is the voice of
my Beloved that knocketh, saying, Open to me, my
sister, my love, my dove, my undefiled : for my head is
filled with dew, and my locks with the drops of the night.
I have put off my coat; how shall I put it on ? I have
washed my feet; how shall I defile them ? My Beloved
put in His hand by the hole of the door, and my bowels
were moved for Him. . . . . I opened to my Beloved, but my Beloved had withdrawn Himself and was
gone : my soul failed when He spake ; I sought Him,
but I could not find Him ; I called Him but He gave
me no answer. . . . I charge you, O ye daughters
of Jerusalem, if ye find my Beloved, that ye tell Him
that I am sick of love." v. 1-8. The intensity of her
desire, arouses the interest of those she questions, and
they ask, " What is thy Beloved more than another be·
loved, O thou fairest among women ? What is thy Beloved more than another beloved, that thou dost so
charge us ?" This calls out her ardent praises of her
Beloved, and in praising Him, she is taught of God
where to find Him, and advances a step onward in her
apprehension of the relationship between them. " My
Beloved is gone down into His garden, to the beds of
spices, to feed in the gardens, and to gather lilies. I
am my Beloved's, and my Beloved is mine. He feedeth

among the lilies." vi. 2, 3. Before it was, "My Beloved is mine, and I am His." The chief thought then
was her possession of Him. But now it is, "I am
my Beloved's, and my Beloved is mine." Her soul
has taken hold of the deeper truth here, her Beloved's ownership of her. It is blessed to have Christ
for ours, but infinitely more blessed for us to be His.
If He is ours only, we may fail to keep Him, but if we
are His, He can never cease to keep us. The Shepherd
does in a sense belong to the sheep, but the secret of
their safety lies in this, that they belong to Him. This,
however, is an advanced apprehension of our relationship to Christ. Our first realization is always of our
ownership of Him, and it needs some such exercises of
soul as this Bride had gone through, to teach us the
deeper truth.

In chaps. vi. and vii., the Beloved, whom she has thus
regained, tells out her preciousness afresh in stronger
words than ever. He calls her "My dove, my undefiled," and says, "How fair and how pleasant art thou,
O love, for delights." vii. 6. And He expresses the
intensity of His love in wondrous words that can be received only by that heart which has come indeed to the
utter end of self, "Turn away thine eyes from me, for
they have overcome me!" Can it be indeed possible
that our love is *this* to our Lord? The bride here
believes the words of her Beloved, and exclaims in answer, for the third time, but with a far deeper expression
than before of the amazing yet blessed truth, "I am

31

my Beloved's, and His desire is toward me." vii. 10.
Her possession of the Beloved is left out altogether now ;
it is enough for her that she belongs to Him.   And her
soul has reached the consciousness at last that she is
precious to Him also, " His desire is toward me."   She
has always known that she desired Him, but that He
should desire her is something deeper and harder to
learn.   And yet it is most blessedly true ; as other parts
of the Scriptures abundantly testify.   " Hearken, O
daughter, and consider, incline thine ear, forget also
thine own people and thy father's house, so shall thy
king *greatly desire* thy beauty." Ps. xlv. 11.   " Now,
therefore, if ye will obey my voice indeed, and keep my
covenant, then shall ye be a *peculiar treasure* unto me."
Ez. xix. 5.   " For the Lord *taketh pleasure* in His people." Ps. cxlix. 4.   " Neither shall thy land any more
be termed Desolate ; but thou shalt be called Hephzibah "
(i. e., my delight is in her) " and thy land Beulah "
(i. e., married): " for the Lord *delighteth* in thee, and
thy land shall be married." Is. lxii. 4.

This is the third time that the close union and mutual
affection of the Bridegroom and the Bride are thus mentioned in this Song.   First it was, " My Beloved is mine,
and I am His." ii. 16.   Next it was, " I am my Beloved s,
and my Beloved is mine." vi. 3.   And here it is, " I am
my Beloved's, and His desire is toward me." vii. 10.
St. Ambrose says concerning these three sayings, that
they give us a threefold diversity in the manner of
the Bride's expression, which denote the three stages of

her progress in the love of God ; to wit, her beginning,
advance, and perfection. First she thinks most of
possessing Christ ; next she realizes chiefly that He
possesses her ; and at last she rejoices in the unspeakable knowledge that His desires are toward her, and
that she is necessary to His joy. This latest apprehension is the fulfilment of Paul's prayer for the Ephesian
christians in Eph. i. 17, 18, "That the God of our
Lord Jesus Christ, the Father of glory, may give
unto you the spirit of wisdom and revelation in the
knowledge of Him: the eyes of your understanding
being enlightened : that ye may know what is the hope
of His calling, and what the riches of the glory of His inheritance in the saints." Christians may learn at an early
stage in their experience something of the riches of their
inheritance in Christ ; but it is a far deeper lesson, and
one often learned far later, to know the riches of His
inheritance in us. The bride here had learned it at last,
and the immediate result is, that she who in the beginning
had been invited by the Bridegroom to come with Him,
now invites Him to come with her. "Come, my Beloved, let us go forth into the field : let us lodge in the
villages. Let us get up early to the vineyards ; let us
see if the vine flourish ; whether the tender grape appear,
and the pomegranates bud forth : there will I give Thee
my loves. The mandrakes give a smell, and at our
gates are all manner of pleasant fruits, new and old,
which I have laid up for Thee, O my Beloved." vii.
11-13. She has realized so fully the "riches of His

inheritance in the saints," that she can confidently call upon Him to come with her and enjoy the pleasant fruits she has laid up for Him. This is indeed to know the love of Christ which passeth knowledge. May our Lord Himself reveal it to us!

Chap. viii. appears to be a sort of recapitulation of the whole wondrous story. The longing and the satisfying of that longing, accompanied by a glorious assertion of the might and purity of true love, are here again set forth, 1-7. The "little sister," type of the soul who has but just begun to believe on Christ, and to be fed with milk, is here encouraged to look for and expect an increase, 8, 9. And, finally, in the last verse, the Bride reiterates her invitation to her Beloved. "Make haste, my Beloved, and be thou like to a roe, or to a young hart upon the mountain of spices." Reminding us of the closing verses of Revelation also, "He which testifieth these things saith, Surely I come quickly; Amen. Even so, come, Lord Jesus."

With this book the developing series concerning the heart exercises of God's people as to sanctification, closes, for the soul has made its final discovery, and has learned at last the all-sufficiency of the love of Christ to swallow up and extinguish everything else! And fears, perplexities, disappointments, mysteries, questionings— all are lost in the ocean of Divine love! It has entered here into that realized union with the Lord, which is the consummation of Christian experience, and which includes within itself all possible gift and blessing. Earth can contain no more than this union. And Heaven itself will only be the perfection and completion of it, when the Bride shall sit down forever beside her Bridegroom, upon His throne, and share His eternal glory.

Beloved, have our hearts entered into this "banqueting house" where joy unspeakable and full of glory awaits us? Have we consciously realized this wondrous union, and are our souls rejoicing in its unspeakable delights? Has this blessed "mystery" of our faith been revealed to us, and are our hearts opened wide to receive it? Are we walking, with the step of a possessor, through this marvellous palace of delights, and claiming each fresh revelation of its unutterable secrets as our own? It is a palace open to all, though all do not enter it; it is a union intended for every one, though but few apprehend it; it is a mystery revealed to the babes, but hid from the wise and prudent. For our Divine Bridegroom Himself prayed while on earth "That they all may be one; as Thou Father, art in me, and I in Thee, that they also may be one in us : . . . . I in them, and Thou in me, that they may be made perfect in one ; that the world may know that Thou hast sent me, and hast loved them as Thou hast loved me." "That they *all* may be one !" let us praise the Lord for this little word "all"! And let us act on it with the simple faith of the bride about whom we have been reading, and yield ourselves to its sweet fulfilment. For to such as do, there will begin for them straightway, days of heaven upon earth. And then, in the blaze of this overmaster-

31*

ing and utterly satisfying love, the wonderful prayer in Eph. iii. 14-19 will be fulfilled, and they will be really able at last to "comprehend with all saints, what is the breadth, and length, and depth, and height; and to know the love of Christ which passeth knowledge," and will be filled to the very brim "with all the fulness of God."

"O Jesus, Jesus! dearest Lord! forgive me if I say
For very love, Thy sacred name a thousand times a day.
I love Thee so, I know not how my transports to control;
Thy love is like a burning fire within my very soul.

"Oh wonderful! that Thou shouldst let so vile a heart as mine
Love Thee with such a love as this, and make so free with Thine
The craft of this wise world of ours poor wisdom seems to me;
Ah! dearest Jesus! I have grown childish with love of Thee.

"For thou to me art all in all, my honour and my wealth,
My soul's desire, my body's strength, my soul's eternal health.
Burn, burn, O Love! within my heart, burn fiercely night and day,
Till all the dross of earthly loves is burned, and burned away.

"O Light in darkness, Joy in grief, O Heaven begun on earth!
Jesus! my Love! my Treasure! who can tell what Thou art worth?
O Jesus! Jesus! sweetest Lord! what art Thou not to me?
Each hour brings joys before unknown, each day new liberty!

"What limit is there to Thee, Love? Thy flight where wilt thou
    stay?
On! on! our Lord is sweeter far to-day than yesterday.
O love of Jesus! Blessed love! so will it ever be;
Time cannot hold thy wondrous growth; no, nor eternity!"

CHAPTER XXIII.

THE PROPHETS.

THE LORD'S REVELATION OF HIS PLANS TO HIS CHILDREN.

Keynote: John xv. 15.

PROPHECY is God's revelation of His secret plans and purposes. It was given not for a merely temporary use, but for all ages and all people. Paul says concerning it, "Whatsoever things were written aforetime were written for our learning, that we through patience and comfort of the Scriptures might have hope." Rom. xv. 4. Prophecy it is manifest can only come from the Lord, for He alone knows the end of things from the beginning, and He only holds the threads of destiny in His hands. Therefore we are told concerning the prophets, that, "The prophecy came not in old time by the will of man : but holy men of God spake as they were moved by the Holy Ghost." 2 Peter i. 21. Throughout the books of the prophets, consequently, we read continually. "And the Lord spake," or, "Thus saith the

Lord," or, "The Lord spake, saying;" so that of each one it is manifestly true that "the Spirit of the Lord spake by him," and "His word was in his tongue."

In giving to His people these books of prophecy, the Lord is treating them as friends, for He Himself when on earth said to His disciples, "Henceforth I call you not servants, for the servant knoweth not what His Lord doeth; but I have called you friends, for all things that I have heard of my Father I nave made known unto you." Abraham was called the "friend of God," and when God was about to destroy Sodom, although it was not a matter that concerned Abraham personally, He said, "Shall I hide from Abraham that thing which I do?" And He stopped on His way to Sodom to tell His purposes to His "friend," listening with all the condescension of a real friendship to Abraham's plea for the doomed city, and even yielding everything that he asked. No sweeter picture of the reality of our position as "friends of God" could be given than this story of Abraham. And I feel that when we come to the study of these prophetical books, we should realize ourselves as being in this blessed position of personal intimacy, and should understand that our Father and our Friend is here disclosing to us His secrets. "Surely the Lord will do nothing, but He revealeth His secret unto His servants the prophets." Amos iii. 7.

Written prophecy began about the year 800 B. C., during the reigns of the divided kingdom, when all was outward confusion, and the faith of the Lord's true peo-

ple needed a divine revelation to pierce the gloom that
surrounded them on every hand. With the plainest
declarations of His judgments on the sin that so
abounded in the midst of His people, the Lord, from the
first, joined the most distinct assurances of the coming
of a Saviour, who should usher in a kingdom of righteousness and peace, that would finally " cover the earth
as the waters cover the sea."

The Lord Jesus Christ therefore, and His salvation
form the centre of all prophecy, as we read in 1 Pet. i.
10–13, " Of which salvation the prophets have enquired
and searched diligently, who prophesied of the grace
that should come unto you : searching what, or what
manner of time the Spirit of Christ which was in them
did signify, when it testified beforehand the sufferings
of Christ, and the glory that should follow. Unto whom
it was revealed, that not unto themselves, but unto us
they did minister the things, which are now reported
unto you by them that have preached the gospel unto
you, with the Holy Ghost sent down from heaven ;
which things the angels desire to look into." Again
we read in Acts iii. 24, "Yea, and all the prophets from
Samuel and those that follow after, as many as have
spoken, have likewise foretold of these days." Also in
Acts xxvi. 22, 23, Paul declared that his preaching
was but a "witnessing to both small and great," of
the very things which the prophets and Moses had
said should come ; "that Christ should suffer, and
that He should be the first that should rise from the

dead, and should shew light unto the people, and to the Gentiles."

A recent writer has said concerning these books that, " Parallel with the record of prophecy, runs a historical record of its fulfilment, up to the point when the light of the gospel of Christ is shed over the world. There was a time when all that was known of God's gracious purposes was matter of prediction only; but now an important part of it has become matter of history; and the transference of events from the one record to the other is continually advancing. It is easy to see the advantage of having these records side by side. The fulfilment of any part of prophecy, besides being important in itself, gives the most confident assurance of the completion of the fulfilment. Thus if we have at first a prediction of glory as the result of suffering, the accomplishment of the predicted suffering is the surest pledge of the coming glory . . . The great burden of prophecy is the coming of a Divine Saviour to suffer and conquer for man, and then to share the fruits of His conquest with His people. Now the first part we know is accomplished, and this stands to us the pledge of all the rest."

We are encouraged therefore by the literal fulfilment of all the details of the prophecies concerning the first coming of our Lord in humiliation, to look towards an equally literal fulfilment of the prophecies concerning His second coming in glory, and we shall find a careful study of that which is here written in reference to it, of deep interest and great practical value.

There are seventeen books of prophecy. Hosea, Amos, Joel, Micah, Nahum, Zephaniah, Isaiah, Jeremiah and Habakkuk wrote previous to the carrying away of the Jews into Babylon ; Ezekiel, Daniel and Obadiah, wrote during the course of the captivity ; and Haggai, Zechariah, and Malachi, after the restoration of the Jews under Ezra and Nehemiah to their own land. The prophecy of Isaiah is the first in the arrangement of the books in our Bibles, but in point of time Joel, Amos and Hosea are supposed to have written their books earlier. A comparison of the dates at the beginning of each book will make this clear to us. But the opening verses in Isaiah, Amos, and Hosea all point to about the same period of time, with only the difference of a few years. "The vision of Isaiah the son of Amoz which he saw concerning Judah and Jerusalem, in the days of Uzziah, Jotham, Ahaz and Hezekiah, kings of Judah," Is. i. 1. Compare Hosea i. 1 and Amos i. 1. The prophecy of Jonah which is dated 862 B. C., and which had reference to Nineveh only, though containing a hidden type of Christ's death and resurrection, is not taken into accouut here.

I have no doubt the order of these books, as it is given to us in our Bibles, has some spiritual revelation in it, which we have not yet perhaps fathomed ; and so also, I believe, have the meanings of the names of the different prophets. These meanings can be found in chapter ii.

The prophecies deal mostly with the dispersion of the ten tribes, the captivity and restoration of Judah,

and the utter apostasy of the people from the worship of the true God, together with the Lord's final
purposes of grace and mercy. They are full of appall-
ing descriptions of the doom of an apostate nation,
but these are always coupled with exulting descriptions of the mighty Redeemer who was to come, and
of the glory of His reign. Thus Amos says concerning Israel, " I will sift the house of Israel among all
nations, like as corn is sifted in a sieve ; " but adds a
little after, " In that day will I raise up the tabernacle of
David that is fallen ; . . and I will bring again the captivity of Israel, . . . and I will plant them in their own
land, and they shall no more be pulled up out of their
land which I have given them, saith the Lord thy God;"
Amos ix. 11–15 ; a prediction which in Acts xv. 16, 17 is
declared to refer to Christ. Joel also, who predicts the
awful destruction from the Almighty to come upon the
rebellious nation, also declares that " then will the Lord
be jealous for His land, and pity his people. Yea, the
Lord will answer and say unto His people, Behold I will
send you corn, and wine, and oil, and ye shall be satisfied therewith, and I will no more make you a reproach
among the heathen. . . . And it shall come to
pass afterward that I will pour out My Spirit upon all
flesh. . . . And it shall come to pass, that whosoever shall call on the name of the Lord shall be delivered : for in mount Zion and in Jerusalem shall be deliverance, as the Lord hath said, and in the remnant whom
the Lord shall call." All of which is shown us in Acts

ii. 16–21 to have had an incipient fulfilment on the day
of Pentecost; and which also plainly points onward to a
future complete and glorious fulfilment, when Christ
shall come in power to establish His outward millenial
Kingdom. With equal plainness do all the prophets,
whether those before the captivity, or those who shared
it, as well as those who were restored from it, speak of
this coming glory.

These prophecies take no note apparently of the centuries of time which were to elapse between the incipient fulfilment of the promises in Christ's first coming,
and their complete fulfilment at His second coming.
The long period of the Church's history called in Luke
21 : 24 the "times of the Gentiles" were apparently utterly ignored, and our Lord's coming in humiliation to
die, and His coming in glory to reign, are connected
often in the same sentence, as though they were to be
coincident in time. It is essential to the right understanding of prophecy to be aware of this. The reason given
for it by students of Scripture has been, that, with the
death of Christ, and the "cutting off of the Jews," Jewish history ceased; and that the "times of the Gentiles"
which are going on now, until the return of Christ, and
the restoration of the Jews, during which "Jerusalem is
to be trodden under foot of the Gentiles," is not noticed
by anything more than sometimes a slight allusion; the
prophecy for the most part passing right over it, and
taking up the thread of Jewish history at its close, as
though no time had elapsed between. Paul speaks very

32

fully concerning these "times of the Gentiles" in Rom.
xi. 11–27, closing with the words, "For I would not,
brethren, that ye should be ignorant of this mystery, lest
ye should be wise in your own conceits; that blindness
in part is happened to Israel, until the fulness of the
Gentiles be come in. And so all Israel shall be saved : as
it is written, There shall come out of Sion the Deliverer,
and shall turn away ungodliness from Jacob : for this is
my covenant unto them, when I shall take away their
sins."

The passage quoted by our Lord in Luke iv. 16–19 is a
striking illustration of this close connection in the
prophecies, of things, which in actual experience were to
be many centuries apart. He read from the prophet
Esaias in chap. 61 : 1, 2, stopping short however in the
middle of verse 2. The verse reads in Isaiah, " To proclaim the acceptable year of our Lord, and the day of
vengeance of our God; to comfort all that mourn."
But our Lord stopped at the end of the first sentence,
" To proclaim the acceptable year of the Lord, " although only a comma separates it from that which follows, " the day of vengeance of our God." The reason
of this was, that the acceptable year had come, but the
day of vengeance had not come, and has not come yet.
Nearly 1900 years at least have therefore in fact separated
these two things, which in prophecy seemed to be coincident. Following out this prophecy, on from the point
where our Lord closed the book and sat down, to its end,
we find the final restoration of the Jews plainly declared,

their authority over the Gentiles re-established, and Jerusalem again made a " praise in the earth. See Isaiah lxi. 4–11 ; also lxii. which is plainly a continuation of the same prophetical message.

Many devout readers of the Bible have objected to the thought of a literal fulfilment of prophecy, and have been inclined to think that it refers only to the Church in a spiritual sense. But I believe most careful students of the present day take a different view, and agree in thinking that these prophecies refer primarily to Israel and Judah, although they have also a very blessed typical application to Christians. We who now by faith enter into the inward spiritual kingdom of our Lord, enter also into spiritual blessings, which have a wonderful correspondence to the temporal ones here set forth. There is doubtless to be a real outward millennium on this earth, when the "kingdoms of this world shall become the kingdoms of our Lord, and of His Christ;" but there is also now and here, for every faithful heart, an inward millennial experience, which answers spiritually, to the descriptions these prophecies give of the future earthly glory. It is doubtless from this cause that the mistake has arisen in the Church, of monopolizing to herself prophecies, which belong primarily to Israel, and which are plainly to have a literal as well as a spiritual fulfilment.

It is curious however that, in this appropriation, Christians have taken only the blessings to themselves, and have handed the curses over to the Jews, and this fact should have long ago opened every eye to the mistake. For in many places the blessings and the curses are together in one sentence, and cannot be understood by any really intelligent mind other than as referring to one and the same class of people. It is plainly the people who have been cursed, who are to have the blessings. And while, as I say, we may use these glorious prophecies as the typical expression of our present inward millennial joys, we must never lose sight of the fact that they are to be literally and actually fulfilled to the Jews, in their triumphant return to their own land, and their restoration there to acceptance with the Lord, and to true righteousness before Him.

In tracing the course of prophecy I have not space to dwell long upon those prophecies which refer to Christ's first coming, and their literal fulfilment, especially as they are already familiar to every student, and the references in the margins of any good reference Bible bring them all out with great clearness. I will therefore simply insert at the close of this chapter, out of the Bagster Bible, a collection of all the prophecies referring to Christ, with their parallel passages in the New Testament.

In reference to the prophecies referring to Christ's second coming in glory, and the restoration of the Jews, I can only give a general view. The field of unfulfilled prophecy is too vast to be taken up in detail within the limits of a book like this. Moreover, the views of careful and earnest students, concerning its details, differ so widely, that I should feel very cautious about entering into it too minutely or stating anything too positively.

That the Lord Jesus Christ will surely come again to reign in a kingdom of universal righteousness on this world is, I think, accepted by most Christians in the present day. But as to the details of this event there are, as I have said, a variety of views. The two principal are called respectively the Pre-millennial and the Post-millennial Advent. The one states that Christ is to return before the millennium, and is to usher in that blessed time by His redeeming and purifying presence. The other states that He is to come at the close of the millennium, and that the world is to be prepared for His presence by the previous universal reign of righteousness and peace. My own view is the former, as it seems to me most in accordance with Scripture teaching.

The story as I receive it, is simply this :—

I. The Lord will come back suddenly, like a thief in the night, to receive His saints to Himself. Those who are dead will be raised, and the living saints will be caught up with them, to " meet the Lord in the air," as we read,

" For if we believe that Jesus died and rose again, even so them also which sleep in Jesus will God bring with Him. For this we say unto you by the word of the Lord, that we which are alive and remain unto the coming of the Lord shall not prevent them which are asleep. For the Lord Himself shall descend from heaven with a shout, with the voice of the archangel, and with the trump of God : and the dead in Christ shall rise first : then we which are alive and remain shall be caught up together with them in the clouds, to meet the Lord in the air : and so shall we ever be with the Lord." 1 Thess. iv. 14–17.

" Behold, I shew you a mystery : we shall not all sleep, but we shall all be changed In a moment, in the twinkling of an eye, at the last trump : for the trumpet shall sound, and the dead shall be raised incorruptible, and we shall be changed." 1 Cor. xv. 51, 52. See also 2 Thess. ii. 1 ; Luke xvii. 26-37 with Isa. xxvi. 20 ; Luke xxi. 36 ; Matt. xxv. 1-13.

The Lord will not be visible to the world at large at this time, for the saints must first be gathered up to meet Him thus, " in the air ; " and the only thing the world will know about it, will be the sudden and unaccountable disappearance of all the Christians out of it.

" I tell you, in that night there shall be two men in one bed : the one shall be taken, and the other shall be left. Two women shall be grinding together ; the one shall be taken, and the other left. Two men shall be in the field ; the one shall be taken, and the other left." Luke xvii. 34, 35, 36.

II. While still "in the air," the saints will be judged in reference, not to their salvation, but as to their rewards. See 1 Cor. iii. 12-15. The marriage of the Lamb will take place, and the Son will present His bride before the throne with exceeding joy. As we read,

" Let us be glad and rejoice, and give honour to Him : for the marriage of the Lamb is come, and His wife hath made herself ready ; And to her was granted that she should be arrayed in fine linen, clean and white : for the fine linen is the righteousness of the saints." Rev. xix. 7-9 with Matt. xxv. 1-13. See also Jude 24 ; 2 Cor. iv. 14 ; 1 Cor. iv. 3-6 ; Matt. xvi. 27 ; Rev. xi. 18 ; xxii. 12 ; 1 Cor. ix. 24. 25 : 2 Cor. v. 10 ; Rom. xiv. 10-14 ; Heb. x. 35-38 ; 2 Tim. iv. 1-9 ; 1 Pet. i. 7 ; 1 Pet. iv. 13 ; 1 Pet. v. 1-4 ; 1 John ii. 28 ; Ps. lxii. 12 ; Ps. xlv. with Dan. vii. 9-14 ; Jude 24 ; Col. i. 22.

III. Certain events will meanwhile be taking place upon the earth. Antichrist will arise and restore many of the Jews to their own land, making a covenant with them for seven years, which he will break at the end of three and a half years, and will assemble all nations around Jerusalem to besiege it. This siege will at first be successful, and the Jewish nation, in their distress, will at last be brought to know the depth of their need, and to call upon their God for help. As we read,

" For there shall arise false Christs, and false prophets, and shall shew great signs and wonders; insomuch that, if it were possible, they shall deceive the very elect. Behold, I have told you before." Matt. xxiv. 24, 25.

" And he shall confirm the covenant with many for one week" [seven years]; " and in the midst of the week" [at the end of three and one half years] " he shall cause the sacrifice and oblation to cease, and for the overspreading of abominations he shall make it desolate, even until the consummation, and that determined shall be poured upon the desolate." Dan. ix. 27.

" And from the time that the daily sacrifice shall be taken away, and the abomination that maketh desolate set up, there shall be a thousand two hundred and ninety days" [about three and a half years]. Dan. xii. 11.

" When ye therefore shall see the abomination of desolation, spoken of by Daniel the prophet, stand in the holy place (whoso readeth let him understand), then let them which be in Judæa flee into the mountains." Matt. xxiv. 15-29 with Rev. xiii. 1.-8.

" For I will gather all nations against Jerusalem to battle, and the city shall be taken and the houses rifled, and the women ravished ; and half of the city shall go forth into captivity, and the residue of the people shall not be cut off from the city." Zech. xiv. 1, 2, 9. See also Joel ii. 1-32; Dan. ix. 26, 27: Rev. xiii. 1-8 ; Dan. xii. 1 ; Dan. vii. 21-26; Jer. xxx. 4-11 ; Rev. xi. 2; Dan. viii. 11-27 ; Rev. xvi. 14; Is. xiii. 4.

IV. And *now* is the time to which all prophecy points, when Christ shall come again to the earth, bringing all His saints with Him, and His feet shall stand upon the

Mount of Olives, that very mount from which He went up into heaven. As we read,

"And when he had spoken these things, while they beheld, He was taken up; and a cloud received Him out of their sight. And while they looked steadfastly toward heaven as He went up, behold, two men stood by them in white apparel; which also said, Ye men of Galilee, why stand ye gazing up into heaven? this same Jesus, which is taken up from you into heaven, shall so come in like manner as ye have seen Him go into heaven. Then returned they unto Jerusalem from the mount called Olivet, which is from Jerusalem a sabbath day's journey." Acts i. 9–12.

"Then shall the Lord go forth and fight against those nations, as when He fought in the day of battle. And His feet shall stand on the Mount of Olives, which is before Jerusalem on the east." "And the Lord shall be King over all the earth: in that day shall there be one Lord and His name One. All the land shall be turned as a plain from Geba to Rimmon, south of Jerusalem: and it shall be lifted up, and inhabited in her place from Benjamin's gate unto the place of the first gate, unto the corner gate, and from the tower of Hananeel unto the king's wine-presses. And men shall dwell in it, and there shall be no more utter destruction; but Jerusalem shall be safely inhabited." Zech. xiv. 3, 4. 9–11. "And Enoch also, the seventh from Adam, prophesied of these, saying, Behold, the Lord cometh·with ten thousand of His saints, to execute judgment upon all." Jude 14, 15. "When Christ who is our life shall appear, then shall ye also appear with Him in glory." Col. iii. 4. See also on this point, Dan. vii. 21, 22; Joel ii. 1–11, with Rev. xix. 11–21; Is. xiii. 3–6, xxxi. 4.5; Ps. cii. 16, xcvi. 10–13; Mal. iii. 1–5; Ezek. xliii. 1–4; Haggai ii. 21, 22; Is. lxvi. 15; lii. 10; 1 Thess. iii. 13; Is. xxxi. 4, 5.

V. Every eye will now see Him, and all the tribes of the earth will mourn at the sight, and will call on the rocks and the hills to cover them, and hide them from the day of His coming. He will deliver Jerusalem, and destroy His enemies, and will gather together His chosen people, the Jews, from all the lands where they have been scattered, and restore them to their own land, where they will recognize Him, and mourn for their rejection of Him. As we read,

" And then shall appear the sign of the Son of man in heaven ; and then shall all the tribes of the earth mourn, and they shall see the Son of man coming in the clouds of heaven, with power, and great glory. And He shall send His angels with a great sound of a trumpet ; and they shall gather together His elect from the four winds, from one end of heaven to the other." Matt. xxiv. 30, 31 with Is. xi. 10, 11.

" And it shall come to pass in that day, that I will seek to destroy all the nations that come against Jerusalem. And I will pour upon the house of David, and upon the inhabitants of Jerusalem. the spirit of grace and of supplications ; and they shall look upon Me whom they have pierced, and they shall mourn for Him as one mourneth for his only son, and shall be in bitterness for Him, as one that is in bitterness for his first-born." Zech. xii. 8–14.

" And it shall come to pass in that day, that the Lord shall set His hand again the second time to recover the remnant of His people, which shall be left, from Assyria, and from Egypt, and from Pathros, and from Cush, and from Elam, and from Shinar, and from Hamath, and from the islands of the sea. And He shall set up an ensign for the nations, and shall assemble the outcasts of Israel, and gather together the dispersed of Judah from the four corners of the earth." Is. xi. 11, 12.

See also Rev. vi. 15–17; Luke xxiii. 27–30 ; Is. ii. 19–21 ; Zech. viii.; Zech. xiv. 12–15, Ez. xxxix. 11–22 with Rev. xix. 17–21 ; Zeph. iii. 8 ; Mal. iv. 2 ; Dan. xii. 1 ; Jer. xxx. 4–9, xxxi. 8–15, xxxii. 42–44, xxxiii. 14–16 ; Is. lii 10: liii. 1, 2, 9, 10 ; lxvi. 15–21 ; lx.; lxi.; lxii.; 1 Thess. ii. 1–9 with Is. xi. 1–9 ; Haggai ii. 7.

VI. At this time the judgment of the nations who are living on the earth, spoken of in Matt. xxv. 30-46, will take place ; sin will be purged out of the world by the

judgments and rebukes of the Lord, and universal peace
and righteousness will be established.   As we read,

" When the Son of man shall come in His glory, and all the
holy angels with Him, then shall He sit upon the throne of His
glory: and before Him shall be gathered all nations: and He
shall separate them one from another, as a shepherd divideth his
sheep from the goats: And He shall set the sheep on His right
hand, but the goats on the left." Matt. xxv. 31-33.

" And in mercy shall the throne be established: and He shall sit
upon it in truth in the tabernacle of David, judging and seeking
judgment, and hasting righteousness." Is. xvi. 5.

" And He shall judge among the nations, and shall rebuke many
people : and they shall beat their swords into plowshares, and their
spears into pruning-hooks : nation shall not lift up sword against
nation, neither shall they learn war any more." Is. ii. 4.

" And I saw heaven opened, and behold a white horse ; and He
that sat upon Him was called Faithful and True, and in righteousness He doth judge and make war.   His eyes were as a flame of
fire, and on His head were many crowns ; and He had a name written that no man knew but He Himself. And was clothed with a
vesture dipped in blood : and His name is called The Word of God.
And the armies which were in heaven followed Him upon white.
horses, clothed in fine linen white and clean. And out of His
mouth goeth a sharp sword, that with it He should smite the nations :
and He shall rule them with a rod of iron: and He treadeth the
winepress of the fierceness and wrath of Almighty God.   And He
hath on His vesture and on his thigh a name written, King of Kings,
and Lord of Lords." Rev. xix. 11-16. See also Joel iii. 12-16 ; Ps.
ix. 7, 8 ; Ps. lxxvi. 9; lxxxix. 14 ; Is. iv. 3, 4 ; xlii. 4; Matt. xii.
18-21 ; John v. 22; Is. xi. 1-9 with 2 Thess. ii. 1-9 ; Is. xxvi. 21 ;
xiii. 6-11 ; xviii. 21, 22 ; lxvi. 14-16 ; Zeph. i. 14-18 ; Zech. xiii. 8,
9 ;   Is. x. 20-22 with Rom. ix. 27, Micah v. 7-8, Zech. xiv. 16 ; Is.
xix. 22-25.

VII. The creation will now be delivered from the
bondage of corruption, and restored to its original glory.
Jerusalem will become again a holy city inhabited by the

people of the Lord. Satan will be chained for a thousand years, and the millennium will be ushered in. As we read,

" For the earnest expectation of the creature [creation] waiteth for the manifestation of the sons of God. For the creature [creation] was made subject to vanity, not willingly, but by reason of Him who hath subjected the same in hope : because the creature [creation] itself shall be delivered from the bondage of corruption into the glorious liberty of the children of God. For we know that the whole creation groaneth and travaileth in pain together until now." Rom. viii. 19-22 with Is. xi. 6-9. " Then shall Jerusalem be holy, and there shall no stranger pass through her any more." " But Judah shall dwell for ever, and Jerusalem from generation to generation." Joel iii. 16-20. "And I saw an angel come down from heaven, having the key of the bottomless pit and a great chain in his hand. And he laid hold on the dragon, that old serpent, which is the Devil, and Satan, and bound him a thousand years, and cast him into the bottomless pit, and shut him up, that he should deceive the nations no more, till the thousand years should be fulfilled : and after that he must be loosed a little season." Rev. xx. 1-3 ; See also, Is. lx. lxi., lxii., xxxv., lxv. 17-25 ; Zech. xiv. 9 ; Micah iv. 1-5 ; Hab. ii. 14 ; Is. li. 3, 11 ; xxxii. 15-18 ; xxxiii. 20-22 ; Hosea ii. 14-23 ; Joel ii. 21-27 ; Amos ix. 11-15 ; Rom. xi. 26, 27.

VIII. During the millennium the Lord Jesus Christ will reign over the earth, and His saints will share His throne As we read,

" Behold, the days come, saith the Lord, that I will raise unto David a righteous Branch, and a King shall reign and prosper, and shall execute judgment and justice in the earth. In His days Judah shall be saved, and Israel shall dwell safely : and this is His name whereby He shall be called, The Lord our Righteousness." Jer. xxiii. 5, 6.

" And I saw thrones and they sat upon them, and judgment was given unto them : and I saw the souls of them that were beheaded for the witness of Jesus, and for the word of God and which had not worshipped the beast, neither the image, neither had received his mark upon their foreheads, or in their hands; and they lived and reigned with Christ a thousand years. But the rest of the dead lived not again until the thousand years were finished. This is the first resurrection. Blessed and holy is he that hath part in the first resurrection: on such the second death hath no power, but they shall be priests of God and Christ, and shall reign with Him a thousand years." Rev. xx. 4-6.

" For unto us a child is born, unto us a son is given: and the government shall be upon His shoulders: and His name shall be called Wonderful, Counsellor, The mighty God, The everlasting Father, The Prince of Peace. Of the increase of His government and peace there shall be no end, upon the throne of David, and upon His kingdom, to order it, and to establish it with judgment and with justice from henceforth even for ever. The zeal of the Lord of hosts will perform this." Is. ix. 6, 7.

" I saw in the night visions, and, behold, one like the Son of man came with the clouds of heaven, and came to the Ancient of days, and they brought Him near before Him. And there was given him a dominion, and glory, and a kingdom, that all people, nations, and languages, should serve Him : His dominion is an everlasting dominion, which shall not pass away, and His kingdom that which shall not be destroyed. . . . . But the saints of the Most High shall take the kingdom, and possess the kingdom for ever, even for ever and ever. . . . And the kingdom and dominion, and the greatness of the dominion under the whole heaven, shall be given to the people of the saints of the most High, whose kingdom is an everlasting kingdom, and all dominions shall serve and obey Him." Dan. vii. 13, 14, 18, 27. See also Matt. xix. 28 ; 1 Cor. vi. 2, 3 ; Rev. ii. 26, 27 ; Micah iv. 1, 2, 3 ; Zech. vi. 12, 13 ; Ps. lxxii.; Ps. xcvi. 10–13, with Rev. xix. 6. Ps. xcvii. 1–6; Ps. xcix. 1, 2 : Is. xxiv. 23; xxxii. 1 ; Luke i. 32, 33; Rom. v. 17; xv. 12 ; 1 Cor. xv. 25 ; Rev. xi. 15.

IX. At the end of the millennium, Satan will be loosed again for a little season, and will induce men again to rebel. A great army will be gathered against the Lord, and will be defeated. Satan will be cast into the lake of fire. The great white throne will be set up, and the dead will be judged. The new heavens and the new earth will be ushered in, and all sin and sorrow will for-ever flee away. As we read,

"And when the thousand years are expired, Satan shall be loosed out of his prison; and shall go out to deceive the nations which are in the four quarters of the earth, Gog and Magog, to gather them together to battle: the number of whom is as the sands of the sea. And they went up on the breadth of the earth, and compassed the camp of the saints about, and the beloved city: and fire came down from God out of heaven, and devoured them. And the devil that deceived them was cast into the lake of fire and brimstone, where the beast and the false prophet are, and shall be tormented day and night for ever and ever. And I saw a great white throne, and Him that sat on it, from whose face the earth and the heavens fled away; and there was found no place for them. And I saw the dead, small and great, stand before God; and the books were opened; and another book was opened, which is the book of life; and the dead were judged out of those things which were written in the books, according to their works. And the sea gave up the dead which were in it; and death and hell delivered up the dead which were in them: and they were judged every man according to their works. And death and hell were cast into the lake of fire. This is the second death. And whosoever was not found written in the book of life was cast into the lake of fire. And I saw a new heaven and a new earth; for the first heaven and the first earth were passed away; and there was no more sea. . . And I heard a great voice out of heaven say-ing, Behold, the taberncle of God is with men, and He will dwell with them, and they shall be His people, and God Himself shall be with them, and be their God. And God shall wipe away all tears from their eyes, and there shall be no more death neither sorrow, nor crying, neither shall there be any more pain: for the former things are passed away," Rev. xx. 7-15, and xxi. 1, 3, 4.

X. Finally, the Lord Jesus Christ, having accom-plished the purposes of His mediatorial coming and

33

reign, will deliver up the kingdom to His Father, and God will henceforth be "All in All."

" For as in Adam all die, even so in Christ shall all be made alive. But every man in his own order; Christ the first-fruits; afterward they that are Christ's at His coming. Then cometh the end, when He shall have delivered up the kingdom to God, even the Father; when He shall have put down all rule and all authority and power. For He must reign till He hath put all enemies under His feet. The last enemy that shall be destroyed is death. For He hath put all things under His feet. But when He saith, All things are put under Him, it is manifest that He is excepted which did put all things under Him. And when all things shall be subdued unto Him, then shall the Son also Himself be subject unto Him that put all things under Him, that God may be all in all." 1 Cor. xv. 22-28.

Such are the outlines of the story of the latter days, as I have learned it. Of the times and seasons, I believe, it is not meant for us to know, as these God has put into His own power, Acts i. 6, 7. But that our Lord is coming again to this world of ours, and that His coming is to be at a day and an hour when we look not for Him, there can, I think, be no doubt. Therefore it behooves us to be ready, that we may not be ashamed before Him at His coming. And we would do well to take heed to the warning in 2 Pet. iii. 2-14:

'' Knowing this first, that there shall come in the last day scoffers, walking after their own lusts, and saying, Where is the promise of His coming? For since the fathers fell asleep, all things continue as they were from the beginning of the creation. For this they willingly are ignorant of, that by the word of God the heavens were of old, and the earth standing out of the water and in the water: whereby the world that then was, being overflowed with water, perished: But the heavens and the earth which are now, by the same word are kept, in store, reserved

unto fire against the day of judgment and perdition of ungodly
men. But, beloved, be not ignorant of this one thing, that one
day is with the Lord as a thousand years, and a thousand years as
one day. The Lord is not slack concerning His promise, as
some men count slackness, but is long-suffering to us-ward, not
willing that any should perish, but that all should come to repentance. But the day of the Lord will come as a thief in the
night; in the which the heavens shall pass away with a great
noise, and the elements shall melt with fervent heat ; the earth
also, and the works that are therein, shall be burnt up. Seeing
then that all these things shall be dissolved, what manner of
persons ought ye to be in all holy conversation and godliness ;
looking for and hasting unto the coming of the day of God, wherein
the heavens, being on fire, shall be dissolved, and the elements
shall melt with fervent heat ? Nevertheless, we, according to His
promise, look for new heavens and a new earth. wherein dwelleth
righteousness. Wherefore, beloved, seeing that ye look for such
things, be diligent that ye may be found of Him in peace, without
spot, and blameless."

I am well aware that this is a subject which does not
interest all Christians, and which is considered fanciful
and unprofitable by many. But if it is indeed a truth,
as the angel declared to the disciples on the Mount of
Olives, while they looked toward the heavens where a
cloud had just received their Lord out of their sight, that
"this same Jesus which is taken up from you into
Heaven, shall so come in like manner as ye have seen
Him go into Heaven," then it must certainly be important for us to know it, and to enter into the mind of
God about it. And I believe myself that there is hardly
any truth which has so great an effect in making Christians unworldly as this.

For, if we expect one who is absent from us to return

at any moment, we shall surely make ourselves ready for his coming, and will take care to arrange our matters so that when he comes he shall not find us engaged in anything of which we think he will not approve. And it has been very striking to me to notice that the Lord's exhortations to holiness of life are always based, not on the fear of death, but on the hope of His return, and its unexpectedness. As we read:

" Watch, therefore, for ye know not what hour your Lord doth come." "Therefore be ye also ready; for in such an hour as ye think not, the Son of Man cometh," Matt. xxiv. 42, 44. " Let your loins be girded about, and your lights burning: and ye yourselves like unto men that wait for their lord, when he will return from the wedding: that when he cometh and knocketh they may open unto him immediately." " Be ye therefore ready also: for the Son of Man cometh at an hour when ye think not," Luke xii. 35, 36, 40. " Take ye heed, watch and pray; for ye know not when the time is. For the Son of Man is as a man taking a far journey, who left his house, and gave authority to his servants, and to every man his work, and commanded the porter to watch. Watch ye, therefore; for ye know not when the Master of the house cometh, at even, or at midnight, or at the cock-crowing, or in the morning; lest coming suddenly He find you sleeping, and what I say unto you, I say unto all, Watch." Mark xiii. 33-37.

I am convinced that these passages teach us that the thought of the unexpectedness of our Lord's return is a far more powerful incentive to holiness than the thought of death ; and I believe the Church has suffered great loss from having overlooked this. It all depends upon how much we love Him, whether we are longing to see Him back. And our present walk and life will surely be greatly modified by a firm belief on our part, that at any moment we may see Him and hear the voice of the trumpet that calls us to His side. Let us ask ourselves a few solemn questions here. Are we, like the early Christians, waiting for Him to come? Are we *ready* for His coming? We cannot wait until we are ready. What should we think of a housekeeper, who was expecting a visit from a very distinguished guest, and whose house should be all turned inside out with repairs, and painting, and cleaning, with not a quiet room in it, but who should yet say to us, " Oh, yes, I am waiting longingly for my friend to arrive, and am expecting him at any moment?" I am sure we should stand amazed at such waiting as that, and would say, " But how can you wait for him until you are ready? Would not his coming now be, to say the least, very inconvenient and ill-timed; and would you not prefer that he should delay his coming, until you have prepared a comfortable place in which to receive him?"

We may well pause and think, therefore, whether *we* are ready for our Lord's coming. Are our houses, and our lives, and our churches prepared to receive Him? Would His coming just at this present moment be inconvenient or ill-timed to us? If we knew of a certainty that He were coming next week, should we go on with our lives as they are, and carry out our present plans and purposes for the few intervening days? I remember being very much impressed with hearing of John Wesley, that, upon being asked by a friend one morning how he would spend the day if he knew he

33*

should certainly die that night, he replied, after a solemn pause, "I should do just the things I have already
planned to do. I should attend to the business I have
laid out. I should see the friends I have expected to
see. I should go to the places I have arranged for. I
should read the books I have prepared. I should eat
my meals, and take my usual rest, and should quietly
await the hour of my death without one anxious thought."
It seemed to me, when I heard it, grand to be ready
like that! And such, I am sure, was our Lord's thought
concerning us, when He said, "Therefore, be ye also
ready, for in such an hour as ye think not the Son of
man cometh."

We may not perhaps understand all the details.
But enough is plain to teach us that our Lord is surely
coming again, and to stir our hearts with a triumphant
hope of our own personal share in His glory. For if
He *should* come to-morrow, what human tongue could
put into words the unimagined and unspeakable joy and
gladness that would become the portion of all His people! To see Him face to face, the Desire of all nations,
and our own Beloved! To be made like Him! To be
done with sin forever! To have our vile bodies fashioned
like unto His glorious body! To be presented faultless
before His Father's throne with exceeding joy! To sit
down with Him in His kingdom! To be abundantly
satisfied with the fatness of His house, and to drink
forevermore of the river of His pleasures! Ah, who can
tell or dream of what this would be?

"He is coming! and the tidings
  Sweep through the willing air,
With hope that ends forever
  Time's ages of despair.
Old Earth from dreams and slumber
  Wakes up and says, Amen:
Land and ocean bid Him welcome,
  Flood and forest join the strain.
He is coming! and the mountains
  Of Judea ring again;
Jerusalem awakens
  And shouts her glad Amen.
He is coming! and the tidings
  Are rolling wide and far;
As light flows out in gladness
  From yon fair morning star."

The books of prophecy close with Malachi in the year
397 B. C. No prophet was to arise after him, and the
Jewish nation were left from henceforth to wait, for
nearly four hundred years, until "the consolation of
Israel" should come. The closing words are a solemn
and yet blessed warning and promise:

"For, behold, the day cometh, that shall burn as an oven; and
all the proud, yea, and all that do wickedly, shall be stubble; and
the day that cometh shall burn them up, saith the Lord of hosts,
that it shall leave them neither root nor branch. But unto you
that fear My name shall the Sun of righteousness arise with healing in His wings; and ye shall go forth, and grow up as calves of
the stall. And ye shall tread down the wicked; for they shall be
ashes under the soles of your feet in the day that I shall do this,
saith the Lord of hosts. Remember ye the law of Moses, My
servant, which I commanded unto him in Horeb for all Israel.

with the statutes and judgments. Behold, I will send you Elijah the prophet before the coming of the great and dreadful day of the Lord: and he shall turn the heart of the fathers to the children, and the heart of the children to their fathers, lest I come and smite the earth with a curse."

Had Israel heeded this warning, and received Christ at His first coming as their King, who can say whether the world's salvation would not then have been accomplished? But they rejected Him, and the day of triumph has been deferred until the "times of the Gentiles" shall be fulfilled.

But the Lord is not slack concerning His promise as some men count slackness, and the glorious "times of restitution of all things which God hath spoken by the mouth of all His holy prophets since the world began" shall surely come at last. And the day will dawn finally, according to the promise, when in "the dispensation of the fulness of times," God will "gather together in one all things in Christ, both which are in heaven, and which are on earth;" and when "at the name of Jesus every knee will bow, of things in heaven, and things in earth, and things under the earth; and every tongue will confess that Jesus Christ is Lord, to the glory of God the Father."

"He which testifieth these things saith, Surely I come quickly; Amen. Even so, come, Lord Jesus."

The great Prophecies and Allusions to Christ in the Old Testament, which are expressly cited, either as predictions fulfilled in Him, or applied to Him in the New Testament. From Hales's Analysis of Sacred Chronology.

FIRST SERIES:

DESCRIBING CHRIST IN HIS HUMAN NATURE, AS THE PRO-
MISED SEED OF THE WOMAN, IN THE GRAND CHARTER OF
OUR REDEMPTION (GEN. iii. 15); AND HIS PEDIGREE, SUF-
FERINGS, AND GLORY, IN HIS SUCCESSIVE MANIFESTATIONS
OF HIMSELF UNTIL THE END OF THE WORLD.

I. THE SEED OF THE WOMAN.
—Ge. 3. 15. Gal. 4. 4. 1 Tim.
2. 15. Rev. 12. 5.

II. BORN OF A VIRGIN.—Ps.
22. 10; 69. 8; 86. 16; 116.
16. Isa. 7. 14; 49. 1. Mi. 5.
3. Je. 31. 22. Matt. 1. 23. Lu.
1 26–35.

III. OF THE FAMILY OF SHEM.
—Ge. 9. 26.

IV. OF THE RACE OF THE
HEBREWS.—Ex. 3. 18. Phi.
3. 5. 2 Cor. 11. 22.

V. OF THE SEED OF ABRA-
HAM.—Ge. 12. 3: 18. 18;
22. 18. Mat. 1. 1. Jno. 8. 56.
Ac. 3. 25.

VI. OF THE LINE OF ISAAC.
—Ge. 17. 19; 21. 12; 26. 4.
Ro. 9. 7. Ga. 4. 23–28. He.
11. 18.

VII. OF JACOB OR ISRAEL.—
Ge. 28. 4–14. Ex. 4. 22. Nu.
24. 7–17. Ps. 135. 4, &c. Is.
41. 8; 49. 6. Je. 14. 8. Lu. 1.
68; 2. 30. Ac. 28. 20.

VIII. OF THE TRIBE OF JU-
DAH.—Ge. 49. 10. 1 Ch. 5. 2.
Mi. 5. 2. Mat. 2. 6. He. 7. 14.
Re. 5. 5.

IX. OF THE HOUSE OF DA-
VID.—2 Sam 7. 12–15. 1 Ch.
17. 11–14. Ps. 89. 4–36; 132.
10–17. 2 Ch. 6. 42. Is. 9. 7;
11. 1; 55. 3, 4. Je. 23. 5, 6.
Am. 9. 11. Mat. 1. 1. Lu. 1.
69; 2. 4. Jno. 7. 42. Ac 2.
30; 13. 23. Ro. 1. 3. 2 Tim.
2. 8, Re. 22. 16.

X. BORN AT BETHLEHEM THE
CITY OF DAVID.—Mi. 5. 2.
Mat. 2. 6. Lu. 2. 4. Jno. 7. 42.

XI. HIS PASSION OR SUFFER-
INGS.—Ge. 3. 15. Ps. 22 1–
18; 31. 13; 89. 38–45. Is. 53.
1–12. Da. 9, 26. Zec. 13. 6, 7.
Mat. 26. 31. Lu. 24. 26. Jno.
1. 29. Ac. 8. 32–35; 26. 23.

XII. HIS DEATH ON THE
CROSS.—Nu. 21. 9. Ps. 16.
10; 22. 16; 31. 22; 49. 15.
Is. 53. 8, 9. Da. 9. 26. Jno.
3. 14; 8. 28; 12. 32, 33. Mat.
20. 19; 26. 2 1 Cor. 15. 3.
Col. 2. 15. Phi. 2. 8.

XIII. HIS INTOMBMENT AND
EMBALMENT.—Is. 53. 9. Mat.
26. 12. Mar. 14. 8. Jno. 12.
7; 19. 40. 1 Cor. 15. 4.

XIV. His Resurrection on the Third Day.—Ps. 16. 10; 17. 15; 49. 15; 73. 24. Jon. 1. 17. Mat. 12. 40; 16. 4; 27. 63. Jno. 2. 19. Ac. 2. 27-31; 13. 35. I Cor. 15. 4.

XV.—His Ascension into Heaven.—Ps 8. 5, 6; 47. 5; 68. 18; 110. 1. Ac. 1. 11; 2. 33. Jno. 20. 17. Ep. 4. 8-10. He. 1. 3; 2. 9. Re. 12. 5.

XVI.—His Second Appearance at the Regenera-

tion.—Is. 40. 10; 62. 11. Je. 23. 5, 6. Ho. 3. 4. Mi. 5. 3 Ha. 2. 7. Da. 7. 13, 14. Mat. 24. 3-30; 26. 64. Jno. 5. 25. He. 9. 28. Re. 20. 4; 22. 20.

XVII.—His Last Appearance at the End of the World.—Ps. 50. 1-6. Job 19. 25-29. Ec. 12. 14. Da. 12. 2, 3. Mat. 25. 31-46. Jno. 5. 28-30. Ac. 17. 31; 24. 25. Re. 20. 11-15.

SECOND SERIES.

DESCRIBING HIS CHARACTER AND OFFICES, HUMAN AND DIVINE.

I. The Son of God —2 Sa. 7. 14. I Ch 17. 13 Ps. 2. 7; 72. 1. Pr. 30. 4. Da. 3. 25. Mar. 1. 1. Lu. 1. 35 Mat. 3. 17; 17. 5. Jno. 1. 34-50; 3. 16-18; 20. 31. He. 1. 1-5. Ro. 1. 4. I Jno. 4. 14. Re. 1. 5. 6

II. The Son of Man.—Ps. 8. 4, 5. Da. 7. 13. Jno. 1. 51 ; 3. 13; 5. 27. Mat. 16. 13 : 26. 64. He. 2. 7. Re. 1. 13; 14. 14.

III. The Holy One, or Saint.—De. 33. 8. Ps. 16. 10; 89. 19. Is. 10. 17; 29. 23 ; 49. 7. Ho. 11. 9. Hab. 1. 12; 3. 3. Mar. 1. 24. Lu. 1. 35; 4. 34. I Jno. 2. 20.

IV. The Saint of Saints. —Dan. 9. 24.

V. The Just One, or Righteous.—Zec 9. 9. Je. 23. 5. Is. 41. 2. Ps. 34. 19, 21. Lu. 1. 17. Mat. 27. 19-24. Lu. 23. 47. Ac. 3. 14; 7.

52; 22. 14. I Jno. 2. 1, 29, Ja. 5. 6.

VI. The Wisdom of God.— Pr. 8. 22-30. Mat. 11. 19, Lu 11. 49 I Cor. 1. 24.

VII. The Oracle (or Word) of the Lord, or of God. —Ge. 15. 1-4. I Sa. 3 1-21. 2 Sa. 7. 4. I Ki. 17. 8-24. Ps. 33. 6. Is. 40. 8. Mi. 4. 2. Je. 25. 3. Jno. 1. 1-14; 3. 34. Lu. 1. 2. He. 11. 3; 4. 12. I Pe. 1. 23. 2 Pe. 3. 5. Re. 19. 13.

VIII. The Redeemer, or Saviour.—Job 19. 25-27. Ge. 48. 16. Ps. 19. 14. Is. 41. 14; 44. 6; 47. 4; 59. 20; 62. 11; 63. 1. Je. 50. 34. Mat. 1. 21. Jno. 1. 29; 4. 42. Lu. 2. 11. Ac. 5. 31. Ro. 11. 26. Re. 5. 9.

IX. The Lamb of God.— Ge. 22. 8. Is. 53. 7. Jno. 1. 29. Ac. 8. 32-35. I Pe. 1. 19. Re. 5. 6; 13. 8; 15. 3; 21. 22; 22. 1.

X. The Mediator, Inter-
cessor, or Advocate.—
Job 33. 23. Is. 53. 12; 59.
16. Lu. 23. 34. 1 Ti. 2. 5.
He. 9. 15. 1 Jno. 2. 1. Re.
5. 9.
XI. Shiloh, the Apostle.
—Ge. 49. 10. Ex. 4. 13. Mat.
15. 24. Lu. 4. 18. Jno. 9. 7;
17. 3; 20. 21. He. 3. 1.
XII. The High Priest.—
Ps. 110. 4. Is. 59. 16. He. 3.
1; 4. 14; 5. 10; 9. 11.
XIII. The Prophet Like
Moses.—Deu. 18. 15–19. Lu.
24. 19. Ma. 6. 15. Jno. 1. 17-
21; 6. 14. Ac. 3. 22, 23.
XIV. The Leader, or Chief
Captain.—Jo. 5. 14. 1 Ch.
5. 2. Is. 55. 4. Mi. 5. 2. Da.
9. 25. Mat. 2. 6. He. 2. 10.
XV. The Messiah, Christ,
King of Israel.—1 Sa. 2.

10. 2 Sa. 7. 12. 1 Ch. 17. 11.
Ps. 2. 2; 45. 1, 6; 72. 1; 89.
36. Is. 61. 1. Da. 9. 26. Mat.
2. 2–4; 16. 16. Lu. 23. 2.
Jno. 1. 41–49; 6. 69. Ac. 4.
26, 27; 10. 38.
XVI. The God of Israel.
—Ex. 24. 10, 11. Jos. 7. 19.
Ju. 11. 23. 1 Sam. 5. 11. 1 Ch.
17. 24. Ps. 41. 13. Is. 45. 3.
Eze. 8. 4. Mat. 15. 31; 22.
32. Jno. 20. 28.
XVII. The Lord of Hosts,
or the Lord.—2 Sa. 7. 26.
1 Ch. 17. 24. Ps. 24. 10. Is.
6. 1-5. Mal. 1. 14. Rom. 12.
19. Phi. 2. 9–11.
XVIII. King of Kings, and
Lord of Lords.—Ps. 89.
27; 110. 1. Da. 7. 13, 14.
Mat. 28. 18. Jno. 3. 35; 13.
3. 1 Cor. 15. 25. Ep. 1. 20–
22. Col. 3. 1. Re. 19. 16.

www.ingramcontent.com/pod-product-compliance
Lightning Source LLC
Chambersburg PA
CBHW031824090426
42741CB00005B/125